Dearest Andrew,

Here are some interesting thoughts
and ideas to add to the wisdom
you already have about life.
            Much love,
            Mum.

LAW AND PROVIDENCE

BENJAMIN FAIN

LAW AND PROVIDENCE

SPIRIT *and* MATTER,

DIVINE PROVIDENCE *and*

the LAWS *of* NATURE,

and the OPENNESS *of the* WORLD

to GOD *and* MAN

Translated from Hebrew by
KAREN GILBERT

URIM PUBLICATIONS
Jerusalem • New York

Law and Providence: Spirit and Matter, Divine Providence and
the Laws of Nature, and the Openness of the World to God
and Man
by Benjamin Fain

ISBN 13: 978-965-524-058-0
Printed in Israel
First Edition

Book design by Ariel Walden

Urim Publications
P.O. Box 52287, Jerusalem 91521 Israel

Lambda Publishers Inc.
527 Empire Blvd., Brooklyn, New York 11225 U.S.A.
Tel: 718-972-5449   Fax: 718-972-6307
mh@ejudaica.com

www.UrimPublications.com

Contents

Contents

Contents

CHAPTER FOUR
Knowledge of the World from a Jewish Perspective

Part 3   THE HISTORY OF THE WORLD

CHAPTER FIVE
The Creation of the World and the Start of Its Development

Contents

Preface

THIS BOOK IS ABOUT SCIENCE AND ITS PLACE IN JEWISH thought. In a sense, this book is a continuation and development of the ideas in my previous book, *Creation Ex Nihilo*. However, it stands alone, and no prior knowledge of *Creation Ex Nihilo* is necessary. In modern times, a secular outlook has developed that appears to draw its atheistic conclusions from the achievements of science. When these laymen, who know little about either science or theology, come to choose between completely differing views, they prefer the tremendous achievements of science, which rule, so it would seem, clearly in favor of the secular approach. I cannot state categorically that this is the only reason for the popularity of secularism, but I am certain that the preconception that science somehow contradicts faith has made a significant contribution to the prevalence of atheism. The contribution of certain religious groups, due to a lack of understanding of the true interaction of science and faith, has also had a substantial effect. But if a lack of understanding exists amongst observant Jews, perhaps this is due to the unconscious influence of the historical approach of the church, which has been struggling with science since its infancy.

Although the relationship between Torah and science contains many aspects, one particular issue currently stands out. This is the mismatch between the literal meaning of the Torah, especially of the book of Genesis, and what are considered to be the conclusions of the fundamentals of science. In my opinion, reading the literal meaning of the account of creation in the book of Genesis is not the most effective way to understand the Torah and its relationship with science. Jewish tradition has always accepted an allegorical interpretation of the story of creation. Neither Maimonides, Nachmanides, nor Rabbi Yehuda Halevi viewed the literal meaning of the creation story as a direct way to understand the Torah's message. In our own time, Rabbi Joseph B. Soloveitchik, one of the leading Jewish philosophers of the twentieth century, who was steeped not only in the world of Torah but also in the world of science, completely ignores the difference between the scientific account of evolution of the universe and the description of the creation of the world as it appears in the Torah. He wrote, "I have never been seriously troubled by the problem of the Biblical doctrine of creation vis-à-vis the scientific story of evolution at both the cosmic and the organic levels, nor have I been perturbed by the confrontation of the mechanistic interpretation of the human mind with the Biblical spiritual concept of man" (*Lonely Man of Faith*, 7).

The scientific description of the development of the world is on another plane from the biblical description of the creation of the world. The Torah's account has the connotation of a plan or an idea. "The world was created in ten utterances" (*Ethics of the Fathers* 1:5). Then each "utterance" is transformed into reality: "God said: 'Let there be light,' and there was light" (Genesis 1:3). The Torah describes a process of planning – "let there be light," and immediately afterwards the outcome – "and there was light." Science, on the other hand, relates solely to the stage of implementation. Thus I see no contradiction between the Torah, which is the plane of *divine* thought and planning, and the scientific plane of material, physical implementation. They are two different dimensions of reality. If this is the case, then the true contradiction and the real battlefield lie not between science and Torah but between two world views: the secular one and the religious Jewish one. A clear distinction must be made between science itself and the world view that purports to be scientific and science-based. In reality, there is no conflict between science and faith, as people tend to think. There is only a conflict between the two different world views, between two types of faith – secular faith and Jewish faith: faith versus faith! The comparison that we will make in this book between the two types of faith will lead us to the clear conclusion that one faith is blind and irrational, while the other is rational and well-grounded. Materialistic faith – indeed, secular faith in general – is blind and irrational, whereas Jewish faith is rational and compatible with our intellect.

A widespread preconception of scientists and certain philosophers, in particular in the nineteenth and twentieth centuries, is that the world can be explained in a rational, scientific way, without the inclusion of the *divine*. In my previous book, *Creation Ex Nihilo,*[1] I tried to show the inadequacy of this view. It may be stated, without a shadow of a doubt, that it is impossible to explain and describe the world solely using scientific tools. This is in spite of the popular belief among laymen and intellectuals alike that science can explain everything – the creation of the world, its laws and its development and, as part of this, the evolution of life and human history. This notion might lead a confused person to believe that atheism is the truth. Hence, it is crucial to demonstrate the unfoundedness of the atheistic view and the lack of reasoning behind it. It is only out of sheer ignorance that one can believe that this view is supported by science. I feel a sense of obligation to share my thoughts of the unfoundedness of the atheistic view with as large an audience as possible. Indeed, I see it as a kind of mission.

I must emphasize that ignorance of the world in which we live is not just the legacy of the layman but also of those who see themselves, rightly or wrongly, as intellectuals. Many people think that a person who holds an academic degree, or an eminent scientist in a particular field, also has knowledge of the structure of science and of scientific discovery. But even a distinguished scientist may not understand the structure of science and its role in describing the world. One of the goals of this book is to enable us to understand how the world develops under divine providence while being subject to the laws of nature at the same time.

However, this book also has another, no less important, aspect. When we arrive at the reality of God through theoretical reasoning only, our lives are not all that affected. Such a God is transcendental – people cannot comprehend Him, and we cannot understand His relationship with us or even whether He is involved in worldly matters or not. Belief in the existence of God through intellectual reasoning alone cannot be the basis of any religion. Only when God reveals Himself and involves Himself in the lives of human beings can He change them. And there lies the question: are there any scientific tools for researching divine revelations? By its very nature, science researches phenomena that are found in large quantities, such as atoms and molecules. Divine revelation is unique, one-off in nature,

---

1. Although I refer on several occasions to my previous book, *Creation Ex Nihilo*, the present book stands alone, as mentioned above.

one-of-a-kind. Nevertheless, science – or, to be more precise, manner of scientific reasoning – can contribute to our understanding of divine revelations as well as to theology, the science of God. I see this as one of the goals of this book. Science gives us tools to analyze the world and God's creations from a particular perspective.

One may ask whether scientific knowledge can really bring us closer to a better understanding of the world and of God. We could cite many examples of people who possess considerable scientific knowledge, world-renowned scientists, who are far removed from faith. The answer is that scientific knowledge gives us an understanding of a certain aspect of the world. Without more general knowledge and understanding, we do not come closer to God or to the world, His creation. But what is this more general knowledge and understanding?

To answer this question, I will relate a parable cited by Maimonides in his *Guide of the Perplexed* (3:51). A king's palace is located in a certain city. Maimonides divides the people who approach the king into various groups. According to the parable, the closer a person is to the king's house and to the king himself, the closer he is to God:

> Those who seek to reach the ruler's habitation and to enter it, but never see the ruler's habitation, are the multitude of the adherents of the Law. I refer to the ignoramuses who observe the commandments.
>
> Those who have come up to the habitation and walk around it are the jurists who believe true opinions on the basis of traditional authority and study the law concerning the practices of divine service, but do not engage in speculation concerning the fundamental principles of religion and make no inquiry whatever regarding the rectification of belief.
>
> ... Know, my son, that as long as you are engaged in studying the mathematical sciences and the art of logic, you are one of those who walk around the house searching for its gate .... If, however, you have understood the natural things, you have entered the habitation and are walking in the ante-chambers. If, however, you have achieved perfection in the natural things and have understood divine science, you have entered in the ruler's place into the inner court and are with him in one habitation. This is the rank of the men of science; they, however, are of different grades of perfection.

What do we learn from this parable? One may achieve closeness to God and understanding of His world in various ways, each of which is important.

While partial knowledge – whether of *halakha* (Jewish law), mathematics or physics – contributes to one's understanding of the world, it does not provide the complete picture. What unites them is Jewish metaphysics, which helps us understand the world, its laws and its development under divine supervision. This is also the goal of this book – to overcome the ignorance that prevents us from understanding the world in which we live.

If we look at the Bible, we can see that even though it speaks at length about God's revelations and His connection with the prophets, it does not tell us a thing about the essence of God Himself. The Kabbalah, the major work of Jewish mysticism, took it upon itself to comprehend God's essence, if only in a partial way. It is important to emphasize that the kabbalistic objective is to discover the hidden essence that is behind the external forms in reality, and this objective is more important today than ever before. "For as long as nature and man are conceived as His creations, and that is the indispensable condition of highly developed religious life, the quest for the hidden life of the transcendent element in such creation will always form one of the most important preoccupations of the human mind" (Gershom Scholem, *Major Trends in Jewish Mysticism*, 38).

Over the past three centuries, there has been a new divine revelation – namely modern science.[2] I believe that it is extremely important to use these new tools in order to understand anew various aspects of the world that are hidden from us. When I talk of "new tools," I mean not only the content of the various scientific theories, but also the structure of science and its position vis-à-vis our general knowledge of the world – the metaphysics of science. I am talking about both an understanding of the limits of science and our understanding that knowledge of science exists in the realm of the Kingdom of Heaven. "The Kingdom of Heaven is the kingdom of true knowledge, when the light of wisdom will shine on the universe and its contents" (Rabbi Soloveitchik, *And From There You Shall Seek*, 203).

The world is full of mysteries. The routine of everyday life and our mundane view of things prevent us from perceiving the mysteries of the world. In the words of the Psalmist: "How great are your deeds, Lord, exceedingly profound are your thoughts." However, a superficial look at the world can-

---

2.   In both my previous book, *Creation Ex Nihilo*, and in Chapter Four of this book, I show that modern science is a revelation of God.

not help us to understand this: "A simple man cannot know, nor can a fool understand this" (*Psalms* 92:7). When we reach the limit of our understanding and perceive this limit, then we come close to the depth of the issues at hand. To gain a deep understanding is to reach the limits of things that human beings are able to understand. In the words of Albert Einstein, "[The scientist's] religious feeling takes the form of a rapturous amazement at the harmony of natural law, which reveals an intelligence of such superiority that, compared with it, all the systematic thinking and acting of human beings is an utterly insignificant reflection" (*Ideas and Opinions*, 40).

Both the scientific analysis of reality and our understanding of the limit of such analysis enable us to discover the mysteries of the world. The purpose of this book, other than confronting the naturalistic approach, is to find these mysteries and to solve some of them. The name of this book is *Law and Providence*. There is a great mystery in the world – how can the laws of nature be reconciled with the will of God and the wills of human beings? I will attempt both to explain the nature of the problem and to provide a possible solution.

Judaism's constant struggle with idolatry is one of its most important challenges, perhaps the most important of all. Even though idolatry in its ancient form – bowing down to idols, the moon and the stars, and to the golden calf – has disappeared from much of the modern world, its essence still plays a central role in modern civilization. The form that modern-day idolatry takes is secularism. Modern civilization, which has achieved more than all previous civilizations in terms of humanity's control over its vital resources, has replaced faith in God with faith in science. It seemed, at least at first, that if one could formulate a solid world view of nature, man and his place in nature without having to resort to God, then this was proof that God did not exist. This is the essence of secularism and atheism.

The perception of nature and its laws as the ultimate source is the idolatry of our time. In my opinion, the struggle against this new idolatry and the need to expose the weakness and the poverty of the secular world view are of supreme importance. However, I cannot succeed in this mission without some effort from the reader. I am certain that this effort – the active study of this book – will contribute greatly to the reader's inner spiritual world.

The book is divided into three Parts. Part I, *Fundamental Principles*, which serves as an introduction, introduces the terminology, concepts and fundamental ideas needed to understand and describe the world run by God.

Part II, *The Laws of Nature*, is devoted to science and to the scientific account of the developments of the world. There I present my understanding of the laws of nature as one of the elements of the spiritual, divine world. This spiritual world is a kind of divine operating system, a tool of divine providence, while the laws of nature are simply a part of it. This view enables us to gain a deeper understanding of the nature of modern science and its place within an account of divine management. These are the laws of the world from the Jewish perspective.

A few words about Chapter Two, which is devoted to physics, the foundation of science. It is a good idea to read it in order to become familiar with the principal concepts of modern physics. These concepts help us gain a better understanding of nature, which is a part of the divine creation. It is possible that certain parts of Chapter Two will seem too complex and intricate to some. If so, the reader may omit these parts, but Chapter Two should not in any way discourage the reader from reading the parts that follow, as these parts contain the main themes of the book.

In a sense, one may view the first two parts as a kind of prologue to Part III, *The History of the World*. The development of the world is described here as a process that takes place under divine supervision, which uses the laws of nature, which are themselves a component of the divine, spiritual world. Therefore, I use modern science to describe the development of the world while pointing out the unique, creative, one-off events which indicate God's intervention, divine providence.

I divide the history of the world into three eras: the physical era – from the creation of the world to the creation of life; the era of life – from the creation of life to the creation of man, and the era of history – from the creation of man to the present day. In the era of history, alongside the will of God, the will of human beings also affects the development of the world. In Part III, *The History of the World*, I present the development of the world from a Jewish perspective.

* * *

I would like to express my gratitude to the first readers of the manuscript of this book (Hebrew edition); to my wife, Shoshana, for her support and valuable comments; and to Yaakov Gantz, of blessed memory, for his many helpful remarks. I would also like to thank Shalom Baruch for his comments on the content of this book and its significance. I am grateful to Levi Kitrossky for our interesting discussion about the development of the world, which helped me formulate my ideas more precisely, and to Dr. Baruch Podolsky for Hebrew linguistic consultation. Special thanks to Rabbi Yaakov Ariel for his encouragement and for emphasizing the importance of the subject.

This English edition is a corrected and abridged translation of the Hebrew edition – *Hok ve-Hashgaha*. I would like to thank the translator Karen Gilbert for her fruitful cooperation.

—Benjamin Fain
Herzliya, Israel
5770/2010

Part 1

FUNDAMENTAL PRINCIPLES

CHAPTER ONE

God and Man

1. THE UNIQUENESS OF MAN

The *thaumatic* shock that liberates man from looking only at the routine and regular features of experience opens his soul to the unique and transcendent.

(A.J. Heschel, *Between God and Man*, 29)

THE ROUTINE OF EVERYDAY LIFE MAKES US LOSE THE ability to discern the depth of reality. A little boy, or even a grown man, can watch television without seeing anything odd or special about the characters on the screen. A large amount of knowledge is needed to acquire even a partial understanding of the processes that lead to the moving pictures on the television screen. Now, the reality to which we are exposed is immensely more complex, sublime and mysterious than a simple television. Therefore we must invest a monumental effort to detach ourselves from the dazzling and misleading effect of routine.

Imagine that a creature from another world that is completely different from our own arrives on Earth and observes what goes on here. Let's call this creature *Scientist*, because in the reality that he comes from everything occurs in a strictly scientific way.

On second thought, this character, *Scientist*, who has arrived in our reality from a far-off land, is not so imaginary. In fact, most of the scientists that I know have not yet admitted the complexity of our reality, and are still under the illusion that their scientific tools are all that is necessary to understand the world. I, too, during certain periods in my life, was like a scientist who

19

had arrived from a distant planet. The intellectual routine and a scientist's eagerness in the pursuit of science can distract him from observing reality and from seeing all the wonder and mysteries that may be found in it.

Scientist came across many interesting things on Earth: an almost infinite variety of plants, animals and many types of machines. However, the people impressed him most of all. Here was something that utterly contradicted his world view. The first thing he noticed was that despite the similarity between people, no two were identical. Each was unique and represented a complete world. *Scientist* had already found something here that prevented him from using his usual methods, which were based on the study of uniform items – such as atoms and molecules – that are identical everywhere in the universe. But this was just the beginning. Step by step, *Scientist* discovered the people's different and peculiar characteristics. In the actions and movements of human beings, he observed a thing that might be called "purposefulness." *Scientist* saw an enormous difference between his usual research subjects and people. Incidentally, human beings were not the only creatures who demonstrated purposefulness. The animals and even the plants did so to various extents.

It quickly became clear to *Scientist* that his vocabulary was insufficient to describe the qualities of human beings. He found that his world of concepts was too weak to describe the new reality in which he had found himself, and he had to invent new words in order to report the peculiar and incredible phenomenon called the "human being." Human beings have numerous and varied *feelings*. They *enjoy the beauty* of a view and *the beauty* of other humans. They hear sounds called *music* and become *excited* by them. They have emotions such as *love, brotherliness, friendship, hatred, resentment, jealousy* and many others. These feelings, these emotions, are unique to each person. One human being's love is not the same as another's. And yet people *talk*, and *through talking* they are able to convey their feelings and sensations to one another, even if only partially.

Human beings feel concern for themselves – self-interest – and in this it seems that they are no different from the rest of the animal kingdom. However, they have one thing that is specific to them: a feeling of concern for others (not to be confused with animal instincts, which are expressed in the protection of their young). Human beings are capable even of giving up their lives for each other. This quality amazed *Scientist*. While *self-interest* had a certain logic to it, *Scientist* found it hard to see any sense in self-sacrifice for the sake of another.

More about logic: sometimes human behavior showed evidence of logic, unlike *Scientist's* usual research subjects – atoms, molecules, gases, solid bodies, and so on – which cannot be described at all in terms of logic. There are laws that describe the movements of molecules, but the concept of logic and ideas such as reason, insight and wisdom have nothing to do with the world of materials. They are also irrelevant to other subjects within *Scientist's* field of research, such as electromagnetic fields and gravity.

Man is capable of *creating* new things, such as *music, poetry* and *art*. Man also *creates* science itself. From *Scientist's* point of view, man's most incredible quality is the ability to *create* new things that did not exist previously. Of all the wonders that *Scientist* had seen on Earth, human beings were the most fascinating.

All these discoveries convinced *Scientist* that aside from the material-physical reality that he knew, there was another reality, a *spiritual* reality. *Scientist* arrived at this conclusion from his observations of human beings. The scientific tools that *Scientist* was accustomed to using could not describe this new reality. We will talk about spiritual reality in section 3 below, but first I would like to discuss the concept of logic, which I mentioned above as an example of a concept that belongs to spiritual reality.

2. LOGIC – A TOOL FOR DESCRIBING REALITY

Now let us talk about logic as a tool for describing reality. First of all, let me emphasize that logic is only one of the tools for getting to know the world; it is impossible to understand reality using logic alone. In Chapter Four we will discuss knowledge of the world in more detail. At this point, we will attempt to understand what logic is and why we need to use it to describe reality. It is clear that in order to understand the world, we must know how to infer conclusions about different aspects of reality – how to arrive at conclusions from premises. *The goal of logic is to infer true conclusions from true premises* – or, in other words, logic is the means, the tool, for drawing true conclusions. When I use the word "proof," I am referring to proof according to the rules of logic.

First, we will look at a few examples of *logical inference, deduction* and *drawing correct conclusions*. The concept of logic was developed in ancient Greece, in particular in the work of Aristotle, as the art of reasoning and argument. So let us take an example from the Greeks:

– All people are mortal. Greeks are people. Therefore, Greeks are mortal.

From the true premise that *all people are mortal*, the correct conclusion is drawn that *Greeks are mortal*. It is important to note here that the correctness, or truth, of the conclusion derives from the fact that all Greeks are people, and from the valid premise that all people are mortal. If we had been able to find only one Greek who was not a person, then the proof would not have been correct. The drawing of a conclusion, deduction, is valid only if no *counter-example* exists.

Here is an example of an erroneous deduction because of the existence of a counter-example:

– All men are mortal. Socrates is mortal. Therefore, Socrates is a man.

We have here a true premise – *all men are mortal*, and a true conclusion – *Socrates is a man* – but the inference is not correct, and this is because there is a counter-example. Let us say that Socrates is the name of a dog. Hence, from the inference, it is derived that a dog is a man, and this is a wrong conclusion. This inference brings us both to a correct conclusion – that the philosopher Socrates is a man, and to an incorrect conclusion – that the dog Socrates is a man. Therefore, this inference is not valid since using it may lead to incorrect conclusions.

We have determined that inference, the rule for drawing conclusions, is valid if and only if there is no counter-example that contradicts it or if it is possible to show that this example does not exist. The two examples cited above are simple ones. Mathematics provides us with more complex examples for drawing conclusions. It is interesting to note that Maimonides refers to mathematics and the ingenuity of logic together: ". . . so long as you are engaged in studying the mathematical sciences and the art of logic . . ." (*Guide of the Perplexed*, 3:51). At the foundation of geometry lie a few basic premises, called *axioms*. From these axioms, many conclusions are inferred using logic – these are *theorems*. For example, the angles in any triangle add up to 180 degrees; in an equilateral triangle all the angles are equal. Arithmetic also provides countless inferences that are derived from certain premises.

We do not always notice that arithmetical assertions are also the results of logical inference. So, for example, while the statement "Two plus two equals four" appears self-evident to us, it is actually the result of a logical operation.

Logic deals with the analysis of drawing correct conclusions for certain premises, which are also considered correct. "Considered" – this is where the connection to reality comes in. What do I mean? In mathematics, the premises – the axioms – are given, as statements that are true and that do not need to be proven. From a purely mathematical perspective, correctness, or truthfulness, of the axioms is guaranteed by the very declaration that they are true. Sounds strange? Not really. In fact, mathematical claims are always *conditional*: if an axiom is true, then it is possible to prove that a particular statement is also true. However, gaining a *true description* of reality, and aspiring to draw conclusions about it are another matter entirely. Hence, we must determine the relationship between the premises of logic or mathematics and the facts of reality. In fact, mathematics provides us with a language for describing reality. But I will discuss this in more detail in Chapter Three, section 2: *Mathematics – The Language of Science*.

What is important to us at this point is to understand the limitations of logical proofs. Basically, logical proof does not create anything new; it simply brings to light that which is already inherent in a fundamental premise. Take a look at the example discussed above:

– All people are mortal. Greeks are people. Therefore Greeks are mortal.

Here the premise "*All people are mortal*" is talking about *all* people, including Greeks, Romans, Jews, Persians etc. This means that Greeks are latently included in the premise that *all people are mortal*. The conclusion, "*Therefore Greeks are mortal*," only highlights something that already exists in the premise. Therefore, on the one hand, logical proof is a solid, secure tool, but on the other hand, it does not actually produce anything new.

3. SPIRITUAL REALITY

In section 1 above, we talked about an imaginary scientist (although, as I pointed out, he may not be quite so imaginary. Many of my colleagues are similar to that scientist). *Scientist* arrived at the existence of spiritual reality through his observation of human beings. We are used to the reality, the practicality and the objectivity of material reality, of the physical world, the world in which the laws of physics operate, as well as the reality of the animal kingdom. To a certain extent, the material reality forces itself upon us. When we open our eyes, we see trees, grass, buildings, cars, other people, and so on. To a rational person who does not involve himself in philosophical ruminations, there is no doubt that this reality exists independently of him, his perception of it or his presence. This reality exists with or without us. It also exists even when nobody is observing it.

On the other hand, from a purely intellectual perspective, it is possible to imagine that all of this reality is just a figment of my imagination. One cannot logically prove the falsity of this point of view, which is known as *solipsism*.[1] Just as it is impossible to prove logically the incorrectness and falsity of the solipsistic view, it is not possible to prove, from a logical perspective, the realistic view, according to which reality exists objectively and is not dependent on us. In fact, this is our *belief* (and that of almost all people) in the existence of the material reality. Perhaps it is worth emphasizing that we see and feel only a small part of the physical and biological reality. Only a small part of reality *imposes* itself upon us. In the physical reality, those things that we are unable to grasp with our senses are much more abundant. We do not feel various physical fields (other than the gravitational field, and the electromagnetic field in a limited range of frequencies – in the optical, visual ranges), nor can we feel the various particles within matter. We only know about all these things indirectly through studying them, but we have no less confidence in their existence than in the existence of the things that we perceive with our senses.

I should mention one more thing. A person might believe that the material reality is real and nevertheless think that he is not dependent on his material environment, that he is *self-sufficient* – he does not need any external support. But this would be incorrect. Human beings cannot exist without the air that they breathe. Human beings need food and water from their environment. They need heat, and can only survive within a fairly narrow range of temperatures. The sun provides the necessary heat as well as the energy essential for life on Earth. So we can conclude that man is dependent on the solar system. One might think that this would be enough man is

---

1. Solipsism is a philosophical view that there is no reality other than myself alone.

capable of existing in a relatively small world. The size of the solar system and the enormous remote places of our universe do not affect his existence. However, modern science shows us otherwise: only a very large universe such as ours can make the existence of man possible. In order to produce the basic elements of life – carbon, nitrogen, oxygen and phosphorous – the simple elements, hydrogen and helium, which were present at the initial stage of the Big Bang, needed "to ripen" by way of thermonuclear reactions that took place inside the stars. When stars are extinguished, they explode into supernovae, and vital elements scatter in space and come together to form planets – and, eventually, to form us. This planetary "alchemy" requires a period of more than ten billion years.

> [F]or there to be enough time to construct the constituents of living beings, the Universe must be at least ten billion years old and therefore, as a consequence of its expansion, at least ten billion light years in extent. We should not be surprised to observe that the Universe is so large. No astronomer could exist in one that was significantly smaller. The Universe needs to be as big as it is in order to evolve just a single carbon-based life form.
> (J.D. Barrow & F.J. Tipler, The Anthropic Cosmological Principle, 3)

Hence, man does not stand alone and is not *self-sufficient*. The whole world sustains him.

However, there is another reality – a *spiritual reality* that requires a high level of sensitivity and scrutiny to understand it. It is here that opinions are divided. Some people believe in the objective existence of a spiritual reality – in this they are realists, since they believe in the real-ness of a spiritual reality. Others are *solipsists* with respect to the spiritual reality. They believe that the source of any spiritual existence is within man himself. That is to say, there is no objective spiritual reality the source of which is external to man.

I will clarify what I mean by the expression *"spiritual reality."* Emotions, will, desires, thoughts, creative actions, free will, the laws of ethics, and so on – all these are completely unconnected to the characteristics of matter, which has no feelings, thoughts or will. They belong to a different reality – a spiritual reality. In stating this, I am not making any claims about the essence of this reality or its source. As I have mentioned, some people believe that the spiritual reality belongs to man alone (and even that this reality has no independent status, but is solely derived from matter), while other people believe in the substance and objectivity of spiritual reality and see God as its source. We will devote a significant portion of this book to explaining the essence and nature of the spiritual reality.

4. THE DIVINE

A six-year old boy once asked his father: Is there a God? Perhaps because his father was not prepared for this question, or perhaps because this was really what he thought, he replied: "I don't know. Maybe there's a God." This was enough for the boy. It was as if his father had unequivocally solved the question of God's existence. A few days later, the boy's parents found him fervently praying. They were shocked and tried to stop him from praying, but only for a time.

I was that child. Since then, I have not been able to leave this issue alone. For the six-year-old boy, this was not a simple philosophical question, but an existential issue – there is someone to pray to, someone to talk to, man is not alone in the world.

But as time goes by, we lose the innocence of childhood. Along with our education and knowledge we also acquire preconceptions, and they stand in the way of our understanding the world in which we live. We tend to underestimate the value of feelings and to overestimate the roles of reason and logic, and especially the role of science. It is commonly believed that science can explain everything, and if there are still a few things that we cannot understand and explain, it is just a matter of time until we will eventually understand them. If, over time, science has explained things that were not previously understood, then – according to this way of thinking – the same applies to the present, for one day a new science will explain whatever we do not understand today.

However, this is not so. There are things which, by their very nature, science is incapable of understanding and explaining, and there are questions to which science will never be able to provide answers. Science deals with the description of the laws of nature and explains, through those laws, a range of various phenomena. Still, it is unable to answer questions such as: What is the source of the laws of nature? Where does the order in the world come from? Where does the world itself come from?

Nor is logic able to provide answers to questions of this kind. We therefore have no choice but to choose between two possible, diametrically opposed answers: (a) The world itself, by its nature, contains the cause of everything, the cause of the spiritual reality and the people and their creations that lie within it; and (b) The world has a rational basis, a source of reason and spirit, which is external to it – an ultimate spiritual entity. God is the source of everything, the source of spirit and matter; He created the world and He oversees it constantly. These two answers represent two different world views – the secular and the Jewish-religious.

The God of the Bible is *transcendental, personal* and *normative*.

We will discuss the personal and normative aspects of God in due course. God's transcendentalism is expressed in the fact that people do not have any way of grasping His essence. The Torah does not give us any hint as to God's essence, it only tells us about His revelations. When Moses asks God for His name, God's answer only indicates His existence in the world: "God said to Moses: 'I shall be who I shall be,' and He said: 'Thus shall you say to the children of Israel: I shall be has sent me to you.'" (*Exodus* 3:14).

Even though it is impossible to grasp the essence of God, many people believe in Him. But where does this belief in God come from? Is it possible to prove God's existence through logic? From our discussion in section 2 about the nature of logical proof, it is absolutely clear that it is impossible to prove God's existence. The term "to prove" means to infer a correct conclusion from a certain premise or fact. From a particular thing, which is assumed to be true, another thing is derived by logic – a correct conclusion. Logical proof connects two things, A and B, and states that B results from A, but in fact, B is already included in A. Thus, if a particular mathematical statement is derived from another statement, the former statement is already included in the latter one. Logical proof does not create any new truth. In a particular axiomatic system, all the statements (the theorems) that derive from these axioms are already included in them. However, in our world, we have nothing, no divine revelation, that is equal to God and that "includes" Him.

To prove the existence of God would mean to infer His existence from something that exists in our known reality. The absurdity of this enterprise is obvious. A logical syllogism only brings to light and clarifies something that is already included in the premise, something that already exists in our world.

Nevertheless, those who believe in God have a very high degree of certainty. First of all, I would like to point out that there are many things (perhaps most things are like this, in fact) that cannot be proven, but we humans have a deep faith in their existence. For example, it is impossible to prove that I have free will, but I have no doubt that I am always able to choose between various options available to me. Nevertheless, there are people who do not believe that man has free will. There is absolutely no way to prove the veracity of the *belief* in free will, just as there is no way to prove that a person does not have free will. To a person who claims that he *does* have free will, one can argue that his actions are a result of a sequence of causes and effects that began at the creation of the world, and the illusion of free will comes from the lack of knowledge of all the causes that led to a particular choice. Conversely, to a person who claims that he *does not* have free will because everything is pre-determined by the sequence of cause and effect, one can argue that there is no way to prove that there is a causal, deterministic connection between all the events in the world. There is no scientific experiment that is capable of establishing or refuting the existence of free will – it is not a matter of proof but an issue of belief. In section 7 we will elaborate more on the topic of free will. Another example that I have already mentioned is that there is no way of proving, solely through the use of logic, that the external world – everything except for me – truly exists. But any rational person *believes* in the existence of the world, and furthermore, this belief guides him in all his actions.

I would now like to show that faith in God is as solid as the examples above. Our accumulated experience teaches us that all things that have a particular order and sense, such as computers, clocks, pictures, musical works, articles, and so on, are always produced by somebody. When we study nature, clouds, mountains or sand on the beach, for example, sometimes we can discern an image of a person or an animal. Yet here, there is no creator or author. The thing is created "on its own," or, in other words, one might say that here, nature is the author. But this cannot be said of complex things. In such cases, there is always a creator. Now let us take a look at man, the most complex creatures we know: in order to record his entire genetic code in ordinary letters, we would need dozens of thick volumes, like those of the *Encyclopedia Britannica,* and on top of this, the human being also has a soul and free will! No one can prove that this was all created "by itself" without any creator. It would take a great deal of ignorance to think that any law of evolution proved the spontaneous creation of man from the inanimate world. In Chapter Six, we will return to this subject in a clearer and more organized way, but first, let us take a look at the inanimate world itself. A layman may think that there is no complexity here, but we have already seen in the Preface the testimony of Albert Einstein: "[The scientist's] religious feeling takes the form of a rapturous amazement at the harmony of natural law, which reveals an intelligence of such superiority that, compared with it, all the systematic thinking and acting of human beings is an utterly insignificant reflection" (*Ideas and Opinions*, 40).

Scientists discover complexity, sophistication, harmony and consistency in the inanimate world. A researcher who is examining nature is as if he is discovering hidden texts, which are not visible to the naked eye but are an inseparable part of the essence of nature – the laws of nature – the equations of Newton, Maxwell, Einstein, Schrödinger, and so on (see Part II: *The Laws of Nature*). It is such a sophisticated and complex world that in comparison, the most complex things that we are able to produce ourselves are like an "utterly insignificant reflection." What does all of this mean? If we always attribute man-made things to human creators, then surely we have a far greater reason to attribute the production of infinitely complex and sophisticated things, and the creation of the world itself, to a creator. I want to stress that this is not a proof of the existence of God, just as there is no proof for the existence of the external world. However, if we *believe* in the existence of our complex and sophisticated world, then we have an excellent reason to *believe* in its creator.

As Rabbi Soloveitchik wrote:

Just as consciousness of the world in general, and of the self in particular, do not involve logical demonstrations but constitute the spiritual essence of man, so too with the experience of the divine. It is totally aboriginal, the beginning and end of man's reality. *It is forever prior to inference or deduction.*[2] It is the most certain of all certainties, the truest of truths. If there is a world, if anything at all is real – and no one who has not been ensnared by vain sophistries has any doubt about this – then there is a God who is the foundation and origin of everything that exists. If there is a self, if man exists – and this, too, all

---

2. The emphasis here and in the citations throughout the book are mine. – B.F.

human beings know with certainty – then there is a living personal God who fills the consciousness of the self. It is impossible to think, to speak, to discuss the reality of the world and the reality of man without living and sensing the source of being: "I am that I am."

(And From There You Shall Seek, 12)

God is the most primary; He is greater than we can possibly think Him to be. Therefore, no logical proof of His existence can be possible. He is the most general, the most comprehensive entity, from which everything is derived. As Maimonides states:

> It is the most basic of basic principles and a support for wisdom to know that there is something [namely God] that existed before anything else did and that He created everything that there is. Everything in the skies, on the ground and in between exists only because of the fact that He created them. Let it be known that if the Creator did not exist then nothing else would, for nothing can exist independently of the Creator. Let it further be known that if everything ceased to exist, the Creator alone would exist and would not have ceased to exist like everything else had. All things in creation are dependent upon the Creator for their continued existence, but He does not need any of them [for His continued existence]. (Mishneh Torah, The Book of Knowledge, Fundamentals of Torah 1:1–3)

God is the creator and the source of all the reality in the world, both spiritual and physical. Therefore, the spiritual reality has an objective standing that is not dependent on the consciousness of any man, since its source is God. Just as we believe that the physical reality has an objective standing, that the physical world is not a hallucination or an illusion, in the same way, the spiritual reality has an objective source. This is the same sole source of all reality – spiritual and physical, the same. This is the source of all reality – an absolute, ultimate spiritual entity – namely, God.

It is worth mentioning here that, recently, several books and papers on the subject of the anthropic principle (*anthropos* is the Greek word for "man") have been published.[3] It is possible to show that even the most minute changes in the parameters of the laws of nature, such as the charge and mass of an electron, the constant of gravity, and the like, would make any life in

---

3. See Chapter Five, section 2, and the comprehensive work *The Anthropic Cosmological Principle* by J.D. Barrow & F.J. Tipler.

God is the Subject of Everything

There is another important aspect to the discussion of the possibility of proof of the existence of God. Scientific research of reality is based on the premise that it is always possible to isolate a part of the physical reality and to treat it as an object of research. The scientist detaches a particular section of the world and treats it as a closed, isolated system. Thus, he is able to predict the movements of the system. Of course detaching and isolating the system from the matter means also disconnecting it from the spirit, from the spiritual reality and, most of all, from the scientist himself and from his spirit. Only then are we capable of discussing the existence of the object of the research. When I talk about the existence of my external world, I divide the whole world into two parts: me and the *rest of the world*, without me. The external world (without me) is the object, while I am the subject. But it is not always possible to make this division, especially when we are talking about *spiritual* reality. I am not able to divide my "self" into two separate parts – the object self and the subject self. My self is not an entity that can be divided into separate parts. We are used to the fact that a physical thing can always be divided into parts, but it is difficult for us to think of spiritual reality being divided into two parts: the self and the rest of the spirit. My self cannot be isolated from the world of the spirit. Thus, it is all the more impossible to separate my self and God. God is not an object; He is the subject of everything. The existence of God precedes the existence of all reality, including my self and other people's selves. The existence of all reality is dependent on God. A god that we can talk about as our object and whose existence we can talk about is not a god but an idol.

the universe impossible, including, of course, human life. One might say that our world is fine-tuned in the most subtle of ways to the goal of life – in order that animals and people will be produced. When we argue against the anthropic principle, we take into account the possibility (which has a certain plausibility) that many, or even infinite, parallel worlds that have different laws of nature exist. If so, it is no wonder that we exist specifically in the world that is fine-tuned to the existence of life. Once again, this example shows that it is not possible to prove the existence of the tuner, of the Creator of the world, just as it is impossible to prove His non-existence.

One could argue that when we arrive at the reality of God by theoretical reasoning, it does not change our lives. A God such as this is a *transcendental* god – people are not capable of understanding Him, and we have no way of knowing His attitude towards us or whether He is at all involved in worldly matters. The intellectual inference that God exists cannot be a basis for any religion. Only when God reveals Himself and becomes involved in people's lives does He change them. And herein lies the question: are there any scientific tools with which we can investigate divine revelations? The answer is unequivocal: science is not capable of contributing anything to the subject of divine revelation. By its very nature, science investigates things that exist in large quantities, such as atoms and molecules, and repetitive events like the four seasons. In contrast, every meeting between people is a one-off event that does not repeat itself. All the more so, every meeting with God is a unique event.

Many people have felt God's presence in a very profound way, but we, the Jewish people, have a collective memory of His revelations. We owe the essence of our peoplehood to our connection with God and His revelations, a connection documented in the ancient annals of history of the People of Israel. This book, the Bible, is a book of testimonies of numerous revelations that occurred to the nation, and to individuals within the nation, over a fairly long period of time. The Bible does not deal with proofs of the existence of God at all, but rather it tells of people's encounters with Him. Because of its content, this book has been preserved and passed on from generation to generation with the utmost fidelity. The God of Israel is the God of Abraham, the God of Isaac and the God of Jacob. He is both a *transcendental* and a *personal* God, with whom we can have a connection. He is also a *normative* God, setting norms of behavior for us and commanding us to comply with them.

Many people are prepared to recognize a transcendental God but are not prepared to recognize His personal nature. We have inherited from the Greeks the metaphysical idea of God as a pure entity that is not capable of any change or action. The tendency of "modern" thought, which is influenced by the achievements of science over many centuries, is to turn our thought process into something mechanical rather than human, to instill the idea that personality is something subjective and therefore not real, and that reality, represented by science, is impersonal, lacking spirituality and lacking spirit. This is the price of the viewpoint that science is capable of describing and explaining everything. In the words of Martin Buber:

> The description of God as a Person is indispensable for everyone who like myself means by "God" not a principle (although mystics like Eckhart sometimes identify him with "Being") and like myself means by "God" not an idea (although philosophers like Plato at times could hold he was this): but who rather means by "God," as I do, him who – whatever else he may be – enters into a direct relation with us men in creative, revealing and redeeming acts, and thus makes it possible for us to enter into a direct relation with him. This ground and meaning of our existence constitutes a mutuality, arising again and again, such as can subsist only between persons. The concept of personal being is indeed completely incapable of declaring what God's essential being is, but it is both permitted and necessary to say that God is also a Person.
>
> (I and Thou, 135)

I have no doubt that many people, many more than one might imagine, have had religious experiences, and furthermore, that very many more people have had and continue to have contact with God, even if they do not know this. Later on in this book (Chapter Four, section 5) and in *Creation Ex Nihilo*, I demonstrate that scientific discoveries also have a quality of divine revelation. Incidentally, Martin Buber relates that his book, *I and Thou*, is in fact a testimony to the revelation that he himself has felt over a fairly prolonged period of time. As I mentioned above, Jews have a collective memory of divine revelations, which is documented in the Bible. I have been involved in science all my life, and scientific skepticism is deeply ingrained in my consciousness. Therefore, I can understand the skepticism that hampers many people's acceptance of the testimonies in the Bible. However, that very same scientific meticulousness demands that we do not approach that book with preconceptions, selectively accepting "historical" testimonies while denying the spiritual, divine issue that is at the very crux of the Bible.

The Jewish standpoint with respect to God's connection with the world can be summarized in the words of Rabbi Soloveitchik: "God reveals Himself to His creation above and beyond nature, bringing prophecies to human beings. This is the new Torah that was given at Sinai to slaves who had become free, and who then gave it to the rest of the world" (*And From There You Shall Seek*, 29–30).

I have not exhausted the subject of God here. We will return again and again to various aspects of the subject below and throughout the rest of the book.

5. THE MESSAGE OF THE TORAH AND THE BIBLE

Our world, the world in which people live and of which they are a part, is extremely complex and contains innumerable facets. It has "routine" events that repeat themselves over and over. As we have already mentioned, by its very nature science can deal with things and events of this type. It deals with *regular* things, things to which some sort of *rules* apply. However important these things and the science which deals with them are, they do not comprise the whole of our world, and from a certain perspective they are not the most important things in it. Perhaps the unique, one-of-a-kind events are the most important. Indeed, every real creation is a unique event, a new thing that does not come from something that already existed, *creation ex nihilo* – for if this were not the case, then it would not be a creation.[4] Each of us human beings is a new, unique phenomenon, even though we all have much in common. While the shared attributes can be the subject of science, our most precious possession, that thing which is special to me, to you, to all human beings, does not belong to science.

The study of creations, of unique things, is on a different plane from scientific study. Take, for example, a musical work. When the composer created it, the work was a one-off, unique action. But how do other people comprehend it? The performer reads its score and performs it. People listen to performances of it in a concert hall or on the radio, and the act of listening gives them a good feeling. Hundreds of years can pass from the writing of a particular musical work, but its performance continues to have an effect, reaching more and more people. This is the "proof" of the genuineness of creation. I write the word in quotation marks, since this is not logical proof but rather support, which is completely different. "Proof" of creation lies in

---

4.   This is not a proof that these are the qualities of the creation, but rather the search for a definition of creation. The question of whether a true creation exists at all is a metaphysical one. In a deterministic world, there is no place for new creations or anything new at all, but the question of whether our world is deterministic or non-deterministic is on the metaphysical plane. I will address this later on.

its effect on many people over a long period of time. The effect of a genuine creation does not fade with time.

This characterizes all types of spiritual creations. Man himself is capable of affecting his fellow man, of arousing different emotions in him and of bringing him to a certain mental state. But the *creation* of man is capable of affecting many people at various times.

Now let us turn to the most important creation in human history: the Torah and the entire Bible. This book constitutes a detailed report of the various aspects of the encounter between man and God. Many thinkers have discussed this subject, including Rabbi Judah Halevi in his work *The Kuzari*, as well as modern-day Jewish philosophers such as Eliezer Berkovits in his book, *God, Man and History*, and Emil Fackenheim in his books, *What Is Judaism?*, *Quest for Past and Future* and *God's Presence in History*.

It is clearly not possible to prove through logic alone the occurrence of the encounter with the Creator, just as it is impossible to prove the existence of the Creator Himself. I have already explained in *Creation Ex Nihilo*, and will explain further later on, that it is impossible to attain an understanding of reality and knowledge of the world, including scientific knowledge, through human reason alone. God's involvement and revelation are crucial.[5] Both The Torah and the entire Bible contain evidence for the encounter with God. This evidence has been preserved meticulously and passed on through the generations. A whole people, the people of the Book, stands guard over it. But this is not just a technical matter. As with other genuine creations, a kind of unbroken transmission exists through the generations: "Neither with you only do I make this covenant and this oath; but with him that stands here with us this day before the Lord our God, and also with him that is not here with us this day" (Deuteronomy 29:13–14).

The relationship between Jews and the Torah is a special one. Torah study is not the academic study of a book, like the study of history. In addition to its cognitive aspect, Torah study has the status of holiness, prayer and worship. In the daily prayer book, in the second blessing before the recitation of

---

5. There is an apparent contradiction here. On the one hand, without God's involvement, there is no knowledge of the world, but on the other hand, we are not able to prove the existence of God. Knowledge of the world is like a miracle. We will address this further in Chapter Four.

the Shema in the evening service, it is written: "... and we will rejoice with the words of your Torah and with Your commandments for all eternity. For they are our life and the length of our days, and upon them we will meditate day and night." Every sentence of the Torah is open to interpretation. The interpretations are innovative insights (*hiddushim*) that are drawn based on an understanding of the period in which they were written. There is a dialectic integration of *hiddushim* of the Torah together with the meticulous preservation of every single letter in the Torah text, and each generation adds its own insights. On Mount Sinai, the Jews received both the words and the spirit of the Torah. The prophets' successors were the sages, who interpreted the words of the Torah and defined their meaning, but with the passage of time a new understanding and new interpretations were needed. The Torah continues to reveal its meaning to people. The spiritual process continues.

The Torah can be divided into two main parts: the narrative part and the normative, legal part. In Hebrew, the word "Torah" means "law" or "norm." The narrative part includes stories about the creation of the world, the beginning of humanity, the history of the nation of Israel until just before they entered their land. The normative part includes commandments and laws that prescribe how one should act. The two parts are connected to each other, and often one cannot understand one part without taking the other into account. When we talk about the narrative part of the Torah, the question immediately arises: what is the purpose of this part? One might suppose that it is related to the natural sciences and history, as many people believe to this day. As a result of some people's adherence to this view in the past, others were persecuted and even burnt at the stake. In other cases, it prevented people from engaging in scientific and historical research for fear of retribution. However, this view did not originate with the Jewish people. Its chief proponent was the Catholic Church.

It is well known that the narrative part of the Torah is not a textbook of the natural sciences. But in the modern age, many people who regard themselves as intellectuals believe that Judaism, and in particular the Torah, contradicts modern science. In the twenty-first century, how can any intelligent and educated person believe in Bible stories?

In my opinion, views such as this originate in a misunderstanding of both the nature of science and the nature of the messages in the Torah. We will discuss how this relates the nature of science and its limitations in later chapters. Here, I would like to mention that there is no contradiction between the foundations of science and the messages in the Torah. There is nothing in the equations of quantum mechanics or in the general theory of relativity that can contradict the Torah. The application of science to areas that are not relevant to it may be the source of the misunderstandings. For example, the attempt to use science to examine things and events that are unique, such as different creations, may lead to apparent contradictions with the Torah. But we will discuss this further in due course. At this point, let us talk about the nature of the messages in the Torah.

What is it about the Torah – and the Bible as a whole – that is so special compared with any other work? The significance of the Torah is in its presentation of man facing God, since it is the only documentation of its kind of such an encounter. This is presented in a number of different ways: through narrative, poetry and symbolism. It is clear that the messages in the Torah, by their very nature, must be eternal, and this is where we encounter a problem. As it must, "The Torah speaketh in the language of the sons of man." (Maimonides, *Guide of the Perplexed*, 1:26; *Berachot* 31b; *Yevamot* 71a and others).This means that the Torah must use concepts and terminology with which people at the time of the giving of the Torah were familiar. The Torah could not use, for example, concepts taken from modern mathematics or from the general theory of relativity because people at that time would not have understood them, just as most people do not understand them even today. (Likewise, people in the future will know concepts and terminology that we would find incomprehensible.) But the messages of the divine revelation must be understood by people throughout the generations.

Thus, in its description of creation, the Torah uses words and concepts that were familiar to people at the time that the Torah was given. "And a wind from God moved over the surface of the waters" (*Genesis* 1:2). Rabbi Yehuda Halevi explains the concepts that appear in the verse: "... which, by the will of God encompassing [the primary matter], assumed a certain character and the name 'Spirit of God.' The comparison of the primary matter with water is most suitable, because no compact substance can arise from a material which is finer than water ..." (*The Kuzari*, Part Four, 25). In other words, the concepts "water" and "wind" should not be understood according to their literal meaning, but allegorically.

It is clear that in order to understand the deep meaning of the messages in the Torah, we must do some kind of "filtering" and "adjusting," and we must ignore certain things that are related to the period in which the Torah was written. Thus, when the book of Genesis gives an account of the great flood, there is no *hiddush* here. The peoples of ancient orient also have stories of the flood. In those stories, the flood is caused by the will of certain gods and against the will of other gods. One person for whom the gods have special affection is saved from the destruction. According to the Torah, the flood was caused by the will of the one and only God, who performed a just and righteous act: He brought punishment on mankind, which had become corrupt, and saved the only family that had kept its integrity. What is important is not what the Torah says in accordance with commonly-held beliefs, but what it teaches us that is in contrast to these beliefs. It aims to teach us that a singular, just God rules over the world, that everything that happens in the world and that seems to be supernatural is a result of direct action by God, and that there is no place for magic or witchcraft. It is important to understand that the Torah does not teach its lesson in a simple, theoretical manner, but in a way that was acceptable according to the beliefs and knowledge of the people of the generation in which the Torah was given ("according to the state of science" of that generation). If the people of that generation had not believed that a flood had occurred – and this has nothing to do with whether the story of the flood is true or not – the Torah would not have used that story to teach its lesson. The important thing here is not the historical accuracy of the particular event, but rather its conclusions and the lessons that it teaches. Such an approach to the narrative of the Bible was accepted amongst the Amoraim (Talmudic scholars), as stated by the scholar who claimed in the presence of Shmuel Bar Nahmani, "Job never existed at all. He was just a parable" (*Bava Batra* 15a), and "There never was a stubborn and rebellious son [Deuteronomy 21:18–21]. Rather, this was written merely that we might study it and receive the reward for studying."

The Torah does not teach in a philosophical, abstract way. It uses things that are familiar to and accepted by everyone. *What the Torah teaches is not dependent on what is known or generally accepted.* If the Torah had been given at a different time or under different circumstances, it would have based what it said on other ideas and assumptions, *but its spiritual message would have been no different.* Everything that is mentioned in the Torah about nature and mankind, based solely on the state of scientific knowledge at the time of the writing of the Torah, is of no absolute value. Only that which is stated about God and His actions toward nature and man has absolute value. The Torah and the entire Bible are a unique account of man's encounter with God – and herein lies the Torah's special importance to humanity as a whole.

Now let us turn to an issue that has troubled many people – believers, non-believers and those who are unsure – the issue of the creation of the world and its development as described in the Book of Genesis versus the cosmological and cosmogonical modern-day scientific theories. I should point out that eminent thinkers are not troubled by this issue. As we mentioned in the Preface, Rabbi Soloveitchik, one of the pre-eminent thinkers of the twentieth century, completely ignores the difference between the scientific theory of evolution of the universe and the description of creation in the Torah. He wrote, "I have never been seriously troubled by the problem of the Biblical doctrine of creation vis-à-vis the scientific story of evolution at both the cosmic and the organic levels, nor have I been perturbed by the confrontation of the mechanistic interpretation of the human mind with the Biblical spiritual concept of man" (*Lonely Man of Faith*, 7).

The scientific description of the development of the world is on another plane from the biblical description of the creation of the world. The Torah's account has the connotation of a plan or an idea. "With ten utterances the world was created" (*Ethics of the Fathers* 5:1). The "utterance" is transformed into reality: "And God said 'Let there be light,' and there was light" (Genesis 1:3). The Torah describes a process of planning – "Let there be light" – and then, directly afterward, the result – "and there was light." In contrast, science relates solely to the stage of implementation. Thus I see no contradiction between the conceptual, designed, *divine* path of the Torah and the scientific, material, physical path of implementation. They are simply on two different planes.

While our understanding of the universe and the physical world, our knowledge and science, all change with the passage of time, the metaphysical messages inherent in the Torah never change. At various periods in the past, before the twentieth century, both scientists and philosophers believed that the world had not been created but had always existed. Today, the Big Bang Theory (see Chapter Five), a theory that apparently supports the premise that the world was created, is widely accepted. However, as with all scientific theories, the Big Bang Theory has its limitations, and many scientists expect that a more precise theory will back up the version that the world has always existed. But it is not the role of science to determine whether the world was created or has always existed. Indeed, the creation of the world, the creation of the laws of nature and the laws of time and space are all outside the scope of science. They cannot be tested experimentally. These are metaphysical issues that belong to the Torah, while science describes phenomena and events in the world that has already been created.

Some people, including some rabbis, insist upon understanding the Torah literally and extracting seemingly scientific information from it. They perform simple arithmetic: the world was created in six days, which is one hundred and forty-four hours. (Each day has twenty-four hours, and 6 × 24 = 144 hours.) Here comes the contradiction between Torah and science: science claims that the development of the world up until the appearance of man took approximately fifteen billion years, compared with the Torah's 144 hours of creation, including the creation of human beings. We have already said that the Torah is not a physics, cosmology or cosmogony textbook and that the message of the Torah is a spiritual message of divine planning. Incidentally, the lack of logic in the above calculation becomes apparent when we take into account the fact that according to the Book of Genesis, in the first three days the solar system had not yet been created, and therefore there is no reason to think that one day was twenty-four hours long. On the other hand, according to modern-day cosmological theory, approximately ten billion years passed between the Big Bang and the formation of the solar system. This would mean that based on the literal interpretation here, the first three days took ten billion years!

Do not think that the insistence on a literal interpretation of creation is typical of Jewish philosophers. We have already mentioned Rabbi Soloveitchik's view. The *rishonim* (medieval commentators), including Maimonides in the *Guide for the Perplexed* and Rabbi Yehuda Halevi in *The Kuzari*, were prepared to discuss the possibility of an eternal world in order to match the philosophical theories that were commonly accepted in the period in which they wrote. Below is the commentary of a twentieth-century thinker, Rabbi Eliyahu Eliezer Dessler, who quotes Nachmanides. He writes in his book, *Michtav me-Eliyahu*:

"Because six days did God make Heaven and earth . . . ." The days referred to here relate to the period before the completion of creation, when the concept of time was different from that which applies now. But the Torah was given to us in accordance with our own concepts: "Moshe came and brought it down to earth." This is the meaning of the dictum, "The Torah speaks as if in human language"; it speaks to us in accordance with our own perceptions of matter and our own concepts of space and time. And everything discussed in the Torah with respect to matters preceding the end of creation were brought by Moshe from God, using concepts that we are able to understand. Just as we explain to a blind person that which he cannot see using descriptions from the sense of touch and the like, the spiritual matter is brought to us in a material form which, with some imagination, has some connection to the spiritual matter, and through this we can comprehend it as much as possible.

See Nachmanides, Genesis 1:3:

". . . .in the profounder sense, the Emanations issuing from the Most High are called 'days,' for every Divine Saying which evoked an existence is called 'day.' These were six, for Unto God there is the greatness, and the power, etc. [the six spheres from] The explanation of the order of the verses in terms of this profound interpretation is sublime and recondite. Our knowledge of it is less than that of a drop from the vast ocean."

We see from this that in the simple meaning of the text – that which is conveyed to us in accordance with our own conceptual capacity – we are to understand actual days made up of hours and minutes. But in its real essence, that is to say, in its inner meaning, the text has quite a different connotation. It refers to six spheres, which are modes of revelation of the divine conduct of the world and it was only written for our benefit as if it were six days. And how do the six days hint to the six revelations? This is "sublime and recondite," in the words of Nachmanides.

In the excellent book by Rabbi Nehunya ben Hakana, the question is asked why it is written, "Six days God created the heaven and the earth," when it should have been written "In six days . . . ." He explains that this teaches that each day has its own power. This means: each day in itself is a separate creation; hence it says "Six days," namely, the days themselves were created then. This teaches that every day has its own power, its own substance – its own revelations, as at that time the concept of the special revelation explained to us in the Torah in the name of a certain day, and which alludes to the fact of that particular revelation, was created. This illustrates how the six days are six powers and six revelations by which the heaven and earth were created. (Michtav me-Eliyahu, Vol. B, 151)

I should add one more thing that is often ignored. Hebrew word *yom* which is used in Torah is translated by English word *day*. However, the word *yom* in general has different connotations than the word *day*. Thus it is written in Exodus, "Six yom shall you work, but on the seventh yom you shall rest; in plowing and in harvest you shall rest" (34:21). The Ibn Ezra explains here: "Since the full yom that is commonly known is the movement of the upper sphere from the east to the west in twenty-four hours. And the yom of the sun is three hundred and sixty-five days . . . ."

The Torah itself is "aware" of possible arguments regarding how one is to understand the concept of "day," (*yom*) and it therefore gives a precise definition: "And God called the light yom (Day), and the darkness He called Night . . ." (Genesis 1:5). Rabbi Saadia Gaon explains: "God called the periods of light yom (*day*) and the periods of darkness *night*." The Radak (Rabbi David Kimche) also supports this explanation. Hence, the Torah uses the word yom-"day" as the period of time of the action of light – the *illumination* period. It is clear that when the Torah talks about light, this is not just physical light, but it is first and foremost spiritual light. According to the Kabbalah, the projection of this light – illumination – is the emanation of light from God: the spheres are the illumination of the infinite.

Since creation is primarily a spiritual act, the spiritual content of the days of creation is what determines the relative importance of each of the six days. The Torah allocates three days to the first essential ten billion years, according to scientific estimates, while one day was allocated to the creation of living creatures and man. The Book of Genesis is not a chronology, nor is it a history or an information booklet on nature and the world. It presents man opposite God. The order of priorities of the Book of Genesis, which was determined according to the spiritual value of the various elements of creation, is expressed, *inter alia*, in the amount of space devoted to those elements. Thus, everything that the Torah says about the formation of the world is written in thirty-four verses, whereas it devotes more than three hundred and fifty verses to the building of the sanctuary and its dedication.

We have devoted our discussion thus far to the relationship between Torah and science. What about the relationship between Torah and philosophy?

It is generally accepted that western civilization is based on two sources, Greek philosophy and the Bible. The formation of western civilization is often described as "Athens meets Jerusalem," an encounter between Greek philosophy and the Jewish world view. This view was adopted by Christianity and Islam in different ways.

Neither Greek philosophy nor its legacy, western philosophy, is uniform. In fact, both include various materialistic and idealistic philosophical doctrines. All of these doctrines are based on certain metaphysical assumptions, such as determinism or non-determinism, free will and the like, which cannot be proved or confirmed through logic or experimentation. This begs the question: how can we discern, from all the different metaphysical assumptions, which of them are "true"? This will be discussed in the next chapter.

At this point, I would like to summarize my opinion regarding the nature of the message of the Torah. It is a spiritual message, complex and open to interpretation by people in every generation. But in this world, in our world, there is no choice other than to wrap a spiritual message in a physical covering. It is not just that every word of the message is made up of written or printed characters or that materials are used in this endeavor, but that these words, sentences and concepts are taken from man's accumulated day-to-day experience – *the Torah speaks according to the language of man*. It is therefore vital that we distinguish between the *spiritual message*, *spiritual content*, and the *physical wrapping* of the message. Any attempts to verify or deny the facts related to the physical wrapping fail to touch on the spiritual message of the Torah.

6. METAPHYSICAL PRINCIPLES AND THE TORAH

> The homo religiosus ... is not concerned with interpreting God in terms of the world but the world under the aspect of God.   (*Halakhic Mind*, 45)

At the basis of our understanding of our world and our behavior within it lie several metaphysical principles, such as:

(a) The existence of the world and its lawfulness
(b) The unity and uniformity of the laws of nature
(c) Causality versus the appearance of new things, creation *ex nihilo*
(d) Determinism versus non-determinism and free will

All these are examples of metaphysical principles. How do we adopt certain metaphysical principles and reject others? Even if it seems to us that a certain metaphysical principal is self-evident, we cannot prove it. This brings us to a situation of arbitrariness. I believe that we have free will, but I know people who do not believe in free will at all. It is impossible to decide one way or the other, either by experiment or by reason. It is the same with all metaphysical assumptions. In this book I take an unequivocal view: *the Torah (and the Bible in general) is the source of the metaphysical principles.* This view is derived from belief in God – that He is the source of all existence. It is clear that the Torah contains metaphysical messages. In fact the whole Torah is one big metaphysical message. What this means is that the Torah's messages cannot be achieved through intellectual reasoning or experimentation. If they could, mankind would not have needed divine revelation, which is the substance of the Torah. Hence, whenever we must choose between various metaphysical possibilities, we turn to the Torah to find the solution.

Now we will take a look at the problem of understanding the world. One aspect of this problem is the issue of Torah versus science. Sometimes this is presented as a problem of reconciling Torah and science, while in fact we use the achievements of science to prove the truth of the Torah. As mentioned above, this an impossible task. It is an attempt to draw general conclusions from a limited number of data and from the specific to the general, known as the induction principle. In Chapter Four, we will see the falsity of the induction principle: it is impossible to infer a generality from a specific. The different levels of knowledge are presented in the following diagram:

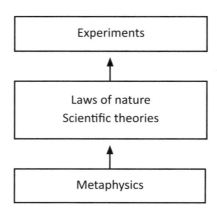

The first level is the level of experiments. In Chapter Four, we will prove that it is impossible to infer a scientific theory from experimental data, though, conversely, it is possible to test a scientific theory that has the status of conjecture – a hypothesis – using experiments. In addition, all scientific theories are based on a number of metaphysical principles; however, it is impossible to infer a scientific theory unequivocally from metaphysical axioms since different scientific theories can have the same metaphysical basis. Likewise, different experiments can be suitable for one theoretical basis.

As we have explained, we have no interest in scientific proofs of religious truths. That would be impossible, just as it is impossible to prove science by experimental statements. In fact, the opposite is true. We will look in the Torah, as an expression of divine revelation, for a justification of the metaphysical axioms that lie at the basis of scientific theories as shown in the following diagram:

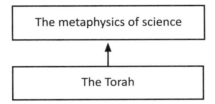

We will go from the metaphysics of religion to the metaphysics of science. At the beginning of this chapter, I included a partial quotation from Rabbi Soloveitchik. Below is the full text of the quotation:

> The prime problem of the philosophy of religion is not theosophy or theology but the understanding of the sensible world. The homo religiosus is not only theocentric but also ontocentric. He is not concerned with interpreting God in terms of the world but the world under the aspect of God.
>
> (*The Halakhic Mind,* 45)

I would like to stress the change in direction. We have explained above that it is wrong to search for proofs that the statements of the Torah regarding nature can be reconciled with the results of scientific research in each generation, and that it is wrong to try to reconcile the Torah with different philosophical doctrines, as if these proofs would prove the truth of the Torah. According to the new approach that we received at Mount Sinai, the source of all reality, including our very existence, is in the divine. Rabbi Soloveitchik presents Maimonides's doctrine as follows:

> [This is the new teaching that was given to Moses with the statement "I am that I am," as Maimonides interpreted it: I exist necessarily, and any attribution of existence is only a metaphor for My infinite existence, whose necessity is its essence [essence = truth = existence]. True existence is divine existence and everything that exists "depends on it" for its existence. This theory is one of the most wonderful and profound thoughts that our great teacher put at the center of his world.   (And From There You Shall Seek, 158–159, n. 4)

Let us summarize by saying that one cannot reinforce the Torah by reconciling it with science and philosophy. And there is no basis for the common converse tendency to refute the Torah by showing its apparent incompatibility with science or with a certain philosophy. I should point out that laymen are not the only ones who make this mistake – philosophers sometimes do so as well. In fact, the Torah is the source of metaphysical principles, of science and of philosophy.

7. FREE WILL

During my life, I have made several choices that have had major effects not just on me and my own life, but also on the lives of many others. In my youth, I chose science as my goal in life. It was not easy to realize my choice given the anti-Semitic policies of the former Soviet Union, but I succeeded nonetheless. Articles and books that I have published have had an effect on others. I published a book that provided a theoretical basis to a new field that was just starting to develop: quantum electronics (the physics of lasers). The book was the first in its field, and eleven thousand copies were sold in the Soviet Union. It was translated into English and German and it had a significant impact on the development of the field. Other important choices in my life include the decision to join the Jewish national movement in the Soviet Union and the decision to immigrate to Israel. Still other significant choices connected with the previous ones, such as the choice to arrange, together with friends, unofficially and against the will of the authorities, a symposium on Jewish culture in Soviet Russia in Moscow in 1976. That choice and its implementation had many repercussions on the Soviet Union and the rest of the world. On December 24, 1976, the New York Times published an editorial about the Soviet authorities' actions to suppress the symposium:

> If it were not fundamentally so serious, there would be much that is comic about the frenzied Soviet reaction to the unofficial symposium on Jewish culture this week in Moscow.
>
> It seemed at times as though all the non-nuclear forces of the Kremlin had been mobilized to halt this fearsome threat to Soviet power . . . .

Our entire lives are a string of choices and decisions, some more important than others. If my ability to choose, my free will, is taken away from me, I will cease to be *me*. I will cease to be a person, and I will also cease to be a creative being. I am absolutely convinced of this. But philosophers who have devoted a great deal of time and effort to the issue of free will have concluded that there is no logical or scientific proof of the existence of free will, just as there can be no proof of the non-existence of free will. Our knowledge of the existence of free will is not based on logical inference. Free will is a direct, unmediated human experience.

The concept of free will is a metaphysical concept. This means that it is impossible to prove the existence of free will through experiment or by logic. Nonetheless, no rational person doubts his ability to make decisions, to choose, to change his mind, to overcome his inclinations and his weaknesses and to act against his strongest instincts. But a word of caution: sometimes people confuse free will with the freedom to achieve certain goals. I am free to choose between various options, but I am not free to achieve whatever I want. For example, let's say that I am offered a better job that the one I currently have. I am free to choose whether to stay at my current job or to accept the offer of the better job. But when I decide, out of free will, to accept the job offer, there is no guarantee that it will actually turn out to be better – in other words, I do not have the absolute freedom to achieve. Our choices do not always lead us to our expected goals.

From a religious perspective, free will is a matter of faith. Judaism's standpoint is clear: free will, which is one of the principles of our faith, is ingrained in the consciousness of every believing Jew. The principle of free will is a necessary condition of the Jewish ethical system. As Maimonides writes in the final chapter of *Eight Chapters – Introduction to Commentary on Ethics of the Fathers*: "Were a man compelled to act according to the dictates of predestination, then the commands and prohibitions of the Law would become null and void and the Law would be completely false, since man would have no freedom of choice in what he does. Moreover, *it would be useless, in fact absolutely in vain,* for man to study, to instruct, or attempt to learn an art . . ." (*Eight Chapters*, Chapter Eight). And later, in the same chapter, "In reality, the undoubted truth of the matter is that man has full sway over all his actions. If he wishes to do a thing, he does it; if he does not wish to do it, he need not . . . God said: See, I have set before thee this day life and the good, death and evil . . . therefore choose life." In the Babylonian Talmud (*Berachot* 33b), Rabbi Hanina states: "Everything is in the hands of heaven except for the fear of heaven." This means that man is given the freedom to choose to serve God or not. *Without the infrastructure of free will, Judaism becomes no more than a collection of parables without normative validity.*

The Midrash relates that the creation of humanity was a kind of revolution. This man, for whom the entire world was created, at first was not created with a consensus:

> At the time that the Holy One, Blessed Be He, came to create Adam, Benevolence said: Create, and Truth said: Don't create. He picked up Truth and cast her to the ground. The ministering angels said: Lord of the World, why do you curse your Truth? While the ministering angels were arguing, God created him. (Bereshit Rabbah, 5)

What was the nature of the objection to the creation of man? The entire creation, without man functions in complete harmony with the Creator's will. There is only one part of creation that is not compelled to act specifically according to the will of the Creator, but is free to act according to its own will. This exceptional case is man, the possessor of choice. Here God is on the brink of bringing into the world a new entity that is liable to violate the harmony in creation. It is this innovation that arouses the objection to his creation.

The ministering angels saw creation as a perfect composition that was liable to be spoiled by man's involvement. This was not God's intention. He viewed creation as a work that needed completing, as the Torah states: "which God created to make," and the only creature able to complete it is man (not an act of "perfecting" but rather of "completion," according to Rabbi Kook).

The principle of free will is not a scientific principle, but an "unscientific" principle. We cannot prove its existence through scientific experiment or logical inference. It is a metaphysical principle without which no ethical system could exist. Free will is actually a *belief* without which the concepts of good and bad would have no significance, the life of man would be pointless and the concept of "morality," based on the concepts of good and bad, would be meaningless.

This is all well and good, but how is free will compatible with general causality, with the fact that everything has a cause? In other words, since there are scientific laws that determine everything in the world, where does free will come from? If everything is determined by the laws of nature, we do not, in fact, have free will. All of our behavior can be predicted in advance,[6] and what we see as free will is simply an illusion: we are not free. We will discuss determinism – the idea that everything in the world is determined in advance – in greater detail later, but at this point I can identify the metaphysical assumption that lies at the basis of these conclusions. The assumption is that science, and physics in particular, describes everything in the world and all the phenomena within it.

Of course, there is absolutely no chance of proving the premise that science is capable of describing and predicting all the phenomena in the world. This is a metaphysical assumption. We have already stated that in this book, we are examining metaphysical principles based on their compatibility with the Torah. Based on this, as we have learnt from the discussion in this chapter, free will is completely compatible with the Torah. But let us take a look at the assumption that contradicts free will, the premise that all phenomena can be described by science. It is not just that this is a metaphysical assumption that is unprovable; it also contradicts our entire experience. A key characteristic of science is that it can predict things, whereas our day-to-day experience teaches us that science cannot describe or predict most of the phenomena around us. It is worth remembering that scientific prediction

---

6. While it is true that according to quantum mechanics precise prediction is not possible, that does not change matters. The uncertainty of quantum mechanics has no connection with free will. We will discuss this in greater depth later on.

is always well-defined – even if there is inaccuracy in the prediction, it is known about in advance.

Now let us place ourselves in the shoes of the scientist who is trying to carry out scientific research with the utmost objectivity. We step outside and look at everything that moves and changes with time. We see many cars moving around the city streets. When I examine the movement of the cars, I quickly come to the conclusion that it would be absolutely impossible to make a scientific prediction about it. Concepts of scientific accuracy, including defined inaccuracy, do not apply to the movement of cars. One cannot scientifically predict the route of any particular car. The problem is that all of these cars are driven by people who determine their routes. There is no way to use scientific laws, the laws of nature, to determine the people's routes, whether they are driving in their cars or walking around the city streets. I have no doubt that the laws of nature also apply to people and the cars driven by them. But the issue is that in addition to the laws of nature, there is another factor that influences the people's movements: free will. Human behavior is determined both by the laws of nature and by their free will, and this is why the scientist is unable to predict human beings' actions scientifically.

According to the view that I am presenting here, free will has an independent status. According to the opposing view, free will does not exist: what we see as free will is actually, first and foremost, a derivative of the laws of nature and the laws of physics. It only seems to us that we are free to choose between the various options available to us, while we should actually consider all the causes that preceded that particular decision and all the causes that preceded those causes, all the way back to the creation of the world (and if the world was not created, then the chain of causes would continue all the way back into the infinity of time). Clearly, this kind of theory has no practical significance – it gives no tools for predicting the routes of cars, animals or people. As we have already mentioned, this is a metaphysical assumption.

It is worth noting that there are people who, in their day-to-day lives, behave in accordance with the assumption that they have free will but deny its existence on a philosophical level. They feel free will directly, but the determinist world view seems to them to make more sense. By the same token, it is difficult to expect someone who believes in the solipsist view to behave as if reality did not exist.

One way or another, we adopt the view that free will has an independent status, that it characterizes the human self, and that it is an important attribute of the mind – perhaps the most important of all. But from a naturalistic perspective, according to which everything in the world develops and changes solely according to the laws of physics, man's purposeful behavior and free will are a mystery. We will deal with this further in Chapter Three. Now we come to the matter of the mind.

8. THE SELF — A CONNECTION WITH GOD

The spirit is the man one knows. He must have continuity through periods of sleep and coma. I assume, then, that this spirit must live on somehow after death. I cannot doubt that many make contact with God and have guidance from a greater spirit. But these are personal beliefs that every man must adopt for himself. If he had only a brain and not a mind, this difficult decision would not be his.   (Wilder Penfield, quoted from *The Self and Its Brain* by K.R. Popper, J.C. Eccles, 558)

If we had trouble understanding the nature of free will, which is just one of the mind's attributes, it will be that much harder to grasp the nature of the mind itself. Throughout his life, from childhood to old age, man has to deal with two different, contradictory tendencies – the materialistic and the religious-spiritual. Apparently, experience tips the scales in favor of the materialistic. A child's first work of art is a house built from solid, material blocks. The cars that travel through the city streets and inter-city highways are made of material parts, as are computers. The most complex mechanism in the world is man, whose organs and brain are composed of matter. And above all, the basic assumptions and the findings of scientific research, which has made some monumental achievements in modern times, do not include the spirit.

On the other hand, all my life, even from childhood, I have felt and experienced my self. I feel the self instantaneously and in an unmediated way. I do not need any proofs, neither logical nor experimental, for the existence of my self. Bertrand Russell, one of the great philosophers of the twentieth century, wrote: "I hold that whatever we know without reference is mental" (*Human Knowledge, Its Scope and Limits*, 240).

The reality of *self* is primary for me, and I grasp the external world with my intellect, through my *self*. This is not a metaphysical-philosophical claim but a fact of my life. My consciousness, my *self*, perceives everything that takes place in the world, be it in my own life or in the lives of my family and friends, as a part of its internal experience. When I consider myself, after a period of time in a state of unconsciousness – in sleep or under general anesthetic – I wake up and I determine that my *self* has not changed. Likewise, when I consider my life and the important moments in it, I come to the conclusion that my *self* has **continuity**. My child-self and my adult-self are the same self. *I have no doubt whatsoever regarding the existence and reality of my self.*

I will expand on this topic in a more general direction. Our world is so complex that human beings cannot understand it completely. When humans reach the limits of their understanding and comprehend these limits, they approach profundity. True understanding is to stand on the brink of things that we have no capability of comprehending. As the Psalmist writes: "How great are your deeds, Lord; exceedingly profound are your thoughts. A simple man cannot know, nor can a fool understand this" (Psalms 92:7–8). However, this does not mean that a wise and intelligent person understands God's thoughts and the greatness of His deeds. Rather, the psalm says that a wise person "will understand *this*" – *how great and profound are his deeds*, while he does not have the ability to grasp and to understand them, though a fool does not even "understand *this*."

I now return to the dilemma at hand. In our day-to-day lives, we become used to routine, and as a result, we do not see one of the greatest miracles, if not the greatest, in the whole world: the miracle of the self of every single person in the world. Human beings are foreign objects in the physical world. It is not just that one cannot predict humanity's appearance on the planet based on the laws of physics, but it is also impossible to explain and understand the phenomenon of man in the time frame given. Science can describe and "explain," in a certain sense, all the physical parts comprising human organs, including the most complex organ, the brain. But the self is not comprised of material parts, nor is its behavior determined by the laws of physics or chemistry.

Awareness of the fact that I am composed of – if the term "composed of" is appropriate here – two entities, material and spiritual, is not simple at all and may even be even impossible. Perhaps this is the threshold between the comprehensible and the inconceivable discussed above. *We have difficulty categorizing a mundane, everyday experience as wondrous. The human soul is one of the mysteries of the world.* As an analogy, consider a child who is so accustomed to television that he sees nothing strange about it. The child must mature and learn a great deal in order to understand how a television works. The limitation of this metaphor is that television can be learned about and understood through science, while my inner world, my self, does not belong to the field of science at all.

We must make an enormous mental effort in order to overcome the childish approach that takes everyday experiences for granted. Let us take a look at various machines, such as a car or a sophisticated computer. The common thread in these examples is that a human must always operate these machines. Now, biologists "state" that the human brain is similar to a sophisticated computer, a very sophisticated computer. However, no machine or computer works on its own. *Someone* needs to steer the car or the plane. *Someone* needs to program the computer, operate it and read its data output.

Here we reach the critical point that requires serious intellectual effort to detach ourselves from our ordinary thinking. My brain has a master who programs and operates it, and that master is my self. The mystery lies in the fact that I have no tools with which to describe the self and how it operates the body and the brain. We have become accustomed to the fact that everything in the world, such as various machines, biological organs and the brain, can be described using scientific tools. We have become accustomed to the fact that everything is made of matter. But here we must step out of our regular way of thinking and understand that there is a mystery here. The self, which is spiritual, uses the brain as is its personal computer.

Two eminent scientists of the twentieth century, Karl Popper and John Eccles, wrote a book called *The Self and Its Brain*. The book does not touches upon this mystery. It accepts as fact that the mind operates the brain and, through it, the entire body. How? The authors intentionally avoid these questions. Something that is not biological, not material, exists, and that is the self, which uses the human body (and brain). *Recognition of the spirituality of the self is a stage on the way to opening the door to belief in God.*

In books about western philosophy, it is common to view René Descartes (1596–1650) as the man who distinguished between the two different entities or between the two substances: the substance represented by the physical world, which Descartes called "the substance that extends in space," and "the thinking substance," which is represented by man's consciousness. He says the following:

> ... I have a clear and distinct idea of myself inasmuch as I am only a thinking and unextended thing, and as, on the other, I possess a distinct idea of body, inasmuch as it is only an extended and unthinking thing, it is certain that this I [that is to say, my soul by which I am what I am], is entirely and absolutely distinct from my body, and exists without it.
> (Descartes, Key Philosophical Writings, Wordsworth, 1997, 181)

Descartes states here what we have already mentioned, namely: that it is "easier" to know the mind than to know the body – since man does not need proof for his thoughts or his feelings, whereas he only knows his body though research and study.

It is worth emphasizing that the idea of the two substances, body and soul, which have a reciprocal relationship and interact with each other, has a long-standing tradition in Jewish thought. In fact, Descartes also drew his ideas from his religious tradition, which included the Bible. In the first verses of the Book of Genesis, we read: "And the Lord God formed man out of the dust of the ground, and breathed into his nostrils the breath of life; and man became a living soul." Nachmanides, the eminent Jewish philosopher and commentator who lived in the thirteenth century (1194–1270), explains this: "And the verse says that He breathed into his nostrils the breath of life in order to inform us that the soul did not come to man from the elements .... Rather it was the spirit of the Great God: out of his mouth comes knowledge and discernment. For he who breathes into the nostrils of another person gives into him something from his own soul" (*Nachmanides's Commentary on the Torah*, Genesis 2:7). God gives man a part of His soul, so to speak. Nachmanides continues: "and the whole man became a living soul since by virtue of this soul he understands and speaks and does all his deeds ...." Onkelos translates the words "living soul," the soul that apparently characterizes every living being as "talking spirit," and emphasizes the uniqueness of man. Following him, Rashi explains: "Cattle and beasts were also called living souls, but this one of man is the most alive of them all, because he was additionally given intelligence and speech." Rabbi Soloveitchik summarizes: "A spark of the Creator is concealed in him" – in man. This spark exists within the self of each of us. As Maimonides writes in the *Guide of the Perplexed* (1:1):

> Now man possesses as his proprium something in him that is very strange as it is not found in anything else that exists under the sphere of the moon: namely, intellectual apprehension. In the exercise of this, no sense, no part of the body, none of the extremities are used; and therefore this apprehension was likened unto the apprehension of the deity, which does not require an instrument, although in reality it is not like the latter apprehension, but only appears so to the first stirrings of opinion. It was because of this something, I mean *because of the divine intellect conjoined with man*, that it is said of the latter that he is in the image of God and in His likeness . . . .

The connection between man and God is continuous, at least as a possibility, but the option is given, there is free will. Man can strengthen his connection with God or weaken it: "You have the choice: if you wish to strengthen and to fortify this bond, you can do so; if, however, you wish gradually to make it weaker and feebler until you cut it, you can also do that" (Ibid. 3:51).

The mind-body problem is highly complex and difficult to comprehend, if indeed it is comprehensible at all. The greatest difficulty is in grasping the interaction between the body and the mind. As Nachmanides writes: "A material thing [man] cannot fully comprehend how the separate entity [the intellect, which is spiritual rather than physical] can affect this physical reality . . . ." (from Y. Leibowitz's *Body and Mind*, 32) Even though man is an intelligent being, and can understand many things, there is one thing that is beyond his comprehension: how can a spiritual entity be an active agent in the physical reality.

Approximately three centuries after Nachmanides, Rabbi Moshe Isserles, who compiled the *Shulhan Aruch,* interpreted the wondrous nature of the connection between body and mind. The blessing "who fashioned man with wisdom . . ." talks about man's body and its physical functions. The blessing ends with the words: "Blessed are you, God, Who heals all flesh and acts wondrously." After this comes one of the most sublime prayers to be found in the prayer book, which opens with the words: "My God, the soul you placed within me is pure," after which come the blessings of the Torah, which bring us to the world of the spirit. The words "acts wondrously" stand between the two worlds – between the reference to bodily functions and the reference to the life of the spirit and the mind. What is Rabbi Moshe Isserles's interpretation? Acts wondrously in what? According to the structure of the prayer book, it seems that these words refer to the part that comes before them, to the biological functions. One could also say, in accordance with what comes after these words, that they also relate to the great wonder of the psychic reality of humankind. But Rabbi Moshe Isserles says that *the wonder is the connection between the two.* The fact that two entities – body and soul – are connected to each other is difficult to comprehend even for a person who believes that both the world of nature and the world of the spirit were created by God. He *acts wondrously* by connecting a spiritual entity with a physical entity. That is the wonder.

Many concepts that were previously impenetrable barriers to human thought are now taken for granted since the development of theoretical physics in the twentieth century by such seminal scientists and thinkers as Einstein, Planck, Bohr, Born, Schrödinger, Heisenberg and Dirac. In the past, no explanation would have been considered acceptable if it were not sufficiently "concrete." Such was the case with Newton's law of gravity, demonstrated by the falling apple. In contrast, today's physics describes even the most ordinary substance symbolically. We can compare this roughly to Jewish Kabbalah, or mysticism, which also uses symbolic language.

As mentioned above, one of the difficulties of the dualist approach – the view that there are two entities, mind and body – is the problem of the **interaction** between them. The body is material, while the mind is spiritual. How can they interact? It has been argued that two entities that are different in their essence cannot interact with one another. For example, how can we understand the interaction between an electromagnetic field, photons, and atoms and molecules? For a person accustomed to concrete explanations who does not conceive of any other options, even the interaction between matter and photons seems implausible. In Chapter Two I will try to give a succinct account of modern physics. But here, too, I will bring a story that describes an account of interaction between two different entities – atoms and photons. This is the story told by Professor Richard Feynman, one of the twentieth century's great physicists:

> You can imagine to what lengths my father went in order to provide me a higher education. He sent me to study at MIT, I graduated from Princeton,

returned home and my father says to me: "Now you have a good science education. I always aspired to understand something that I could never understand.
My son, will you explain something to me?

I answered, "Yes."

He said, "I understand they say that light is given off by atoms when the
atom passes from one state to another, from an excited state to a state of lower
energy."

I said, "That is correct."

My father continued, "And light is a kind of particle, I think they call it a
photon?"

"Yes, that is correct."

"Accordingly, if the photon is given off from the atom, while the atom is in
its excited state, then the photon has to be inside the atom."

I responded, "Well, that is not so."

My father said, "So how can it be that a photon particle is given off by the
atom and is not there?"

I thought for a few minutes, then answered: "I'm sorry; I don't know. I
can't explain it to you."

He was very disappointed. All these years he tried to teach me something,
and the result was so inadequate.   (The Physics Teacher, 1969, 319)

Here we have a clash of two ways of thinking. One is concrete, demanding
concrete answers in terms of day-to-day experience. The modern physicist,
however, understands that reality is complex and cannot be perceived in
terms of day-to-day experience. The physicist is already accustomed to symbolic language and is comfortable with his way of thinking. Feynman is not
troubled by his father's question. He knows that the spontaneous emission
of a photon can be described by equations of quantum electrodynamics, and
thus he has no need for a more concrete explanation. Moreover, the concrete
"explanation" would not satisfy him at all.

Of course, this is simply an analogy. We have no theory of mind-body
interaction, not in symbolic or any other language. We have no science that
can describe the interaction between mind and body. But we have already
stated that not everything belongs to the realm of science. My interaction
with my inner world does not belong to the realm of science. It exists outside
the public domain, and no science can reach the private domain. In any case,
I have no doubt that interaction, or reciprocal activity, takes place between
my *self* and my body. I know it with certainty as an unmediated experience.

On the other hand, the possibility of interaction between body and mind cannot be logically refuted simply because they are two entities that are different in nature.

We saw in the previous section that there is a gap between the inner feeling of certainty that free will exists and certain views that deny free will. This gap is much greater when we talk about the existence of the mind. The mind is an absolute mystery from the perspective of the atheist, but to deny the mind is to deny my self, my personality. This is precisely the price demanded by the materialist approach. In the next section, we will discuss the essence of this approach.

9. THE MATERIALIST VIEW – MATERIALISM

We have the certainty that matter remains eternally the same in all its transformations, that none of its attributes can ever be lost, and therefore, also, that the same iron necessity that it will exterminate on the earth its highest creation, the thinking mind, it must somewhere else and at another time again produce it. (Friedrich Engels, *The Dialectics of Nature,* Introduction)

Materialism is an ancient philosophical view or philosophical movement. As with the majority of philosophical schools, materialism started to develop in ancient Greece. At its foundation lies the premise of the unity of creation, a monistic premise, that the source of every entity is physical. This source is called *materia*, and from here comes the name materialism. Over time, views have changed, as has our knowledge of the essence of *materia* and its fundamental components – the elements of matter. Different ancient Greek philosophers dealt with the "problem of matter" in a purely intellectual way, as was common at that time, and offered various solutions. There were those, such as Parmenides, who thought that matter was continuous and could be broken up into infinitely smaller and smaller parts. Any piece of matter, however small, can always be broken down into even smaller pieces. Others, such as Leucippus, Democritus, Epicurus and the Roman philosopher, Lucretius, believed that matter is an atomic structure and that the smallest parts of matter, atoms, cannot be divided. Throughout the ages, people have understood matter as something that can be felt and seen, that has color and that offers resistance when one pushes against it. Matter is stones, rocks, and earth as well as gases. Our biological organs and body parts, as well as those of animals, are also made of matter. The most complex and sophisticated device in the world, the human brain, is made of matter as well.

But what does modern physics say about the nature of matter? We will talk further about modern physics in the second part of this book. From the modern physicist's perspective, matter has lost the simplicity and tangibility of previous generations. Matter is made up of particles: electrons and nucleons – protons and neutrons. It would seem that there is nothing in between these particles – namely, a vacuum, though in fact a physical entity called an electromagnetic field exists in the space between the particles. Both the particles and the physical fields are fairly abstract entities. Generally, we do not see or feel physical fields, but through various experiments they can be detected and the presence of the field can be determined throughout the space. A physical particle is no less an abstract entity than a physical field. According to the principles of the theory of relativity, a particle has no dimensions and no structure. It is a point, like a geometrical point. According to another, fairly commonly accepted view, the elementary particle is a one-dimensional string in an eleven-dimensional space-time! We should take into account that physical fields have quantum properties, and therefore a quantum electromagnetic field is also represented by particles known as photons.

The picture painted here is very far from traditional, tangible matter. There is a huge gap between the scientific, physical description of a particular crystal and our grasp of that crystal through our senses. Modern physics has come a long way from the classic concept of matter, *materia*. The *materia* of the ancient Greeks and today's physical matter have nothing in common. However, we are not going to make life easy and say that materialism is wrong. Instead, we will redefine the concept of matter, a physical concept. We will define *materia* as a physical substance. From a purely linguistic perspective, it is somewhat difficult to refer to a photon as "matter," but one can use the philosophical term *materia* to define anything physical such as elementary particles, sub-particles such as quarks; physical fields such as the electromagnetic field and the gravitational field, and the quanta of these fields – photons, gravitons, and so on. What all these entities have in common is that they are subject to the laws of physics. Therefore, the modern version of materialism is called *physicalism*. It is certainly a long way from the classical Greek materialism to modern physicalism, but the basic idea remains: that every entity has a uniform source that is physical and not spiritual.

This monist approach, which attributes a physical foundation to all entities, is rather appealing. Moreover, materialism serves as a working premise of all scientific research. When a scientist plans to investigate a particular object, he makes sure to isolate it from anything spiritual. It is therefore no wonder that scientific research does not include the spirit or discover it, though the proponents of the materialist world view try to use the impressive achievements of science to "prove" or reinforce their view. In order to do this, materialism must explain how spiritual entities exist at all. According to materialism, all spiritual entities came into being during the development of the world. I should point out here that the materialistic view is not uniform. Some proponents of materialism do not recognize the existence of a spiritual entity like the mind. According to their view, what we see as the mind is only the movement of molecules in the brain. However, I am of the opinion that even the most extreme materialists recognize the existence of spiritual entities. If so, one needs to explain how the letters, words and sentences, and especially the content and the ideas, of a philosopher's book, for example, came into being. Clearly this cannot be explained by simply applying the laws of nature. We are left with the option of explaining spiritual creations, as well as other aspects of the spiritual world of humans and even human beings themselves, in the material world, through a chain of causal links in the development of the world, including the evolution of life. An entire part of this book is devoted to the subject of the development of the world, but I will say here that, in my opinion, it is impossible to prove the existence of spiritual entities in the material world. This is a metaphysical assumption, like the belief in materialism, that everything can be explained by material causes, or to be more precise, by physicalism. It is clear that in the material world, which is subject solely to the laws of physics, there is no true creativity and no true spirituality.

Classical materialism also includes the messages of determinism and reductionism. What is determinism? It is the metaphysical view that everything in the world is pre-determined by causal connections, by the laws of nature.

Materialism professes to explain everything. Hence the term *reductionism*, in which everything in the world can be reduced to and derived from physics. So, for example, physics is considered the basis for chemistry. All the chemical elements and processes can be explained according to the principles, equations, formulas, and laws of physics. Despite the fact that chemistry deals with extremely complex forms such as the proteins of molecular biology, in principle we can describe all chemical processes using physical formulas. Chemistry can be *reduced* to physics. The concept of *reduction* means that all chemical properties and processes can be derived from physical laws, though to be precise the possibility of the reduction of chemistry to physics is only a belief based on the many achievements of quantum chemistry.

The list below is a simplified representation of the different parts of the world:

1. Elementary and sub-elementary particles and physical fields
2. Atoms
3. Molecules
4. Liquids and crystals
5. Plants, primitive organisms
6. Living organisms with senses
7. Self-conscious humans
8. Community, society, state
9. Economy, free market
10. Science, art, religion, faith

The presumptuous claim of materialism is the claim of *reductionism*, namely that everything emanates from the properties and movement of *materia*. Every development in this world, including the development of life, is determined according to the laws of physics. In the list above, each row follows from the row above it, and each row determines its successor. According to the reductionist claim, society and sociology can be analyzed and understood according to psychology; psychology can be analyzed in terms of physiology; physiology can be comprehended based on biology; biology is understood through chemistry; and chemistry is derived from physics. This means that, according to the reductionist approach, it is possible, in principle, to explain everything in terms of physics: life, human beings with feelings and desires, society, economics, and so forth.

Materialism cannot be proved, but it is clearly not compatible with rationalism. The outcome of materialism is that the results of any intellectual argument can be determined by neither logic nor rational reasoning, but only by the movements of molecules and atoms within our brains. I devoted a section of my book, *Creation Ex Nihilo*, to this subject. Here, I would like to quote Karl Popper, from his book *The Self and Its Brain*, which he co-authored with John C. Eccles:

> I do not claim that I have refuted materialism. But I do think I have shown that materialism has no right to claim that it can be supported by rational argument – argument that is rational by logical principles. Materialism can be true, but it is incompatible with rationalism, with the acceptance of the standards of critical argument; for the standards appear from the materialist point of view as an illusion or at least as ideology.[7]

Let us return to determinism. In the quotation at the start of this chapter, we have Friedrich Engels's statement regarding the "iron necessity" of the processes of development of the world. However, the new version of materialism is physicalism. At the basis of modern physics lies quantum theory.[8] Quantum theory is a non-deterministic, *statistical* theory. Quantum laws only determine probabilities, the chances of possible physical processes occurring. Unlike in classical physics, in the quantum world there is room for chance occurrences. In this world there is room for *laws* and *regularity*, but there is also room for *chance*. Not everything is determined by the laws of nature. There are processes that are not fundamentally deterministic. They are not pre-determined and they cannot be predicted in advance. There is no law that can precisely determine the location of a certain particle in a certain experiment, though it is possible to predict that after numerous repetitions of the same experiment, a fairly ordered picture will emerge whereby the distribution of electrons will be predictable. This sentence may not be particularly easy to understand, and we will talk in more detail about this in the second part of this book. The important thing is to understand that modern physics does not claim that everything in the physical universe behaves according to a law. There is also room for *chance* and the *absence of law*.

---

7. *The Self and Its Brain*, 81.
8. We will discuss quantum theory in depth in Chapter Two.

Modern materialists, the heirs and successors of classic materialists, start with the premise that evolutionary development is based specifically on the combination of regularity and chance. This combination is implemented in the theory of evolution of life. They therefore come to the conclusion of the insignificance and haphazardness of the appearance of humanity as a result of evolution. As George Gaylord Simpson wrote in the epilogue of his book, *The Meaning of Evolution*:

> Man is the result of a purposeless and materialistic process that did not have him in mind. He was not planned. He is state of matter, a form of life, a sort of animal, and a species of the order primates, akin nearly or remotely to all of life and indeed to all that is material.

Needless to say, Simpson's claim that humanity "was not planned" is not the result of any scientific analysis. Jacques Monod, the Nobel prize-winning biologist, supports a similar, perhaps more up-to-date view in his book *Chance and Necessity*: since the molecular processes of evolution are random, the end result (including humanity) must also be random: "The universe was not pregnant with life nor the biosphere with man. Our number came up in the Monte Carlo game" (*Chance and Necessity*, 145). And of course, mind-body dualism is simply an illusion (ibid., 159).

Opinions such as these lead to philosophical, ideological and ethical anarchy. Another Nobel prize-winner, Francis Crick, suggests the following in his lecture *The Social Impact of Biology*:

(a) It is not right that religious instruction should be given to young children . . . .

(b) We cannot continue to regard all human life as sacred. The idea that every person has a soul and his life must be saved at all costs should be not allowed.

(c) If a child were considered to be legally born when two days old it could be examined to see whether it was "an acceptable member of society" (otherwise it would be destroyed).

(d) It might also be desirable to define a person as legally dead when he was past the age 80 or 85 . . . . (From *Challenge*, 452)

The approach that supports the supremacy and primacy of matter and the negation of the spirit leads not only to ethical and ideological arbitrariness, but also to practical arbitrariness. In the twentieth century, Nazi Germany wrought the Holocaust on the Jewish people and a disaster for all of humanity. The anti-religious regime of the Soviet Union caused millions of deaths among its people. An inclination of this kind is also mentioned in our sources. While there was law in Sodom, it was unethical law that led to the suffering of many innocent people.

10. THE THREE WORLDS OF KARL POPPER

Y. Leibowitz proposes that "a person attached to the physicalist world view, which is based on natural science, and which attempts, justifiably or unjustifiably, to explain the world in its entirety, is not prepared to believe in the existence of something that is outside the scope of description according to the categories of physics" (*Body and Mind,* 44). On the other hand, when people observe themselves and their inner worlds, they have difficulty accepting the view that the self has no independent status and that the self is only a derivative of physical laws. This contradiction disappears if we recognize two worlds, an inner and an outer one, existing as two separate, independent entities. As Popper writes: "I am a realist. I claim, like any naïve realist, that there is a physical world and there is a world of conscious states, and between them exists a reciprocity of influence."

I will present here an abstract of Karl Popper's concept of three worlds. World one is the physical world: the world of *materia*, in which the laws of physics rule. World two is my inner world, your inner world, their inner worlds. This is the world of self-awareness, the private realm; the world of personal, subjective knowledge and our thoughts. Karl Popper claims that besides these two worlds exists another world, world three, the world of objective knowledge. This is the world of science, religion, philosophy, ideology, the arts, and so forth. Objectivity, for our purposes, refers to anything with independent existence – that is, independent of the thoughts of the individual. But this does not mean that objectivity is necessarily truth, nor can we always determine the truth.

World three, the objective world, influences world two. There is interaction and reciprocity between worlds two and three. In reality, world two cannot exist without world three. For example, psychologists know of several isolated cases in which a toddler has grown up without any contact with human civilization. In such cases, tragically, after a certain period of isolation, the child ceases to behave like a human being. World three also influences world one, the physical world, in an indirect manner. Because of the reciprocal relationship between worlds one and two, we can conclude logically that world three influences world one. Physical theories (in the category of world three) may cause nuclear weapons in world one. The following diagram represents Popper's three worlds:

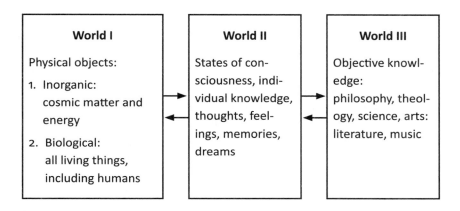

According to Popper, world three is man-made, although everything within it is autonomous and exists independently. After a piece of music is created it has a "life" of its own, and has its own interpretation, independent of its creator. It is no longer dependent on its composer. In a certain way, Popper's theory is a synthesis of Descartes's dualistic approach (two independent entities) and Plato's world of ideas. World three is similar to Plato's world of ideas in that it is not in space or time. Similarly, we cannot define the space that Einstein's theory of relativity occupies, or its duration. The difference between the two theories is that Plato's world of ideas has a divine source, while the source of Popper's world three is human, having a history and development.

We have said that world three is objective. We could try to imagine that most of world three is destroyed: our entire knowledge base – books, manuscripts, computer software and so forth. It is all gone. But we cannot stop there: a large amount of knowledge is stored in our minds – I personally could reconstruct from my memory classical mechanics, the law of gravity, the theory of electromagnetic fields, quantum theory and the special and general theories of relativity. Therefore, let us try to imagine that we are also erasing personal memories. If this were to happen, humanity would go back ten thousand years!

When we consider this new structure, a world made up of three worlds, the question of whether these worlds are actually real immediately arises. I would assume that all of us, or at least the vast majority of people, believe in the reality of world one – the world of material objects, the physical world. In fact, for us, the physical world is a paradigm of reality. However, it is not so clear that world two and especially the abstract world three are real worlds. Something can be defined as real only if there can be interaction between it and world one. Materialism, or to be more precise, physicalism, claims that only world one, the physical world, has reality, whereas common sense tells us that world two is also real. A toothache can be very real indeed. However, Popper's reasoning is quite different.

The fundamental rationale for the existence of world two, the world of personal, mental experience, is that prior to acting on world one we generally need to comprehend, to grasp, the theory that belongs to world three. However, the comprehension of the theory in world three is a mental matter – and that is a process that belongs to world two. World three acts on world one through world two, through a particular person or people. An example of such a process can be illustrated using the example of the design, production and operation of bulldozers used to build an airport. In this case, all the documentation that describes the making of the bulldozers and the directions to operate them, namely all the relevant documents, are things that belong to world one. The paper, the ink and the electronic methods of documentation are physical items that belong to the physical world. But the important thing here is not what kind of paper the documents are printed on or what kind of ink is used. Rather, it is the content of the documentation that is key, and that content belongs to world three. The physical means, items belonging to world one, can change – instead of paper, magnetic tape or a CD could be used, but the content itself, which is a world three item, does not change. Human beings have a special, unique ability to compre-hend the content of world three. When the content of the documentation is comprehended by the person, then this person, or a team of people, can build machines – in our example, bulldozers – and then use them in world one to build things in world one – in our case, to construct an airport.

Now let us return to our question about the reality of worlds two and three. The answer is clear. The reality of a spiritual thing, a world three item, the content of a particular theory, is proven by the fact that the item affects the physical world, world one, and causes significant changes in it, such as the explosion of a hydrogen bomb. Hence, there is no other way than to infer the reality of world two, without which world three would not be able to affect the physical world, world one.

Up until now, the subject has been discussed in the context of the view of Karl Popper – a secular philosopher, who tried to build a picture of the world without God or any spirit other than that of man, though, in contrast to the various schools of materialism, he recognized the existence of the human spirit. From the above account, one could get the impression that world three, a world of human culture in the wider sense, is an independent spiritual entity, like world one, the world of matter, and world two, the world of human minds. However, this is not the case. It is true, as stated above, that world three is *objective* – it exists independently in the sense that it is not dependent on the mind of the individual. However, world three does not exist separately and independently of humanity as a whole; the existence of world three is dependent on worlds one and two. Without the physical apparatus of world one, world three cannot exist. We have seen that if the repositories of human knowledge were eradicated – books, manuscripts, computer software and so forth – then world three would cease to exist.

Without human beings, world three has no independent existence. According to Popper, the source of world three is humankind, and it has a history and development. However, it is clear that before humankind appeared on the face of the earth, world three did not exist either. It is true that it is objective, in the sense that it is not dependent on a particular person, but it is not objective in the broader context – it is dependent on humanity as a whole. World three is an inseparable part of humanity and its development. A person keeps a large amount of knowledge in his brain; this knowledge has come to him during the course of his life, throughout his development, from the general knowledge base – world three. At any moment, the information that is available to a particular person is divided between that which is kept in his brain and that which is kept in various information devices of world three. Later on, we will return to the nature of the status of world three in the context of a divine, spiritual world.

In his argument against materialism, or physicalism, Popper emphasizes the point that the physical world, world one, is not closed, which is in contrast to the materialist view. It is open to world two, the world of my self and the selves of each and every one of us. In Part II: *The Laws of Nature*, we will see that physical laws are compatible with world one's openness to world two. From a secular perspective – and Popper is indeed a secular philosopher – no difficulty arises when we speak in the here and now. As opposed to the materialistic principle, which states that the physical world is closed, we can claim that the world in its entirety (worlds one + two + three) is closed, while the physical world is open just like worlds two and three. World one is directly open to world two, and therefore indirectly open to world three. But a philosopher cannot be satisfied with a momentary representation of the world. He must also consider the development of the world.

Like all scientific theories, secular belief assumes a stage in the development of the world when only the physical existed. *At that point, life did not exist – and, according to secular belief, neither did the spirit.* I emphasize this because it characterizes, and actually defines, the secular belief in contrast to the religious belief. Clearly, the recognition of the existence of the spirit outside of human life does not belong to the secular belief system. It is a religious belief, and therefore, it is the antithesis of secularism.

Let me explain my use of the term *secular belief*. It is possible that there are people who genuinely think that the terms *belief* and *faith* belong to the religious realm, while secular concepts are in the realm of proven knowledge. These people talk about knowledge, proofs and facts on the secular side, and belief on the religious side. But based on what we have discussed and will continue to discuss further, it is clear that secular theories, such as materialism, are actually metaphysical assumptions – or, in other words, *secular beliefs*. As I noted in the preface, we are talking here about faith versus faith – secular faith versus religious faith.

At that stage in the development of the world, before there was life – and, according to the secular belief, before there was also spirit – the entire world was world one, the physical world. According to Popper's scheme, world two is connected to life and to the human spiritual world, while world three is man-made. Now we must conclude that *the world was open from the very beginning*. Otherwise, it would be impossible to explain the development that brought us to our current state, which includes worlds two and three. At certain stages of the development of the world, new entities appeared that were created *ex nihilo* – namely, worlds two and three. If the world was open in its primary stages, we cannot reasonably assume that it ceases to be open in the current stage of combined worlds one, two, and three. What is openness of the world? By this, we mean that something can be derived from nothing (*creatio ex nihilo*). Things that did not previously exist can be created. This is the opposite of materialistic reduction. In due course, we will discuss the place of Popper's three worlds in the overall context of Jewish thought.

11. A SPIRITUAL WORLD

Enormous intellectual effort is required to comprehend the concept of a spiritual world. In section 8, we came across the difficulty of understanding the existence of the mind as a spiritual entity. In general, we have great difficulty understanding anything spiritual. We mentioned earlier that people have always grasped things in a tangible, concrete way. Understanding the divine, a completely spiritual entity, the source of everything, is a huge challenge for human beings. The Psalmist describes the clash of the two world views – the spiritual and the physical:

> Wherefore should the nations say: 'Where is now their God?' But our God is in the heavens; whatsoever pleased Him He hath done. Their idols are silver and gold, the work of men's hands. They have mouths, but they speak not; eyes have they, but they see not; They have ears, but they hear not; noses have they, but they smell not; They have hands, but they handle not; feet have they, but they walk not; neither speak they with their throat. They that make them shall be like unto them; yea, every one that trusts in them. O Israel, trust thou in the Lord! He is their help and their shield! (Psalms 115:2–11)

But let us not delude ourselves – the believing Jew is also not guaranteed to have a pure grasp of spirituality. Jewish history is full of deviations into idolatry, which is tangible and easily understood. Maimonides struggled uncompromisingly (especially in his *Guide of the Perplexed*) against any grain of materialism in his view of God. The difficulty is objective – people do not have the tools for imagining anything spiritual. One requires a very high level of abstraction just to grasp the necessity of the existence of spiritual entities, and perhaps this is where the limit to our understanding lies. The human intellect and mind are connected to the divine intellect (see section 8 above), which can explain how people are nonetheless able to grasp new, abstract things that are not directly, tangibly accessible. On the other hand, our inner world is spiritual, and we do not need any proof or evidence for the existence of our selves, which are, in fact, pure spiritual entities.

In the previous section, I presented the three worlds of Karl Popper. From a certain perspective, this is the pinnacle of understanding of our world that can be achieved in secular philosophy. Popper recognizes the objectivity of the spiritual world, world three in his terminology, but this world is an outcome of humanity's intellect. All the items in world three are man's inventions. Without humanity, a spiritual world would not have existed. It is not only the source of world three that lies in humanity; its objectivity is also dependent upon the presence of human beings. This is a typical idealist approach – a continuation of Immanuel Kant's line of thought,[9] which is expressed in the idea of a man-centered universe, a world in which humanity is at the core. Let us consider an important item of world three – the laws of nature and the scientific description of them. According to Popper (see also Chapter Four, section 4), scientific theory and the laws of physics are a man invention, and their appearance in world three is dated at the time of publication of the theory. But what was there prior to the creation of Newton's or Einstein's theories? Did the laws of nature and the laws of physics not exist? There is no doubt that the wording of this particular law of nature is dependent on human beings, but the law itself and its scientific implications have an objective existence that is not dependent on any person. While every person speaks his own language, the content of his words is not dependent on any given language.

According to my view – which I draw from our sources, from Jewish thought – the spiritual and the physical worlds together are a divine creation that develops over time – "*In the beginning God created the heaven and the earth*," where the word *heaven* symbolizes the spiritual world and *earth*, the physical world. Rabbi Soloveitchik writes: "'*Heaven*' and '*earth*' symbolize . . . matter and spirit of which the world is composed. This means that at the

---

9.   In Chapter Four, I will review Kant's theory in detail.

start of creation God created the two principal components of our world: '*heaven*' – spirit, and '*earth*' – matter" (*Man and His World*, 231).

Professor Yehuda Levi mentions in his book, *Torah and Science* (161) that the Hebrew word "*shamayim*" (heaven) sometimes refers to spiritual worlds only (like the word *heaven* in English). For example, according to Nachmanides (in his commentary on Genesis 1:9), in the first verse of Genesis, the word *shamayim* refers to spiritual values only and does not include the spheres, the heavenly bodies, such as the sun, moon and stars. All of these are included in the word "*eretz*" [earth] (BT *Berachot* 12b).

The spiritual world includes, *inter alia*, the laws of nature, which God imposes on the physical world. According to the Jewish view, which is based on the Bible, God is the creator of the world, of its laws and its order, and He watches over it. God is the creator of a world comprised of two parts, of two worlds – the spiritual and the physical. In fact, the vast majority of the Bible is devoted to the spiritual world.

The word "spirit" is defined by the dictionary as an abstract realm, a realm of the intellect and ethics, while the concept of "spiritual" is defined as belonging to the abstract realm or to the realm of the intellect and ethics, theoretical, belonging to the spirit (the opposite of material, physical).

The concept of a spiritual entity is deeply rooted in the Jewish tradition. Rabbi Yehuda Halevi, in the *Kuzari*, mentions the "Book of Creation": "The Book is constructed on the mystery of ten units ...: 'Ten Sefirōth without anything else; close thy mouth from speaking, close thy heart from thinking ...'" (Part Four, 27). Rabbi Shlomo Aviner explains: "The expression '*belima*' [without anything] means 'without essence.' Namely, there is no physical thing here that can be felt. Human pettiness has brought man to think that only that which can be felt is reality, is real, whereas the holy, the spiritual, the supreme have no substance, they are not reality. But the opposite is true: the more abstract something is, the more '*belima*', the stronger than reality, the more substantial" (*Commentary on the Kuzari*, Part Four, pages 269–270). Maimonides says of those who do not believe in spiritual reality: "That which is not body, nor a bodily event [anything related to the body or descriptions of it, such as strength and weakness, meanness and kindness, etc.] cannot be found amongst the foolish .... It was clear to [wise people] that everything that is distinct from matter has a stronger reality than material things. In fact, it is not correct to say 'stronger,' rather that the distinct reality is more real, since no change can affect it [as all objects are constantly changing and their existence is temporary. But the spiritual that is distinct from the physical – that is permanent and eternal] (*Treatise on the Resurrection of the Dead*, 353).

Rabbi Moshe Chaim Luzzato, in his book *Derech Hashem* (*The Way of God*), writes: "Creation in general consists of two basic parts: the physical and the spiritual. The physical is that which we experience with our senses . . . and the spiritual consists of all entities which are not physical, which cannot be detected by physical means . . . ." (Part One, beginning of Chapter 5).

Rabbi Eliyahu Dessler connects spirituality with the laws of nature and with the essence of nature.

> The plan and purpose of creation are its spiritual content. Everything that exists in the physical world has a spiritual source. Its development, its activity, how it affects other things and is affected by them – all these take place according to spiritual needs, and to serve the spiritual ends that the Creator set for His creation. This is how our sages interpret the verse, "If not for My covenant day and night, I had not established the laws of heaven and earth . . . ." Even the laws of nature depend on the spiritual purpose contained in the covenant of the Torah. What appears to us as a self-contained system of natural laws is only an illusion. Many sayings of our sages illustrate this principle; above all the twice-repeated statement in the morning blessings for light: "He who renews each day, continually, the works of creation." By this, they teach us that we are not to consider the principle of creation as something created once at a point of time in the past and since then existing by its own power, but as something that needs to be "re-created" each day and each moment – "continually".
>
> (Letter from Eliyahu – Published in English as Strive for Truth, 252)

The physical and spiritual worlds are not of equal standing. The existence of the physical world is dependent on the spiritual world at every moment: "The root of its existence is in spirituality." Later on, I will attempt to clarify the nature of the dependency of the physical world on the spiritual world. In Chapter Four, section 8, "**The spiritual world and the physical world in light of science**" – which summarizes Part II: The Laws of Nature – we will look in detail at how we can understand this dependency using scientific concepts. Throughout the book, we will often come across the concept of a *spiritual world*. I would like to emphasize here that the spiritual world has a definite level of reality that is no less than that of the physical world. Of course, a telltale sign of the reality of the spiritual world is the fact that there is interaction, reciprocity, between spirit and matter. Thus, in section 12, we will turn to the subject of this interaction.

First, however, we must clarify the connection between the spiritual, divine world and Popper's world three. As we have stated, world three is populated by humanity's creations and discoveries, including the laws of nature and scientific theories. The appearance of a new item – for example, a new scientific theory or a new work of art – in world three occurs at the time that it becomes known. Therefore one can say that world three is the *accessible* part of the entire spiritual world. Starting from the introduction of a new creation, it begins to be *accessible* to all of humanity. From our perspective, the reality of world three is derived from the reality of the spiritual world as a whole.

12. INTERACTION BETWEEN SPIRIT AND MATTER

Clearly, there must be a link, a connection, between the physical and the spiritual worlds. Without this link, without interaction, without the reciprocal actions between matter and spirit, spirit could not act on matter, and it could not cause it to move. We are familiar with numerous examples of this kind of action in our everyday lives. Let us start with an example that we mentioned in section 10 above. A particular theory of physics includes a basis for the building of a nuclear reactor or an atomic bomb. This theory, which exists in the spiritual world, is documented by way of items in the physical world – books, articles, computer software, and the memories of scientists. The theory itself is not able to bring about any benefit or cause any damage. In the absence of a link between spiritual entities – the physical theory that exists in the spiritual world – and the world of matter, matter would not be affected by it. However, a scientific theory can affect matter when human beings act as the "intermediary" between them, taking them from theory to practice. The human being, the scientist, the engineer, studies the theory of physics, the engineering software and the relevant documents and builds the nuclear reactor, operates it and *supervises its operation.*

People affect matter through all kinds of actions of their biological limbs, which are also part of the physical world. But ultimately, it is a person's mind that activates the connection between the spiritual, scientific entity and matter. We see countless examples of this in our day-to-day lives. People tap into reservoirs of knowledge and produce tools, machines, cars, computers and so on. After a certain device or a certain machine is made, a person *operates* and *supervises* it. A person drives the car, and while the car's functioning is ensured by the precise implementation of its design, constant supervision of its activity is essential – someone needs to hold the steering wheel so that the car will not veer off the road, and someone needs to control the speed using the accelerator and the brake pedal. Without this supervision, an accident would be unavoidable. So it is with man's control over his body. Once a person, who is the spiritual entity, decides on this behavior, he must supervise the device and its actions constantly. Now we come to the three-part model: man's mind creates a link between the spiritual entity and the physical entity and monitors its continued existence. In other words, the mind uses a particular spiritual entity as an operating system for a particular physical entity. The mind can take this spiritual entity from the spiritual world (in particular from the accessible spiritual world – world three), or from a built-in spiritual world within a man. We all have a complex and sophisticated spiritual system, the nervous system, including the brain itself. We call it a *spiritual system* because the nervous system is primarily a spiritual entity, and its content is expressed using the physical means of a person's limbs. In relatively simple actions, such as walking or moving the hands, the mind uses the complex and sophisticated operating system that exists within man.

In more complex actions, such as building machines, the mind also uses the content and theories of the spiritual world that is external to man. This connection is illustrated at the top of the diagram below.

I claim that the three-part model also describes the nature of divine creation and providence. I should point out here that I am not anthropomorphizing God's actions; rather, I am deifying the actions of man. Man was *created in the image of God,* and his actions described above can give us a clue about the nature of divine providence. A look at man's behavior and actions may lead us to a deeper understanding of divine providence. God created a world comprised of a spiritual world and a physical world, and He creates a connection between them. The laws of nature are a part of the divine spiritual world. God operates the laws of nature and imposes them

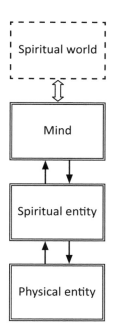

on matter. This sentence requires clarification. The movement of lumps of matter, just like the movement of Earth or of other planets around the sun, complies with the laws of nature, the laws of physics. However, the existence of these objects and of any physical object, of a ballistic missile or the minutest particle of matter, is subject to the laws of nature. Their existence is conditional on the spiritual world, which operates on them. As we mentioned above, we will return to this topic after we study Part II: *The Laws of Nature.*

The following diagram represents the nature of the operation of the divine spiritual world on the physical world. One might say that it is the constant providence that operates the world. In the example above, a person produces the car, operates it and supervises its actions. An outside observer of the car as it travels at a fixed speed on a straight road might think that it moves solely according to the laws of physics, but the truth is that the driver is in control of the car's movements at every moment. In the same way, we also mistakenly think that the world develops solely according to the laws of nature, without God's supervision, but divine supervision is constantly acting, and the laws of nature are simply tools for God's providence.

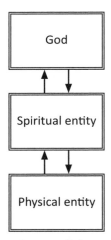

In the two models above, the parallel was drawn between man's soul and God. This parallel has a strong basis in our tradition. The Babylonian Talmud tells of five similarities between man's soul and body and the power of God in the world.

> Just as the Holy One, blessed be He, fills the whole world, so the soul fills the whole body. Just as the Holy One, blessed be He, sees but is not seen, so the soul sees but is not seen. Just as the Holy One, blessed be He, sustains the whole world, so the soul sustains the whole body. Just as the Holy One, blessed be He, is pure, so the soul is pure. Just as the Holy One, blessed be He, sits in the innermost chambers, so the soul dwells in the innermost chambers.
>
> (BT Berachot 10a)

The supervision and the involvement of the spirit in the actions of matter do not contradict the laws of physics. They operate in addition to the laws of physics. This subject is by no means simple, and we will study it in more depth in Chapter Three. At this point, I will just bring examples of the movements of objects that are influenced both by the laws of nature and by the involvement of the spirit. Take, for example, a man-made satellite, which is navigated by a team of people. After the satellite enters its orbit, it moves precisely in accordance with the laws of physics. Its movement is determined by its mass, speed and the like. Suddenly, the object – which, based on all the signs is a closed physical system – starts moving in ways that are impossible to predict by the laws of physics alone. The explanation is simple: the system is not closed. It is open to the minds of the people who are navigating it. It is the human mind that determines the satellite's deviation from its path. The functioning of man, and his movements – this is a different example altogether, one with which we are much more familiar. Our movements are the result of our decisions – the spiritual cause – as well as the laws of nature.

The physical world is not closed[10]; it is open to the spirit of God and man. It would appear from this that the use of science, and physics in particular, is limited. When we look at the movements of an object such as a satellite or a car, we cannot determine in advance that it moves solely according to the laws of nature. When man controls the body, we must take man's decisions into account, as well as the laws of nature. Similarly, when we attempt to explain the development of the world, whether on the cosmic level or the organic level, we cannot do this solely by reference to science – divine supervision is also acting here.

Spiritual reality changes and develops; it is rich and varied. As well as the changing elements of divine providence it also includes laws that are permanent and fixed. We can assume that the development of the world and the development of life occur through gradual, evolutionary change.[11] In every development of this type there must be something that can be called a *preservation system*. New things appear against the background of a constant and fixed infrastructure. Human beings, who were created in the image of God, can fulfill their tasks as partners of God if they (and their intellect) can stand in front of the external world and study its complex actions. This is possible when the changes are gradual and when there are fixed laws.

In nature and its development, the laws of nature fulfill the role of the *preservation system*. They exist in parallel to divine providence, or to be more precise, they are the preserving part of providence. In the development of life, the genetic material recorded in the genetic code (DNA) is uniform for every animal and plant. The changes and the innovations which determine the direction of evolution occur under the supervision of God and are passed to future generations by the genetic mechanism which is the preservation system. Likewise, the commandments and Jewish law (*halakha*) preserve

---

10.   Remember that according to the materialist dogma, the physical world is indeed closed and complete. However, we do not follow this view.

11.   This does not contradict the possibility that such gradual development may take place sporadically and unevenly.

the Jewish way of life. This preservation system passes from generation to generation: "And you shall teach them diligently to your children, and you shall talk of them when you sit in your house, and when you walk by the way, and when you lie down and when you rise up" (Deuteronomy 6:7). Another example of this is human language: the rules of grammar are its preservation system.

God blessed man saying: "Be fruitful and multiply, replenish the earth and subdue it" (Genesis 1:28), and He instructed him to conquer nature. Knowledge of the world enables humanity to have control over nature. When preservation systems exist in the changing and developing world, then in principle the possibility of understanding the world exists. This possibility is dependent on the will of God (See Chapter Four which is devoted to Knowledge of the World), but it is also dependent on man's readiness to accept revelations of the laws of nature. A person who is not equipped with the necessary knowledge cannot grasp the message of the revelation.

The three-part model described above and the examples of the connection between the human mind and matter are just an analogy to the connection between God and our world, spiritual and physical alike. As with every analogy, this one has its limits. The spiritual world of human beings, their accessible spiritual world (world three), is in fact only an *image* of the divine spiritual world. The functioning of the accessible spiritual world is dependent on man. Until man operates it, it is actually "dead." The content of a particular book has meaning only when there are people who are capable of reading and using it.

Likewise, a person's body operates and lives all the while that it has a connection with the soul. When the bond between the soul and the body is broken, the body stops functioning. It remains with all its physical organs, but without a soul, the human body is nothing but a corpse. Without the soul, man does cannot exist – he is dead. The same can be said for the world as a whole and for us who live in it – namely that it exists solely on condition that there is a ceaseless connection with God. Just as man's existence is contingent on the connection with his soul, so the world's existence is contingent. It is not immanent – depending on the world itself, but it is dependent on the connection with God. *Just as my existence is dependent on my soul, the existence of the world is dependent on God.*

While the world is connected to God, it "lives," exists and acts. The laws of nature act on matter all the time. Man operates the car and supervises its operation only for a limited period. After he ceases to operate the car, the car is "dead" – it does not function. The connection between the "spiritual" and the physical is broken. In contrast, a real spiritual world is constantly operated by God and constantly acts on matter. Such a spiritual world "lives" all the time. Of course, when I say that the spiritual world lives all the time, I mean all the time that God is with us.

The spiritual world is real and objective in the sense that it is not dependent on human beings. Of course, it does not include only the laws of nature – they are merely a part of it. The spiritual world is a constantly changing and developing entity; the laws of nature are a constant element of the spiritual world – they are the preservation system. We will devote the next part of the book to the laws of nature.

13. CONCLUSION: THE REALITY OF SPIRITUALITY

Part I of this book, *Fundamental Principles,* contains just one chapter – *God and Man.* A look at the content of this chapter shows that the subject of spirituality is prominent in each of the twelve sections. Even section 9, which deals with the materialistic approach, is part of the discussion on spirituality. The materialistic approach, which denies the independent status of spiritual entities, regards them as being derived from matter.

People talk a great deal about spirituality, especially in religious circles. But only few understand that spirituality is no less solid and real than corpo-reality. It is extremely difficult to grasp the reality of any spiritual entity. This difficulty is particularly pronounced when we compare spiritual entities with physical objects. It is hard to doubt the physical reality, which imposes its tangibility on us. We are able to sense, touch and feel a physical object and we ignore it at our peril, just as a driver who ignores traffic lights is liable to end up in an accident.

In contrast, spiritual things seem abstract and lacking in substance. It is extremely difficult for us to imagine any spiritual entity. In fact, we do not even have the tools to do so, since the tools that we have are all physical, and we cannot imagine a spiritual entity through physical means. However, our inability to imagine a spiritual entity does not prevent us from determining that it is real and from describing its qualities. Modern-day physics provides us with many examples of real things that are impossible to imagine but whose qualities can be described. Even though we cannot imagine elementary particles such as electrons, we have no doubt that they are real, and we are aware of many of their qualities.

The spiritual entity with which we are the most familiar is each of our own *selves*. I should emphasize that the experience of the *self* is primary for us. We have said that physical reality imposes its reality on us – on *us*, on my *self*, your *self* and that of every person. The most primary thing for me is not matter, nor is it the objects around me. Rather, it is my own *self*. I grasp the reality of things that are external to me through my mind. My mind is a fact of my life, more certain than anything else. My self is an essential link in the chain of events that leads me to comprehend everything in the world. Without it, without my self, I have no connection with anything in the world.

While I cannot capture the essence of my self with physical terminology, I have not a shadow of a doubt that it is real. This is not a proof of the existence of the self. It is simply a fact of life. I have complex relationships with many individuals. I feel love and affection towards some, and less warm feelings towards others. I have an almost constant concern about whether I am fulfilling that which is imposed on me from above. I have my own inner spiritual world. I am not a solipsist; I am certain that other people also have their own personal inner worlds, and I am convinced of the reality of these worlds. However, I also understand that there is no logical proof for the existence of these independent inner worlds, nor can there ever be such a proof. It is also impossible to logically disprove the claim, somewhat absurd in my opinion, that my inner world is derived from matter, or *materia*.

The routine of everyday life and the childish approach that takes reality for granted stand in the way of our being amazed by the wonder of the human mind. But comprehending the phenomenon of man is even more complex and astonishing than the concept of the mind. If it is difficult to grasp the concept of a spiritual entity, how much harder it is to grasp the existence of an entity that combines matter and spirit which interact with one another – namely, the human being. Here, the problem of the openness of the physical world arises. If my spiritual self can have an effect on the actions of my physical limbs, this means that the physical world is not closed – a spiritual entity, the self, can affect it. The openness of the physical world, the possibility of interaction between mind and matter, is one of the central problems, if not the central problem, in understanding the world in which we live, and it also lies at the center of this book.

It is interesting to compare the idea of the reality of world three with that of the spiritual world in general. According to Popper, the reality of world three is derived from the fact that items in it, such as scientific theories, are able to influence the physical world, world one. But this influence is contingent on the mediation of a human being. In other words, whenever human beings are not mediating between world three and world one – not using world three items to affect world one – world three has no reality. Without human beings, without humanity, world three is "dead." To put it another way, human beings are the source of the reality of world three. This is the idealistic approach that comes from the secular, God-less view of Karl Popper. However, this is not the case, from our point of view – in other words, from the point of view of Jewish thought. God is the source of the reality of all things. God created the spiritual world, and it is God who imposes it on the physical world. God is the source of the reality of both the physical and the spiritual worlds. As we mentioned at the end of section 11, the reality of world three is derived from the reality of the spiritual world in general.

Recognition of God's grandeur and his transcendental nature should not detract from the issue of providence, of God's involvement in matters of the world, physical and spiritual alike. Understanding the world's openness to God is a central element of this book. Divine providence uses the spiritual world as a complete operating system, of which the laws of nature are a part. In Chapter Three, section 4, we will continue the discussion of the nature of the physical and the spiritual worlds with the help of the scientific knowledge that we will glean through the following chapters.

Part 2

THE LAWS OF NATURE

CHAPTER TWO

Physics – The Foundation of Science: Ideas and People

Ideas...

1. FROM ARISTOTLE TO GALILEO: THE PROBLEM OF MOVEMENT – THE LAW OF INERTIA

AS WE LEARNED IN CHAPTER ONE, THE MODERN VERSION of materialism is physicalism. Physics is a science that deals with the essence of matter, *materia*. To understand what *materia* is we must first become somewhat familiar with physics. As the title of this chapter states, physics is the foundation of science and it is the most developed area of science. When I say "science," I am referring to modern science, which has been around for only the past several hundred years, rather than to human civilization, which has existed for thousands of years. This is not a textbook of physics or of the history of physics. My aim here is to clarify the fundamental ideas, the main concepts, of physics. Matter is one of God's creations, and the more we understand God's work, the closer we can come to God Himself.

If we ask ourselves what it is that characterizes modern physics, from Galileo and Newton to the present day, the answer would be that it deals with motion. The planets revolve around the sun. The sun and the other stars move in a grand cosmic motion. Electrons and protons move inside the atom. Atoms and molecules move within gases and solid bodies. The movement does not stop even at the very lowest of temperatures, absolute zero (vacuum fluctuations).

"A most fundamental problem, for thousands of years wholly obscured by its complications, is that of motion" (A. Einstein, L. Infeld, *The Evolution of Physics*, 17). Aristotle, who lived in ancient Greece from 384 to 322 b.c.e., was fascinated with the problem of motion. At that time, Greece was considered the center of philosophy and mathematics. It would not be an overstatement to say that at the dawn of modern science, in the sixteenth century, the level of knowledge in the fields of mathematics and nature was more or less identical to that of ancient Greece. Hence Galileo, who was born in 1564 and was considered a pioneer of modern science, studied mathematics and nature from the works of Euclid and Archimedes.

Aristotle wrote many books on philosophy (at that time, no distinction was made between philosophy and science) that continued to have a strong influence even many generations later, particularly in the Middle Ages. One of his works was called *Physics*, referring to the science of matter, and thus the word was coined. The majority of that book is devoted to the problem of motion, and Aristotle's main conclusions are as follows:

> A moving body will come to a stop when the force propelling it ceases to act upon it.

And:

> Three factors are necessary for movement: the moved object, the mover and that by which it moves.

Aristotle came to the following quantitative conclusion: If two forces act upon a particular object, they will cause motion at a greater speed that if one force was acting – in proportion to the total forces. The conclusion that the speed of an object is dependent upon the force acting upon it is derived from everyday human experience. Aristotle would often observe, on the streets of Athens where he would spend his time at Plato's academy, that a chariot pulled by four horses traveled at a faster speed than one pulled by two horses.

For approximately two thousand years, this was the accepted law of motion, and it was all the more accepted on account of it having the support of Aristotle. Two thousand years later, in the sixteenth century, the

Italian scientist Galileo came to some fundamentally different conclusions. While, according to Aristotle, if no force is acting on a body, then the moving body will lose speed and "come to rest," Galileo concluded that if there are no external forces acting on a body, then it will continue to move in a fixed motion: at a fixed speed (in a straight line[1]). To understand why these two great minds, Aristotle and Galileo, came to diametrically opposed conclusions based on the very same facts, we will describe a kind of thought experiment (*Gedanken Experiment*). The advantage of a thought experiment is that it helps us to think clearly without having to perform actual experiments. The thought experiment, which was conceived by Galileo, is a key element of modern science. Here is an example of such a thought experiment. Galileo wrote his book, *Discourse Concerning the Two Chief World Systems*, in the form of a dialogue between three men, Salviati, Sagredo and Simplicio. In the excerpt cited below, Galileo, for the first time in the history of science, states the Law of Inertia, upon which Isaac Newton based his mechanics a generation later.[2]

Galileo's Thought Experiment	
SALVIATI	Now tell me: Suppose you have a plane surface as smooth as a mirror and made of some hard material like steel. This is not parallel to the horizon, but somewhat inclined, and upon it you have placed a ball which is perfectly spherical and of some hard and heavy material like bronze. What do you believe this will do when released? Do you not think, as I do, that it will remain still?
SIMPLICIO	If the surface is tilted?
SAL.	Yes, that is what was assumed.

1.   Galileo thought that an object moved in a circular motion. This was a result of the thought experiment described below – if the ball's motion in this experiment were to continue, one could assume that it would move in a circle around the globe. It is simple to understand that this is a result of Earth's force of gravity. Hence, it is reasonable to assume that with no forces acting on it at all, the object would continue in a straight line.

2.   Galileo Galilei, *Dialogue Concerning the Two Chief World Systems*, 145–147.

SIM.   I do not believe that it would stay still at all; rather I am sure that it would spontaneously roll down . . . .

SAL.   Now how long would the ball continue to roll, and how fast? Remember that I said a perfectly round ball and highly polished surface, in order to remove all external and accidental impediments. Similarly I want you to take away any impediments of the air caused by its resistance to separation, and other accidental obstacles, if there are any.

SIM.   I completely understood you, and to your question I reply that the ball will continue indefinitely, as far as the slope of the surface extended, and with continually accelerated motion . . . and the greater the slope, the greater would be the velocity.

SAL.   But if one wanted the ball to move upward on this same surface, do you think it would go?

SIM.   Not spontaneously, no; but drawn or thrown forcibly, it would.

SAL.   Now, tell me what would happen to the same movable body placed upon the surface with no slope upward or downward.

SIM.   Here I must think a moment about my reply. There being no downward slope, there can be no natural tendency toward motion; and there being no upward slope, there can be no resistance to being moved . . . . Therefore it seems to me that it ought naturally to remain stable . . . .

SAL.   I believe it would do so if one set the ball down firmly. But what would happen if it were given an impetus in any direction?

SIM.   It must follow that it would move in that direction.

SAL.   But with what sort of movement? One continually accelerated, as on downward plane, or increasingly retarded as on the upward one?

SIM.   I cannot see any cause for acceleration or deceleration, there being no slope upward or downward.

SAL.   So how far would you have the ball continue to move?

SIM.   As far as the extension of the surface continued without rising or falling.

SAL.   Then if such a space were unbounded, the *motion on it would likewise be boundless? That is, perpetual?*

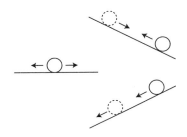

Figure 1.1: A ball on surfaces with an upward incline,
a downward incline and with no incline.

Thus, in 1629 the Law of Inertia, from which modern physics began to develop, was formulated. Two individuals – Aristotle, and, almost two thousand years later, Galileo – arrived at opposite conclusions regarding the question of what would happen to a moving object that was not acted upon by any external force. According to Aristotle, "the moving object would come to rest," while Galileo claimed that it would continue to move at a fixed speed. Who was right? If Aristotle was wrong, what is the source of his mistake? And is it even possible to determine who was right and who was wrong? Three hundred years later, Einstein and Infeld wrote in their book, *The Evolution of Physics:*

> Can it possibly be wrong to say that a carriage drawn by four horses must travel faster than one drawn by only two? . . .
> Suppose that someone going along a level road with a pushcart suddenly stops pushing. The cart will go on moving for a short distance before coming to rest. We ask: how is it possible to increase this distance? There are various ways, such as oiling the wheels, and making the road very smooth. The more easily the wheels turn, and the smoother the road, the longer the cart will

go on moving. And just what has been done by the oiling and smoothing? Only this: the external influences have been made smaller. The effect of what is called friction has been diminished, both in the wheels and between the wheels and the road. This is already a theoretical interpretation of the observable evidence, an interpretation which is, in fact, arbitrary. One significant step farther and we shall have the right clue. Imagine a road perfectly smooth, and wheels with no friction at all. Then there would be nothing to stop the cart, so that it would run for ever. This conclusion is reached only by thinking of an idealized experiment, which can never be actually performed, since it is impossible to eliminate all external influences. The idealized experiment shows the clue which really formed the foundation of the mechanics of motion. (The Evolution of Physics, 7–8)

If we compare the two approaches, that of Aristotle and that of Galileo, it seems that according to Aristotle, the greater the external influence on an object, the greater its speed, whereas according to Galileo, when there are no forces acting on a body it travels at a fixed speed. From a purely logical perspective, we cannot determine which is correct. Aristotle based his conclusion on everyday experience, with all of its shortcomings, while Galileo drew his conclusions from the idealized experiment, the thought experiment, which can never actually be performed.[3]

We cannot determine from a logical perspective which of these is correct. However, we have at our disposal almost four hundred years of scientific development since the time of Galileo, and now we can truly appreciate his view: "The discovery and use of scientific reasoning by Galileo was one of the most important achievements in the history of human thought, and marks the real beginning of physics" (Ibid., 7). However, there is also a hidden danger here. The thought experiment describes an idealized situation. It is an *idealization* of the true situation. Idealization is *simplification* – making something more simple while ignoring certain details that are considered either less important or of no importance at all. But we may be discarding

---

3.   Galileo could have easily explained Aristotle's "thought experiment": the forces of friction of the road are neutralized by the force of the horses, and as a result, the chariot travels at a fixed speed. However, Aristotle cannot explain Galileo's thought experiment, since as far as Aristotle is concerned, an object preserves its speed only if some force is acting upon it.

some crucial things along with the less important ones. My physics professor at university used to say: "All the idealization may come back to haunt you!" In other words, idealization is not the whole truth – it is just an approximation of the truth. Below, we will encounter situations in which a particular idealization is no longer valid and needs to be changed.

The rest of this chapter goes into more detail about the fundamentals of science. Why is it important for us to attain a certain level of understanding of the laws of physics? We aspire to understand the world in which we live. This understanding, while always limited, brings human beings closer to the Creator and to His creation. As we explained in Part I of this book and will continue to discuss throughout it, the laws of nature and the physics that describes them are actually a part of the divine management. Hence, it is important to understand the structure of modern science and the substance of the laws of nature, even if only partially.

2. THE MECHANICAL WORLD – MECHANICS AND THE LAW OF GRAVITY

In Europe, around the sixteenth century, something new began to develop: modern science. An historian would connect the birth of modern science with people such as Tycho Brahe, Copernicus, Kepler and Galileo. However, conceptually, it was Galileo Galilei who truly paved the way to the new scientific way of thinking. In the seventeenth century, Isaac Newton formulated, almost perfectly, the foundation of modern physics, which included mechanics and its law of gravity. Over time, the view of the mechanical world took shape as a mechanistic philosophy. According to this mechanistic approach, everything can be explained by the laws of mechanics and the law of gravity. Essentially, to explain a phenomenon is to identify the mechanism responsible for its existence.

From a conceptual perspective, the starting point of classical mechanics is the law of inertia. According to this law, an object persists in its state of rest or of uniform motion in a straight line until it is forced to change this state by forces acting upon it. This was a new idea – not only did it not derive from everyday experience, but it actually seemed to contradict it. We know with certainty that if we push any object and it starts to move at a certain speed, sooner or later it will lose speed and stop moving. However, in the thought experiment, the new tool that characterized the scientific approach, the scientist tried on a theoretical level to discard all the incidental details and build an idealized picture, which would be impossible to reproduce in practice. In a thought experiment, a scientist constructs an idealization. He talks about an object upon which no forces are acting. No one has ever come across such an object, but to arrive at the fundamental laws, it is crucial to analyze the phenomenon in its simplicity, without any extraneous details. Yet here lies another danger – we are at risk of "throwing the baby out with the bathwater." From a certain perspective, the development of science is expressed in the creation of new idealizations.

The law of inertia describes the situation of an object that is not subject to the effects of any forces whatsoever. What happens when the object in question does have certain forces acting upon it? Newton's second law answers this question.

Newton's Second Law

To understand the essence of Newton's second law, let us look again at the thought experiment. Let us imagine that we are in a spaceship. The movement of an object inside a spaceship can be an excellent example of the law of inertia. We are used to seeing scenes on television that are broadcast from inside a spaceship, where various objects move around, hover at fixed speeds or are at rest. What happens when an object is pushed? The push will cause an object that was at rest to move at a certain speed, and it will cause a moving object to move at a greater speed. Note that the exact same push (the same force) causes different speeds (or speed increases) for different objects. What do these different speed increases depend on? Newton's second law states that the change in speed is a function of both the force's magnitude and the object's mass. The larger the object's mass, the smaller the change in speed that will be caused by the same push.

Newton's second law can be expressed in mathematical terms as follows:

$$F = ma: \textbf{Force } (F) = \textbf{mass } (m) \text{ times } \textbf{acceleration } (a)$$

Acceleration is defined here as the change in speed per unit of time, or the speed of speed (for anyone familiar with calculus, it is the derivative of speed). In fact, this equation, Newton's second law, also defines a new, fundamental concept in physics – mass.

Acceleration is defined here as the change in speed per unit of time, or the speed of speed (for anyone familiar with calculus, it is the derivative of speed). In fact, this equation, Newton's second law, also defines a new, fundamental concept in physics – mass.

So, what is mass? We all seem to understand intuitively what it is. It seems to be the quantity of matter in an object. Initially, Newton himself defined it as "quantity of matter" rather than using the term "mass." But the expression "quantity of matter" is not as clear as it might initially appear. One might imagine, for example, that it refers to an object's weight. However, in a spaceship, as everyone knows, objects have no weight. All the objects hover around inside the spaceship without falling, since there is no force of gravity. If this is the case, does the mass also disappear? Newton's second law of motion defines mass even in the case where the object has no weight at all: Mass is the degree of an object's resistance to the effect of a force acting upon it. When the same force acts on objects of different masses, the object with the greatest mass will have the smallest acceleration (increase in speed per unit of time). According to Newton's second law, acceleration is a function of both the force acting on the object and its mass. The greater the mass, the smaller the acceleration.

In general terms, we can describe the mechanical world as follows: This world includes solid objects, whose interaction occurs by way of the push. This interaction can be illustrated with a game of pool – the movement of the balls on the pool table is a function of their collisions. These interactions can be described using Newton's laws. Between collisions, a ball travels at a fixed speed (the law of inertia, the absence of friction); a collision between the balls causes a change in the speed of the ball that is hit (Newton's second law). However, despite the greatest of efforts, this simple account did not take hold even in Newton's lifetime. His most impressive achievement was in the area of the movement of celestial bodies, where the main factor is the gravitational field that operates at a distance, rather than the push. In fact, in the mechanical world, the gravitational field is a strange and foreign concept. While we can understand the effect of the push in a tangible way from our everyday experience, it is extremely difficult to understand the gravitational field that operates over very large distances. For example, according to Newton's law of gravity, any change in the movement of the sun will immediately be felt on Earth. Furthermore, changes in the movement of objects that are light years away will also have an immediate impact on Earth. But this begs the question: how does an object on Earth "know" that there have been changes in the movement of bodies that are so incredibly far away? Isaac Newton saw something mystical, magical, supernatural, about the gravitational field. As we now know, the gravitational field, just like other types of physical fields, was the forerunner of another, non-mechanistic physics. Incidentally, we encounter the gravitational field in our everyday lives almost constantly. When something falls to the ground, this is the result of Earth's force of gravity. Without it, we would not be anchored to the ground and would float around like astronauts in a spaceship.

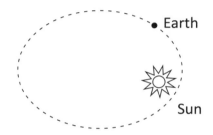

Figure 2.1 Earth's orbit around the sun

To summarize, mechanics enables us to predict the future path of a moving object and to reconstruct it with great precision, if the forces acting upon it are known, and at a particular time, the physical state of the object is known. So, for example, the future courses of the planets can be predicted, where the forces acting upon them are the forces of Newton's gravitational fields. Newton's mechanics, together with his law of gravity, paved the way for great achievements in astronomy and made it possible to perform precise calculations of the courses of the celestial bodies.

The impressive achievements of Newton's mechanics, including in the field of thermodynamics, led to the idea that everything, all natural phenomena, as well as life itself, can be explained using mechanics. However, this aspiration never came to fruition.

3. THE SHAPE OF MODERN SCIENCE

With the exception of certain elements that are important in their own right, the mechanics of Newton and Galileo paved the way to modern physics as a whole. The substance of modern-day physics is different from that of Newtonian mechanics, but the overall structure was established by Galileo and Newton. Science that drew a connection between theory and experiment originated in the work of Galileo. The quantitative nature of science derived from there. The description of quantitative links requires special tools or a special language. In fact, we already have such a language: mathematics. Actually, at that time it was only partially ready – Newton (and, at the same time, Leibniz) invented the new branch of mathematics, mathematical calculus, to describe the laws of nature. In Chapter Three, section 2, we will talk about mathematics as the language of science.

Differential Law

Newton was the first to use the concept of the *differential* law in theoretical physics. The differential law is formulated using differential equations, which link consecutive events that occur one after the other.

For more than three centuries of scientific research, force and matter (and its mass) were the fundamental concepts in all efforts to understand nature.

Let us stop for a moment and reflect on the idea of law and order in the world, since it is science's role to describe this. We are accustomed to the existence of lawfulness in nature, and just as we are accustomed to many other things and fail to see the wonder in them, we do not regard this lawfulness in nature as anything strange or surprising. If we want to understand the essence of things, the essence of the world, then it is specifically the absence of order and lawfulness that would be easier to understand. While their absence would not require an explanation, their existence would. If you leave an empty notebook at home and come back to find that the pages are still empty, you need no explanation. It is another story if you come home to find a passage of text written on one of the pages. Then we would need an explanation – where did the text come from?

Figure 3.1 Objects are thrown from point V on Earth at different speeds

This is an analogy. But what does it illustrate? The order in the inanimate world and the laws of nature that express that order are analogous to the text in the notebook. The order in nature and the laws of nature are not to be taken for granted. It is only our routine way of thinking that prevents us from appreciating the great wonder in the order of nature. The laws of nature formulated by mathematical equations are a comprehensive list of instructions that guide the physical entity in what it must do at every moment. Hence, every law of nature is a particular text that contains a particular message. The existence of order in the world requires an explanation. A world view that does not include God regards this is a great mystery. We will return to this point in Chapter Three.

Here is another important aspect of physical lawfulness. There are many – in fact, infinite – solutions to the mathematical equation that expresses a law of nature. What do I mean by this? The equation that expresses the law of nature does not exclusively determine the movement of the physical objects, the movement of matter. See figure 3.1, which is taken from one of Isaac Newton's works. At point V, different objects are launched in the same direction but at different initial speeds. After the object is sent off, it is subject to Earth's gravitational field. The first object, at a relatively low speed, lands at point D, the closest point to the point of launch. The second object, at a higher speed, falls at point E. The object with an even higher starting speed comes to rest at point F, which is even farther away.

It is interesting that there is a speed at which an object in motion would not fall to the ground at all, but would instead become a kind of satellite. From a mathematical perspective, all of these paths are solutions of the mathematical equation that expresses a particular law of nature. These paths are dependent not only on the law of nature (the mathematical equation), but also on the starting, or initial conditions – the speed and the point of launch. A particular law, therefore, includes an infinite number of possible movements for different initial positions. The laws of science do not provide the initial conditions. They can be determined only from experience.

Hence, for infinite possible movements – each with their own unique initial conditions – the same law of nature applies and the same mathematical equations express that law. One could say that a law of nature is an entity that does not change with the transition from one path to another, from one initial condition to another. The law of nature is fixed – there are numerous, infinite possible paths that obey the same law. However, it is crucial to understand that the law of nature is also preserved within one particular path in each of the paths. What do I mean by this? The path of a particular physical object describes its development over time: at any given moment, it is in another location and traveling at a different speed. The position of the object is dependent on time, but the law of nature itself does not change. It is fixed and is not dependent on time. We can conclude that the law of nature is fixed in two ways: (a) it is fixed and does not change from one path to another; (b) it is fixed within the development of the physical system in time – the system changes with the passage of time, but the law of nature does not change. We can also formulate this as follows: all the physical objects in the world (physical systems) comply with the same law (or laws) of nature, with the law of nature fixed and unchanging for the entire duration of the system's development.

Ultimately, Newton's mechanics was replaced by other theories of physics. But nonetheless a field called mechanics still remains in physics, and is used in the field of astronomy. Mechanics is useful in the calculation of the paths of both missiles and artificial satellites. From a conceptual perspective, to a great extent Newton's mechanics molded the shape of modern physics. The physical quantities also survive, and they remain in the physical theories that replaced it. We have already discussed the concept of *mass*. This concept exists in all physical theories, and is a vital part of them. Another mechanical concept that is used in other theories is that of *energy*. Without going into detail, the concept of energy can be understood intuitively. When an atom bomb explodes, it releases a tremendous amount of energy. When I drive a car, I use the energy of the fuel. In order to function, work, walk, run and swim, I need energy, which I obtain from the food that I eat. Likewise, there is a law of the conservation of energy. The energy that I need comes at the expense of some source of energy or other. It is important to stress that energy is an entirely physical concept, phrased in physical terms. When we use the expression "spiritual energy," we should understand that it has absolutely no connection with physical energy.

4. ELECTROMAGNETISM — THE CONCEPT OF THE FIELD

The theory of electromagnetism brought the concept of the *physical field* to physics. In fact, Newton had already used this concept in his theory of gravity. However, as we have mentioned, from a mechanistic perspective, the gravitational field is an odd, foreign concept. It was only many years later that Albert Einstein came up with a coherent theory of the gravitational field. Now let us try to understand what a physical field is. Nowadays, physics recognizes various different types of physical field, but the theory of electromagnetism was the first to bring to physics a coherent and detailed theory of the physical field – the electromagnetic field. In addition, the electromagnetic field is so frequent in our lives that we can hardly imagine ourselves without the electromagnetic devices that surround us, such as electric lights, radio, television, lasers, etc.

The most fundamental concept of the mechanical world is the concept of matter. Everyone knows (or thinks they know) what matter is. Matter is a stone, a chair, a table, our limbs. Everything that is solid and defined in space is matter. One can see, feel, push or be pushed by the material object. Conversely, the physical field, like the electromagnetic field, is a physical entity that generally cannot be seen or felt and that is not limited, but rather extends across an entire area. This entity seems almost abstract.

How is it possible, nonetheless, to define the field using concepts that we can understand? For example, let us look at the fields of positive and negative electric charges (Figure 4.1). A positive electric charge (+) produces an electric field (static, not time-dependent) in the area around it. In contrast with a material object that is concentrated in a particular place and in a particular volume, an electric field occupies the entire space. What does it mean that an electric field exists at every point in an area? An electric field is a field of electrical forces. An electrical force acts on an electric charge if it is situated at a particular point in that area. A degree of abstraction is required in order to grasp the fact that an electric field exists also in an area without charges. The field's forces exist in every place in the area even if there are no charges upon which they act. In order to test that at a particular point an electric force exists, the charge must be placed at that point. An electric field will repel or attract this charge in the direction of the charge that produces the field: (+) or (-) in Figure 4.1. In the shaded text below, I describe the properties of an electric field. (The fact that the explanation is in shaded text is no indication of any particular difficulty in understanding the example –

A Static Electric Field

On the left side of Figure 4.1, we can see a "picture" of an electric field of a positive (+) electric charge (at the center of the diagram). The arrows show the forces at various points of the field. All the arrows point away from the central charge. This means that if you place a positive electric charge at a certain point, a force of repulsion away from the central charge will act upon it. The length of the arrow in Figure 4.1 is proportionate to the magnitude of the force. One can see that the length of the arrows decreases as the distance from the central charge increases, which reflects the fact that the electrical forces decrease as their distance from the central charge increases. On the right side of Figure 4.1 the electric field of a negative (–) charge is shown. It attracts positive charges. And hence all the arrows are pointing in the direction of the negative charge.

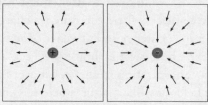

Figure 4.1 Electric fields

(Left)   (Right)

Field of a positive   Field of a negative electric charge

electric charge

99

it is simply to show that one may also continue reading without reading the shaded passage.)

A static electric field, which does not change with the passage of time, is an example of the simplest kind of field. But even in this example we can see the difference between a field and matter. It seems that the physical field exists as an option, as a possibility: If we place an electric charge at a certain point within the area (in the case of an electric field), then the force will act on that charge. The question then arises: is there anything in the area of the field when we do not place any charge there to test the presence of the field? According to the explanation above, we have given an unequivocal answer – a physical field is a new kind of entity, and it exists at every point in the area, irrespective of any tests. As stated, a static electric field is one of the simplest kinds of field. Other fields have a far more elaborate structure as well as a complex dependence on time.

I am sitting in my room. It contains all kinds of material items, but it also contains electromagnetic fields, electromagnetic waves at various frequencies (various wavelengths). To some extent, we are able to "see" optical electromagnetic waves in the visible range. Light from the sun or from electric lights is comprised of electromagnetic waves of this type. In my room, there are also electromagnetic waves in the radio range. It is impossible to see or to feel these waves. However, one can receive radio waves using radio receivers, and shorter waves can be received using television sets. Similarly, in the visible range, our seeing devices, including our eyes, perceive the presence of the electromagnetic field.

In my room, and everywhere, at every point in the area, there exists an entity completely different from matter. But what characterizes the electromagnetic field in places where there are no charges? How is it at all possible to talk about the existence and presence of an entity that is entirely different from matter? The answer is simple – we can attribute energy (or, to be more precise, a concentration of energy) at every point in the area to the electromagnetic field. Just like matter, a field has energy. What follows from this, according to Einstein's formula, is that a field also has mass (a concentration of mass at every point in the area). The electromagnetic field, like other physical fields, is a real entity, no less so than matter.

I would like to add a few words here regarding terminology. We use the word *matter* in reference to atoms, molecules, electrons, protons, and so on.

A physical field is a different type of entity; it is not material. However, we can make our work easier if we deduce from the fact that materialism failed that not everything is matter. We explained above (Chapter One, section 9) that the concept of materialism can be broadened by saying that the foundation of everything in the world is not matter but different physical entities. Today, we also use the term *physicalism* instead of materialism. The Latin word *materia* can also be used to refer to any physical entity – not just matter but also physical fields.

Maxwell's equations describe quantitatively, mathematically, the electromagnetic field and its development through time. The characteristic features of these equations, which also appear in all other equations of modern physics, can be summarized in one sentence: Maxwell's equations are laws that describe the field's *structure* and its development through time. It is important to emphasize the difference between the equations of Newton's mechanics and Maxwell's equations. In mechanics, once you know the position and speed of the object at a certain moment of time and the forces acting upon it, you can predict its entire path in advance. In Maxwell's theory, when we know the state of the field at one particular moment everywhere in the area, we can predict how the entire field will change in space and time. With the help of Newton's laws, we can study the movement of Earth from the force acting between the sun and the Earth. Maxwell's theory does not deal with material objects. Maxwell's equations express the laws that operate in the electromagnetic field. They do not connect two distant planets like Newton's laws do. In Maxwell's equations, the field *here and now* is dependent on the field *closest to it at a time just past*. We can learn about what will happen here through events that occurred at a great distance by summarizing the tiny steps, each of which is described by Maxwell's equations. "The formulation of these equations is the most important event in physics since Newton's time, not only because of their wealth of content, but also because they form a pattern for a new type of law" (*The Evolution of Physics*, 148).

There is another interesting aspect to the laws of the field. Maxwell's equations express a particular law of nature, or, to be more precise, an approximation to that law. *These equations are a fairly complex text that show which changes the field must make at every point in space over a period of time.*

More in the area of metaphysical speculation. A physical field can serve as an analogy to the spiritual world. It exists at every point in space and can contain rather complex information, such as complete texts, dramatic performances, and so on. Via television, it can broadcast events occurring in remote places of the Earth to other locations around the world. However, sophisticated devices are required in order to receive this information, such as television sets and human biological systems. Without these devices, the physical fields cannot be felt or seen. This is precisely the case with the divine, spiritual world. It cannot be seen or felt either, and only human beings, in their great complexity, are capable of connecting with it.

While it is not within the scope of this book to explain and describe the substance of Maxwell's equations, I would nevertheless like to present them here, with no requirement from the reader to understand them:

$$\operatorname{div}\mathbf{E} = 4\pi\sigma$$

$$\operatorname{rot}\mathbf{E} + \frac{1}{c}\frac{\partial \mathbf{H}}{\partial t} = 0$$

$$\operatorname{div}\mathbf{H} = 0$$

$$\operatorname{rot}\mathbf{H} - \frac{1}{c}\frac{\partial \mathbf{E}}{\partial t} = \frac{4\pi}{c}\mathbf{I}$$

To those who are unfamiliar with theoretical physics, these symbols will mean nothing. However, they may assume that there is some kind of message here written in its own language. And there really is an important message written here, but it is not written in one of the spoken languages of the world, nor can it be translated into one of those languages. This is the language of mathematics. Maxwell's greatness lies in the fact that he revealed this message with its many important implications, and they have entered the homes of each and every one of us and made great changes in the world.

These symbols are also a testament to the fact that in the inanimate part of nature, there is an incredible harmony that is expressed in these and other equations. Anyone who wishes can see in this message a mark of divine activity in the inanimate part of nature, even though others may see it as a "natural" phenomenon that requires no explanation.

Max von Laue, an important physicist of the twentieth century, wrote the following about Maxwell's theory. "For me, as for many others, this theory has opened up a whole new world. The understanding of how complex and diverse phenomena can be mathematically reduced to simple, yet beautiful and harmonious equations is one of the most powerful experiences a person could have" (*Geschichte der Physik*).

Boltzmann, another eminent physicist, cites Goethe's *Faust:* "War es ein Gott, der diese Zeichen schrieb?" (Was it a god who wrote these signs?)

This is what Richard Feynman, one of the great physicists of the twentieth century, said about James Clark Maxwell's theory: "From a long view of the history of mankind – seen from, say, ten thousand years from now – there can be little doubt that the most significant event of the nineteenth century will be judged as Maxwell's discovery of the laws of electrodynamics. The American Civil War will pale into provincial insignificance in comparison with this important scientific event of the same decade."

5. THE THEORY OF RELATIVITY

The development of science, and primarily the development of physics, deepens our understanding of the laws of nature. The twentieth century saw the absolute collapse of the mechanistic view. The revolution in physics was led by Albert Einstein, who came up with the special and general theory of relativity and contributed enormously to the foundations of quantum theory. The theory of relativity deepens our understanding of the concepts of space, time and gravity, and connects them all to one another.

The word *relativity* indicates that the theory of the physical reality is dependent on the physical state of the observer describing it – for example, his speed. Or, to be more precise, some physical quantities, such as the speed of an object, have different values for different observers.[4] It is sometimes thought that the statement "Everything is relative" comes from the theory of relativity. This is not at all true. The essence of the theory of relativity is that there are absolute, fixed physical quantities that are not relative and that are independent of the state of the observer.

Here is an example: Speakers of different languages use different words to describe the same reality. The words *table, Tisch, mensa* and *стол* all describe the same thing, a table, in English, German, Latin and Russian.

---

4. Who are themselves traveling at different speeds.

Translation from one language to another makes communication between speakers of different languages possible. On the other hand, translation is possible only for things that are not dependent upon a particular language, things that have the same meaning in all languages. In mathematics we can show the meaning of things using a particular symbol. Hence, the words *five*, *fünf, quinque* and *пять* can all be denoted using the symbol 5.

Albert Einstein studied the concepts of space and time in great depth in his special theory of relativity. In the new picture that arose from his analysis, the duration of an event and the length of a solid body are not absolute. Even an object's mass is not an absolute quantity. These things are relative: they depend on which of the moving systems is being measured, even if it is only possible to observe this dependency at very high speeds, close to the speed of light. Instead of a period of time and the length of an object, which are absolute in Newton's mechanics and in our everyday experience but are relative according to Einstein's theory, there are other absolute things. Space-time behaves as one entity. Both space and time are relative entities, while absolute physical reality can only be attributed to space-time.

We have already seen that the language of science is mathematics. It is difficult to understand the substance of physics without using mathematics, and it is even harder when we are talking about twentieth-century physics. On the other hand, when we focus on the *fundamentals* of the physical theories, they can actually be simpler and clearer in more advanced science. The principle that Einstein exploited fully in his analysis of the physical systems is called the *principle of relativity*. This principle refers to the nature of the laws of physics, the laws of nature.

It is clear that a law of nature should have a meaning that is not dependent on anything relative. We explained in section 3 (Figure 3.1) that the same law "covers" many – in fact, an infinite number – of movements and paths. For an infinite number of initial positions of a physical system, the same law determines the development over time. The laws of nature are not dependent on time and place. For a believing person, a law of nature is a divine command, and as such it is universal, general in nature – it is not dependent on anything special. Even from the scientist's intuitive viewpoint, and most definitely Albert Einstein's, the laws of nature have a distinctive status. The fundamental premise of the scientific account is that the laws of nature operate everywhere and at all times. Physicalism describes these two properties of the physical laws – the fact that they are independent of space and time – as the *symmetry* of nature. "By this usage physicists mean that nature treats every moment in time and every location in space identically – symmetrically – by ensuring that the same fundamental laws are in operation"[5] (Brian Greene, *The Elegant Universe*, 169). The **principle of relativity**, which lies at the heart of the special and general theory of relativity, teaches us that all the physical laws must be identical in all systems, with no connection to the relative movement of the system.[6] Einstein managed to achieve what no one had ever done before him – he discovered the identical, namely symmetrical, laws of nature in all the physical systems. He achieved this with his general theory of relativity.

The principle of relativity also existed in classical physics (up to the discovery of the general theory of relativity) – for all physical systems that move at a fixed speed relative to one another, there are exactly the same laws. It is impossible to discern a fixed movement. When two systems are traveling at fixed speeds relative to each other, one cannot say: "This system is at rest and the other one is in motion." Einstein's great achievement was generalizing the principle of relativity for all types of movements, not just for movements at fixed speeds.

Identical treatment for all systems was achieved in the general law of relativity, by studying the properties of space and time, which led to a deeper understanding of the gravitational field. Einstein came to an astounding conclusion: the gravitational field is actually a field of (geometric) properties of space-time at every place and time. Einstein's equations link the properties of space-time with the distribution of the energies of physical entities at any time and place. Like Maxwell's equations, Einstein's equations describe the development of the gravitational field in tiny steps in space and time. In contrast with other physical fields, which exist in space and time, the gravitational field describes the properties of space-time itself.

---

5.   The author's humanization of nature ("Nature *treats*," "Nature . . . ensuring") is common among scientists. We will discuss this more later on.

6.   The special theory of relativity and classical mechanics include only inertial systems that move at fixed speeds, while the general theory of relativity deals equally with systems whose speeds are fixed and those where they are not fixed.

The Systems of Copernicus and Ptolemy

Right at the initial stages of the development of science, the issue of the choice of system from which we observe and describe physical events was at the center of a ferocious struggle between the Catholic Church and science. Let us imagine two objects, the sun and the Earth, for example. The movement that we are observing and describing is always relative. It can be described by a connection of the frame of reference with the Earth or the sun. Copernicus's great achievement was that he transferred the frame of reference from the Earth to the sun. The frame of reference connected with the sun is much more suitable for a description of the movements of the Earth and the other planets than that connected with the Earth. Therefore, it is preferable to use in the laws of physics (and especially in the laws of physics known prior to Einstein) the frame of reference connected with the sun rather than that connected with the Earth. In terms of simplicity of describing the movements of the celestial bodies, it is better to use Copernicus's system than that of Ptolemy (a world in which the Earth is at its center). However, the Church strongly supported the Ptolemaic system and persecuted any scientists who supported the Copernican system. This vehement debate between the opinions of Copernicus and Ptolemy, which goes back to the early days of science, lost its significance after the discovery of the general law of relativity.

I must emphasize here that we, as human beings, are incapable of imagining a non-Euclidean, curved, three-dimensional space. Two-dimensional curved surfaces, as in figures 5.1 and 5.2, are analogies to three-dimensional curved space. Einstein's equations describe the curvature of space-time at every point in space-time.

These are Einstein's equations (though I will not attempt to discuss them in any depth):

$$R_{\mu\nu} - \tfrac{1}{2} R g_{\mu\nu} + \Lambda g_{\mu\nu} = -\kappa T_{\mu\nu}$$

With the geometrization of gravity, the general law of relativity achieved an incredible conceptual unification. The general law of relativity laid the groundwork for the development of modern-day cosmology – the development of the world after creation from the perspective of physics.

The Curvature of Space-time

In figure 5.1 below, (two-dimensional) space is shown, the geometry of which changes from point to point. In figure 5.2 the effect of matter on the geometry of space is shown.

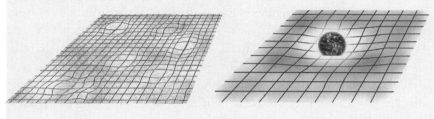

Fig. 5.1 Example of non-Euclidean, two-dimensional space

Fig. 5.2 The effect of a heavy body, such as the sun, on the geometry of space.

Max Born, one of the twentieth century's great physicists, wrote about Einstein's general theory of relativity: "The theory appeared to me then, and it still does, the greatest feat of human thinking about nature, the most amazing combination of philosophical penetration, physical intuition, and mathematical skill."

Einstein and Infeld, in *The Evolution of Physics*, conclude the section of the theory of relativity as follows:

> The theory of relativity develops in two steps. The first step leads to what is known as the special theory of relativity, applied only to inertial co-ordinate systems, that is, to systems in which the law of inertia, as formulated by Newton, is valid. The special theory of relativity is based on two fundamental assumptions: physical laws are the same in all co-ordinate systems moving uniformly [in a straight line and at a fixed speed], relative to each other; the velocity of light always has the same value.... The theory of relativity changes the laws of mechanics. The old laws are invalid if the velocity of the moving particle approaches that of light....

The general theory of relativity gives a still deeper analysis of the time-space continuum. The validity of the theory is no longer restricted to inertial co-ordinate systems. The theory attacks the problem of gravitation and formulates new structure laws for the gravitational field. It forces us to analyze the role played by geometry in the description of the physical world . . . .

6. QUANTUM THEORY

The age of quantum mechanics began at the start of the twentieth century with the work of Max Planck (1858–1947). In order to explain the density of the energy of black-body radiation,[7] in October 1900 Planck suggested a new formula, today referred to by his name. The formula includes the new physical constant – Planck's constant – h. The next step was taken by Albert Einstein in 1905. He suggested that light at a frequency ω (omega) behaves like a collection of quanta, a kind of particle, with the energy of one quantum being $\hbar\omega=\varepsilon$.[8] Einstein called these quanta *photons*. The density of photons in an electromagnetic field is equal to the density of its energy. This hypothesis was tested in a number of experiments which supported it. Thus Einstein discovered for the first time the duality of the wave-particle. Photons have both "particle-like" properties and "wave-like" properties. In certain experiments a photon behaves like a particle, while in others it behaves like a wave. The concentration of the energies of an electromagnetic field is linked to the concentration and distribution of probabilities of the photons. Over time it became clear that it is not only photons that have wave-particle duality. Other particles also do, and in fact all particles, such as electrons, protons and neutrons, have both wave-like and particle-like properties. Einstein's photon theory contained the conceptual seed of quantum mechanics which was to develop in due course.

Electrons behave exactly like photons – quanta of light. The behavior of all quantum objects (electrons, protons, neutrons, etc.), as well as that of photons has one thing in common: all of these particles can be called "wave-particles," not particle-like or wave-like. It is difficult – in fact, impossible – to understand, imagine or sense the nature of quantum particles. Even

---

7.   In physics, a black body is an object that completely absorbs electromagnetic radiation at all wavelengths. This means that all electromagnetic radiation that strikes the body neither passes through it nor is reflected by it but is absorbed into it. This absorption causes a change in temperature of the black body (due to the conversion of the electromagnetic radiation into thermal energy in the body).

8.   Today, the constant $\hbar$, which is equivalent to $h/2\pi$, is more commonly used.

the expression "wave-particle" is rather odd. When we say *particle*, we mean something concentrated in a tiny area of space, while when we use the word *wave* we mean the movement of continuous matter, such as waves of water. We are talking about something that is spread out over a large distance.

Quantum mechanics caused the most major upheaval in our understanding of physical reality, in our understanding of nature. Matter by its very nature has a discrete, granular, non-continuous nature. It is made up of fundamental particles, of the basic quanta of matter. Likewise, an electric charge also has a discrete structure, and this is also the case with energy. A physical field and electromagnetic waves too have a discrete structure. Photons are the energy of light – they are the smallest units of light. All the particles have a **dualistic** property, which expresses the **duality** of the wave-particle, the combination of the wave-like and particle-like properties. We cannot understand duality using concepts from our everyday experience. The reality of the quantum world is completely different from anything that we can grasp with our senses.

There is a significant, radical difference between all the early theories – including the theory of relativity – which we can call classical theories, and quantum theory. The fundamental premise at the basis of the classical theories is that it is always possible to separate the subject from the object, the measuring device and the item being measured. However, quantum particles are so delicate that one cannot ignore the effect of the measurement itself in the position of the particle. Measuring, among other things, is also seeing. In order to see, we must send the photons – at least one photon, the smallest possible unit of light – onto the object being measured. However, a photon has a certain, though limited, amount of energy. When the measured object is large enough, we can ignore the effect of the photon on its movement. But when we want to measure the velocity of something as small as an electron, for example, we cannot ignore the effect of even a single photon on the electron's movement. The measurement itself changes its position. Quantum mechanics, as compared with classical mechanics, is fundamentally incapable of providing a precise prediction of the movement of the quantum object.

Quantum phenomena are strange. They do not sit well with common sense and are contrary to our intuition, which is based on our day-to-day tangible experience. Moreover, with quantum mechanics, we come across a new model of science that we have never encountered before. It used to be perfectly acceptable to think that science was predicated on the condition that *the same cause will always lead to the same outcome.* The classical theories, including the theory of relativity, satisfy this condition. If we know the precise position of a classical physical system at a particular point in time, then we are able, at least in principle, to predict precisely what will happen to that system at a later time. Why do I say *in principle*? I say this because classical physics also has statistical theories which deal with probabilities of events occurring rather than precise outcomes. However, in the case of classical physics, the statistical description is used only because the precise description is too complex and is not practical, even if it is possible to obtain in principle.

This is not the case with quantum theory. Below is a description of the double-slit experiment.

In the double-slit experiment, electrons pass through the plate with two slits and then strike the screen behind the plate. And here is the surprise of quantum theory. When we are talking about a single electron, *there is no law which determines where on the screen the electron will strike,* even though we have as much information as possible about the electron prior to its passing through the double-slit plate. It should be emphasized here that if quantum mechanics is valid – and there are innumerable experiments which indicate that it is – then there is no law that determines the path of the electron. It is not that it exists and we are not aware of it. It simply does not exist. Its existence would contradict quantum theory. From here, we learn that even in the inanimate world, in the material world, not everything has laws. In general, there are no laws that govern a single particle. Conversely, quantum mechanics can give a precise prediction of the development of the probabilities over time. When we send a large number of electrons one after another in the double-slit experiment, we can predict fairly accurately how the wave picture will appear on the screen.

A system of quantum particles is described in quantum theory by a certain function, called wave function. Knowledge of wave function enables us to calculate the possible behavior probabilities of the system. Quantum mechanics offers a new type of physical field. In contrast with the classical physical fields, which describe the existing reality, the quantum field describes the possible, potential reality, the probabilities of different even-

The Double-slit Experiment

We need not be experts in quantum mechanics in order to describe this experiment and understand its implications. We need only know that it can be carried out and that it has been carried out many times, in different versions. A beam of electrons (or other particles) is sent to a screen with two slits. Some of the electrons pass through the slit and hit another screen (see diagram). We may send the electrons one by one or many at once. When an electron arrives at the screen, a black dot appears on it. Quantum theory claims that in principle, we cannot predict a given electron's exact place of contact on the screen. There is no law that governs the path of a given electron. The theory can only calculate the probability that the electron will arrive at a certain place on the screen, but in order to measure these probabilities, we must send a large number of electrons. Since no law determines the arrival point of a single electron, some physicists say (by way of metaphor) that the electron has "freedom of choice."

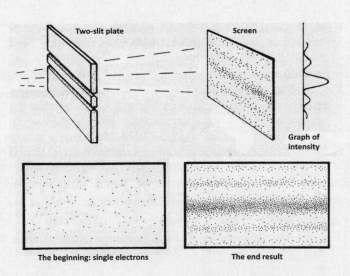

tualities. The equations of quantum theory, like Schrödinger's equations, describe the development of wave function in time and space.[9]

In the classical theories, it is always possible to make a clear distinction between different objects in different places in space. This means that if we affect or exert force on a particular object, another object is not affected by this immediately. Rather, a certain amount of time is required for the object to "feel" the change made to the first object. Therefore, a change in the movement of the sun will be felt on Earth only after the approximately eight minutes required for the gravitational field to extend from the sun to Earth. A flash of lightning produced in one place affects us after the amount of time required for its light to reach us. On the quantum plane, this kind of distinction is not generally possible. The impact of a particular quantum particle is "felt" immediately by other particles located at a distance, even a very great distance, from it. There is no clear distinction between the different parts of the quantum system, and there is reciprocity between them, even if they are enormous distances away from each other and no physical forces are operating between them. This is the non-locality of the quantum entity.

7. NEW DEVELOPMENTS

As science progresses, we move farther and farther away from our simplistic understanding of the material world that is characteristic of the mechanistic approach. The description of matter has become more and more abstract. An illustration of this is shown below in Figure 7.1.

Matter is comprised of atoms, which are themselves made up of protons, neutrons, electrons and quarks. According to string theory, all of these particles are in fact tiny loops in an oscillating string. While these strings are one-dimensional, they move in eleven-dimensional space-time! In fact, the entire volume of matter is full of various types of physical fields. However, the key point is that the movements of the components of matter, such as

---

9. The situation is actually more complicated than this. Wave function describes a field not in regular, three-dimensional space, but in the multi-dimensional configuration space, of all the particles of the quantum system. The phenomenon of non-locality of quantum systems is connected to this fact.

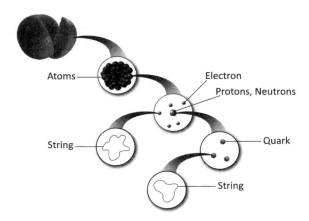

Figure 7.1 A macroscopic object comprised of atoms, electrons, protons, etc.

quarks and strings, behave according to physical laws, which determine their development (statistically, the distribution of probabilities).

8. CONCLUSION: A SCIENTIFIC DESCRIPTION OF THE PHYSICAL WORLD

One might ask – and I have actually been asked this – what Chapter Two, which is devoted to physics, is doing in a book about divine providence and the world's development from the Jewish perspective. What is the point in discussing ideas and concepts of physics in a book such as this? My answer is quite straightforward. It is very difficult, if possible at all, to talk about the divine world without understanding, even if only partially, the laws of nature. Physics is the branch of science that deals with the laws of nature. A study of the laws of nature without any preconceptions is bound to leave a deep impression of the sublime creation and lead to questions about the source of it all. As we have already mentioned, the existence of the Creator cannot be logically proven, and even reality itself cannot be logically proven. We come to know it through the unmediated connection between the self and reality. Likewise, knowledge of God comes about through an encounter between the spirit and divine reality. We have already cited the words of Albert Einstein, who tells of his enchantment by the world: "[The scientist's] religious feeling takes the form of a rapturous amazement at the harmony of natural law, which reveals an intelligence of such superiority that, compared with it, all the systematic thinking and acting of human beings is an utterly insignificant reflection." In other words, the encounter with reality can itself bring us to know God. But it requires a certain degree of humility and wisdom to appreciate the fact that there is also a divine element in our encounter with reality.

We must distinguish the three stages of the development of physics from Galileo to the present day: the mechanistic stage, the electromagnetic stage (this also includes the theory of relativity and its law of gravity), and the quantum stage. These are also the stages of our understanding of the material world.

The mechanistic stage seems to be the easiest to understand. It also fits best with our experience-based intuition. But we must not forget that it took humanity two thousand years, from Aristotle to Galileo, to arrive at an account of the world that seems to us to be fairly simple. A major breakthrough was needed in the way we think and in the way that we study reality. It was Galileo who introduced the *thought experiment* as a way to research reality. The thought experiment, which led to the formulation of the *law of inertia*, marked the beginning of modern physics. According to the law of inertia, if there are no forces acting on an object, then it will continue to move forever at a fixed speed. But it was only Isaac Newton, who was born the year that Galileo died, who produced a near-perfect formulation of the laws of mechanics and integrated them with the law of gravity.

In general terms, we can illustrate the mechanical world using a game of pool – the movement of the balls on the pool table is derived from the collisions between them. These movements can be described using Newton's laws. Between collisions, a particular ball will travel at a fixed speed (the law of inertia), and a collision between balls causes a change in the speed of the ball that is struck (Newton's second law). Even in Newton's day, this simple account did not take hold, despite all efforts. His most impressive achievement was in the field of the movement of celestial bodies, where the main factor is the *gravitational field* acting at a distance, rather than the push. In fact, in the mechanical world, the gravitational field is a strange, foreign concept.

The second stage in the development of physics – and the next stage in our understanding of the world – is connected with the concept of the *electromagnetic field*. An electromagnetic field, and any physical field in general, is a new kind of physical entity, which does not fit with any of our everyday experience. A great deal of abstraction is required to grasp the essence of this entity. In contrast with mechanical objects, which take up a certain amount of space and a limited volume, the physical field is located at every point in space. It cannot be seen or felt, just like a spiritual entity. The electromagnetic stage reached its peak with Albert Einstein's discovery of the special theory of relativity. The general theory of relativity suggested a new type of physical field, a geometric field, a field of geometric properties of space-time at every point in the four-dimensional entity – space-time.

It should be noted that physics develops through the creation of new theories, with the new theory including an old theory as a specific case. This means that all the quantitative conclusions of the old theory are included in the new theory in a more precise way. But that is not all – the new theory also broadens the limits of its application and adds new concepts which were not included in the old theory. Thus, the principles of Newton's mechanics, combined with his law of gravity, give fairly accurate physical predictions in the area to which they apply. The new theory, Einstein's theory of relativity, makes the predictions of Newton's theory more accurate in the area to which it applies, namely in the areas of speeds lower than the speed of light and in relatively weak gravitational fields, while also broadening the limits of its application – to greater speeds and stronger gravitational fields. This is all about application. However, the general theory of relativity also includes new ideas and concepts that did not exist at all in Newton's theories – namely, Einstein's equations, which describe the structure and development of the gravitational field in time. Most important, the general theory of relativity makes a connection between the gravitational field and the geometry of space-time. This is an extremely impressive advancement of our understanding of the world. Newton's theory brought a new concept to the world – the gravitational field – but a deep understanding of this entity was only achieved through the general theory of relativity. As the application of the theoretical basis to technological applications progresses, we are able to broaden our understanding of the world in which we live.

As we approach modern physics, it becomes more difficult and complex to understand the world. The quantum stage is the most difficult to understand. There is no way for us to understand or imagine quantum phenomena by comparing them to something with which we are familiar from our day-to-day experience. All material things that are familiar to us, such as various physical objects, are ultimately made up of quantum particles. Large, macroscopic masses, which consist of a huge quantity of quantum particles, behave in a deterministic way according to the laws of classical physics. This means that their development can be predicted with great accuracy. However, generally speaking, there is no law that can predict the behavior of a single, lone quantum particle. Deep inside the macroscopic object, there is no deterministic lawfulness.

The quantum particle is a new kind of entity that is unlike anything that we know, and we have no tools with which to imagine it. The contradictions that seemingly arise when we attempt to describe this entity are imaginary and derive from the attempt to compare the quantum particle with something already familiar to us. The quantum particle has particle-like properties that manifest themselves in certain experiments and wave-like properties that show up in others. But the quantum particle is neither a wave nor a particle. It is something else. While we can get used to the existence of this entity, we cannot imagine it.

We can learn another thing from looking at the scientific account. The laws of nature are consistent, coherent texts, the contents of which are instructions that guide how a physical entity must develop over time. But the main information about the physical entity is in the initial conditions, while the physical laws describe only the transformation of the initial information.

In Chapter Two, we have attained a certain level of knowledge of the inanimate world. This world is far simpler than the animate world, which also contains human beings – the height of complexity. We can see how complex and sophisticated even the inanimate world is. Its sophistication and complexity are combined with the simplicity and symmetry of the fundamental laws, though many years of study and research, as well as perhaps a touch of genius like that of Einstein, are required to recognize the "intelligence of such superiority" in the structure of the inanimate world and its laws.

People...

9. ISAAC NEWTON

Isaac Newton was born in 1642 in a small cottage on a farm near the village of Colsterworth in Lincolnshire, England. His father, a farmer, died before Isaac was born. In school, Isaac did not stand out as having any particular talents. All that could be said about him was that he was a bright boy with a natural talent for drawing and building models. In 1665, Newton completed his bachelor's degree at Cambridge. That was the year of the Great Plague in England, during which a tenth of London's population perished. Because of the plague, Cambridge University was closed and Newton returned home to his mother in the village, where he stayed until the spring of 1667, when the university re-opened. During those eighteen months of intellectual solitude, Newton was immersed in thoughts of the foundations of physics. When he returned to Cambridge he was ready to lay the foundations for his life work in physics. Many years later Newton wrote in his memoirs: "All this was in the two plague years of 1665 and 1666, for in those days I was in my prime of age for invention, and minded mathematics and philosophy more than at any time since."

Newton was convinced that the laws that govern the movement of the celestial bodies were the regular laws of mechanics that apply to objects on Earth. Before him, the accepted theory in the intellectual world was that the celestial bodies, just like every other body, had their own laws. Isaac Newton was a man of faith. His deep religious faith, which bordered on mysticism, was a driving force in his scientific work, which he saw as deciphering God's mysteries. We can assume that his belief in the unity of the world and in the unity of its laws derived from his religious world view.

He was convinced that the moon acts in accordance with the same laws as a moving object on the ground. But the question was: what kind of force holds the moon on its circular path around Earth, and why does it not fly away from Earth? This is where the apple story comes in. Isaac was sitting under an apple tree next to his house in the village, pondering the Moon's path, when his thoughts were interrupted by the soft thud of an apple falling. The following thought came into his head: perhaps the ground that pulls the apple also pulls the moon and holds it on its circular path around the Earth. Several years later, Newton wrote about this sudden thought: "I compared the force necessary to keep the moon in her orb with the force of gravity at the surface of the earth, and found them to answer pretty nearly."

During the years of the plague (1665–1667), when Newton was staying at home with his mother, he made his most important discoveries in the fields of optics, mathematics and mechanics, and amongst others, his binomial theorem and the principles of differential and integral calculus. This last discovery was a turning point in the history of mathematics. When he returned to Cambridge at the age of twenty-six, the Lucasian Chair was vacant and he was appointed professor of mathematics. His first lecture series was about his theory of optics. He invented and built a telescope built on the principle of reflection – the concentration of the beams was achieved with the aid of a concave mirror instead of a lens (thereby avoiding chromatic aberration). At the request of the Royal Society in London he built another telescope, and as a result, in 1672 he was elected a member of the society and published the principles of the new theory of optics in the society's periodical. In 1675, Newton published the continuation of his article in which he discussed phenomena such as interference and diffraction. (The importance of these phenomena was eventually recognized in the nineteenth century, with the development of the theory of light waves.) In 1679, he returned to look after his mother on her deathbed. When he went back to Cambridge half a year later, he succeeding in deriving Kepler's first and second laws from the premise of gravitation. As a result of his experiments in the field of alchemy, the rest of this research was delayed until 1684. Newton's magnum opus, *Principia* (Principles) was published in 1687. During the years 1689–1690, Newton represented the university in the Parliament of 1689. In 1695 Newton was appointed Master of the Royal Mint and planned England's monetary reform. He served in this position for the rest of his life. In 1701, Newton resigned from his post in Cambridge and moved to London. In 1703, he agreed to be appointed President of the Royal Society and in 1704 published his second major work, *Opticks*. In 1705, Newton was awarded a knighthood by Queen Anne, who knew of his achievements and is said to have declared that she thought it a happiness to have lived at the same time as, and to have known, so great a man. From that point on, Newton was a highly respected national figure in all echelons of English society. This was the first time that this kind of honor was bestowed on account of achievements in theoretical science. Isaac Newton died in March 1727 at the age of eighty-four.

We have already mentioned that Newton was a man of faith. Faith and theology occupied an important, even central, place in his life, and he viewed his work in science as a revelation of the mysteries of God. Newton devoted much time to studying the sources. He read Jewish sources – Josephus and Philo Judaeus – and learned Hebrew so that he could study the Torah, the works of Maimonides, the Talmud and the book of Ezekiel. He considered the study of Jewish works to be vital to understanding the phenomenon of revelation, and he remained committed to the task until his death.[10]

He tried to make an exact replica of the First and Second Temples using the prophecies of Ezekiel, which he read in the original Hebrew. Newton saw a kind of idol worship in the Christianity of the establishment. He could not agree with the concept of the trinity and rebelled against it. Newton was a follower of Arius, who lived in the fourth century C.E. Arius taught that Jesus was a prophet, but that he was a person just like all people. Because of his "heresy," Arius was excommunicated and condemned, and his books were burnt. According to Newton, the word *trinity* appears nowhere in the Christian sources, but was a much later fabrication. In the King James translation the following sentence appears: "And these three are one." Newton discovered that this sentence does not appear at all in the original text.

Immediately after he wrote *Principia*, Newton started writing on religious subjects. It is easy to understand why Newton saw his work in physics and mathematics as a distraction from his mission. "He had committed himself to a reinterpretation of the tradition central to the whole of European civilization."[11] Newton did not simply see the trinity as a mistake, but as a sin of idolatry, and in around 1691, he wrote the paper "An Historical Account of Two Notable Corruptions of the Scriptures," which was published after his death. Had it been published in 1692, Newton would have been branded an outcast and thrown out of both Cambridge and the Royal Society.

Newton left a large collection of papers on matters of religion and history, totaling around one-and-a-half million words (about five thousand

---

10. *Never at Rest: A Biography of Isaac Newton* by R.S. Westfall, Cambridge University Press, 1980.

11. Ibid., 315.

pages)! A friend of Newton's, the philosopher John Locke, wrote that he knew few who were equal to Newton in knowledge of the Bible (*Never at Rest*, 489). Newton likened absolute infinite space to God's sensory system (sensorium) – incorporeal, living, intelligent, omnipresent, belonging to a being who sees all things intimately and connects with us through our little sensoriums, and thus understands our thoughts (*Optics*, Query 28). Newton writes: "The omnipresent God is acknowledged and by the Jews is called Place." (*Never at Rest*, 511)

Newton was convinced that the world as we know it could not have been the result of mechanical necessity, but required the intelligence of a Creator (ibid., 505).

Newton was a shy, withdrawn and ascetic man. He could not stand arguments and did his best to avoid them.

10. JAMES CLERK MAXWELL

James Clerk Maxwell was born on June 13, 1831, in Edinburgh, Scotland, into a distinguished Scottish family. Early in his youth he displayed a propensity for researching phenomena in nature and his environment. At the age of ten, he was accepted as a student to the Edinburgh Academy and his talents were soon widely recognized. At the age of fourteen, he wrote his first paper, which was presented to the Royal Society of Edinburgh. At the same time, he also started to write poetry, and continued to do so until his death. During the years 1847–1854, he continued his studies at Cambridge University, and after graduating he was made a fellow. In 1856–1860, Maxwell served as professor at Marischal College in Aberdeen. One important contribution to science was his kinetic theory of gases. Maxwell discovered how velocities of gas molecules are distributed, which is expressed in a formula which bears his name.

In 1860, he was appointed professor of physics at King's College, London, where he completed his work on color theory. The peak of Maxwell's accomplishments is the development of the electromagnetic field theory. His articles during this period "On Physical Lines of Force" and "A Dynamical Theory of the Electromagnetic Field" laid the groundwork for this theory.

On November 5, 1879, Maxwell died of cancer at the age of forty-eight.

In their book, *The Life of James Clerk Maxwell*, Lewis Campbell and William Garnett paint Maxwell as a pleasant individual. He was a good son, a loving husband and a loyal and sensitive friend. Maxwell was a man of deep faith, which came as a result of serious thought. It was derived both from being convinced intellectually and from something much more important. All his life he was fascinated by matters of faith and religion. From childhood he had an exceptional memory, and his knowledge of scripture was both comprehensive and precise; he could cite chapter and verse for almost any quote from Psalms. A few days before his death, Maxwell said: "I have looked into most philosophical systems, and I have seen that none will work without God" (*The Life of James Clerk Maxwell,* 426).

11. ALBERT EINSTEIN

Albert Einstein was born on 14 March, 1879 in Ulm, in the Kingdom of Württemberg, Germany. Einstein was born in the same year that James Clerk Maxwell died. His father, Herman, was the owner of a small electrochemical plant. In 1889, the Einstein family moved to Munich, and in 1894 to Milan, when Albert attended the Cantonal School in Aarau, Switzerland. From 1896 to 1900 he studied at the Swiss Federal Polytechnic School in Zurich and supported himself by giving lessons in mathematics and physics. After he became a Swiss citizen, he worked from 1901 to 1908 in the Patent Office in Berne. During this period, he completed his studies at the University of Zurich and received a doctorate. He also lectured as Privatdozent at the University of Berne. In 1909, he was appointed associate professor of theoretical physics at the University of Zurich, and in 1911, professor at the German University in Prague. In 1912, Einstein returned to the Polytechnic of Zurich as a professor. In 1914, he was called to Berlin to serve as the director of the Kaiser Wilhelm Institute for Physics, and in the same year he was elected as a member of the Prussian Academy of Sciences, and was given a stipend sufficient to fully support him so that he could devote his time to theoretical research without having any teaching obligations. During this period, he was elected a foreign member of the Royal Society (of Britain) as well as the Academies of Amsterdam and Copenhagen. In 1921, he received a Nobel Prize and was awarded honorary degrees from various scientific institutions. In 1933, after leaving Germany in the wake of the Nazis' rise to power, he was appointed professor of mathematics at the Institute for

Advanced Study at Princeton, in the United States. In 1940 he became an American citizen. On October 11, 1939, Einstein sent a letter to President Roosevelt, warning him that the Germans might use nuclear energy for the purpose of war and suggesting that an American nuclear project be initiated. Albert Einstein died in 1955.

The special and general law of relativity caused a revolution in the accepted views of the nature of space and time and the foundations of accurate science. This work is considered, in terms of its value to the development of science, equal to the work of Galileo and Newton. However, Einstein's thinking was not limited to this one topic; it encompassed the phenomena and fundamental concepts of science in general. Einstein developed the theory of Brownian motion and a series of other theories. He developed the theory of quanta and photons and discovered the photo-electric effect. After Max Planck first discovered the quantum phenomenon, Einstein laid the theoretical foundations of quantum theory.

I would like to digress for a moment and talk about Einstein's religious views. This has particular significance as Einstein himself linked religious feeling with the ability to discover the laws of nature: "You will hardly find one among the profounder sort of scientific minds without a religious feeling of its own" (*Ideas and Opinions*, 49). He connected the scientific accomplishments of Newton, who was a profoundly religious man, with his religiosity: ". . . Newton was a very religious man. Undoubtedly it is from this deep feeling that he drew those superhuman powers, which were necessary for the achievement of all the accomplishments throughout his life."[12]

Einstein was born into a Jewish family, though the family's connection with Judaism was weak. However, up to the age of twelve, Einstein himself was a very religious boy. Einstein describes himself at that time:

Even when I was a fairly precocious young man the nothingness of the hopes and strivings which chases most men restlessly through life came to my consciousness . . . . As the first way out there was religion . . . . Thus I came – despite the fact that I was the son of entirely irreligious (Jewish) parents

---

12. "Zu Isaak Newton 200. Todestage." *Nord und Sued* 50 (1927): 36–40 [Russian] (my translation).

– to a deep religiosity, which, however, found abrupt ending at the age of 12. Through the reading of popular scientific books I soon reached the conviction that much in the stories of the Bible could not be true. (Autobiographical Notes in Albert Einstein – Philosopher – Scientist, ed. P.A. Schilpp, 1945)

We can infer from some of Einstein's comments that from the age of twelve, he did not believe in traditional Judaism and, in particular, he did not believe in a personal God. However, if we look at some other things that he said, we see that the picture is not so clear-cut. This is what Einstein says about the meaning of life:

What is the meaning of human life, or for that matter, of the life of any creature? To know an answer to this question means to be religious. (Ideas and Opinions, 11)

And here are two other quotations, one of which also appears in the Preface to this book, which describe Einstein's view of religiosity:

His [the scientist's] religious feeling takes the form of a rapturous amazement at the harmony of natural law, which reveals an intelligence of such superiority that, compared with it, all the systematic thinking and acting of human beings is an utterly insignificant reflection. (Ibid., 40)

The most beautiful experience we can have is the mysterious. It is the fundamental emotion that stands at the cradle of true art and true science. Whoever does not know it and can no longer wonder, no longer marvel, is as good as dead, and his eyes are dimmed. It was the experience of mystery – even if mixed with fear – that engendered religion. A knowledge of the existence of something we cannot penetrate, our perceptions of the profoundest reason and the most radiant beauty, which only in their most primitive forms are accessible to our minds: it is this knowledge and this emotion that constitute true religiosity. In this sense, and only this sense, I am a deeply religious man . . . . I am satisfied with the mystery of life's eternity and with a knowledge, a sense, of the marvelous structure of existence – as well as the humble attempt to understand even a tiny portion of the Reason that manifests itself in nature. (The World As I See It, 1931)

The following quote from Einstein is extremely close to a description of divine providence:

In every naturalist there must be a kind of religious feeling; for he cannot imagine that the connections into which he sees have been thought of by him for the first time. He rather has the feeling of a child, over whom a grown-up person rules. (Cosmic Religion, 1931; 100–101)

It is reasonable to say that in Einstein's soul there was a struggle between two diametrically opposed orientations, religious and materialist, and his outstanding achievements in formulating a deterministic, physicalist theory forced him to come to a deterministic explanation of all the phenomena of the world:

> The spatiotemporal laws are complete. This means, there is not a single law of nature that, in principle, could not be reduced to a law within the domain of space-time concepts. This principle implies, for instance, the conviction that psychic entities and relations can be reduced, in the last analysis, to processes of a physical and chemical nature within the nervous system. According to this principle, there are no nonphysical elements in the causal system of the processes of nature. In this sense, there is no room for "free will". . . .[13]

I would also add here that perhaps it is true that "in this sense [of scientific thought] there is no room for free will," but it is not obvious that scientific thought exhausts all the phenomena of the world. Such a claim does not come from science at all. It is a metaphysical claim, a kind of belief.

In order to justify his metaphysical claim of determinism, Einstein uses a theological argument: "God does not play dice." If we assume the metaphysical premise that everything in the world is determined by the laws of physics, then we can understand what Einstein says. When randomness is built into the laws of physics, this means that the order in the world, which according to Einstein is fixed exclusively by the laws of physics, can also be random, and this is not something that Einstein can accept.

To summarize Einstein's world view, I will bring testimony from the man himself. On one of the occasions in which Einstein was asked to define God, he provided the following allegorical response:

---

13. "Physics, Philosophy and Scientific Progress." *Journal of the International College of Surgeons* 14 (1950): 755–758.

I'm not an atheist and I don't think I can call myself a pantheist. We are in the position of a little child entering a huge library filled with books in many languages. The child knows someone must have written those books. It does not know how. It does not understand the languages in which they are written. The child dimly suspects a mysterious order in the arrangements of the books, but doesn't know what it is. That, it seems to me, is the attitude of even the most intelligent human being toward God. We see the universe marvelously arranged and obeying certain laws but only dimly understand these laws. Our limited minds grasp the mysterious force that moves the constellations.

According to his own testimony, Einstein believed in a transcendental God. However, as we have explained above (Chapter One, section 4), the God of Judaism is also a personal God with whom we can have a connection, and a normative God who commands that we live by certain norms of behavior. It is this God in whom Einstein did not believe.

12. NIELS BOHR

In the opinion of many scientists, for several decades the undisputed leader of quantum theory was Niels Bohr (1885–1962). The Danish physicist, whose full name was Niels Henrik David Bohr, was the son of Danish physiologist Christian Bohr and Ella Adler, the daughter of a Jewish banking family. Niels Bohr studied physics in Copenhagen and completed his studies in this field as a student and assistant of J.J. Thompson in Cambridge (1911) and Ernest Rutherford in Manchester (1912–1913). In 1913, he was appointed lecturer at the University of Copenhagen. From 1914 to 1916, he was guest lecturer at Manchester University, and from 1916 onwards he was professor of theoretical physics in Copenhagen. In 1922, Bohr was awarded a Nobel Prize. In 1943, when Denmark was in the hands of the Nazis, Bohr fled to England and from there to the United States. There he took part in the atomic bomb project in Los Alamos. After the liberation of Denmark in 1945, he returned to Copenhagen. It is interesting that in October 1941, when Denmark was under German occupation, Heisenberg, a famous German physicist, visited that city. With great excitement, he told of Germany's attack on Russia and emphasized how important it was for Germany to win the war.

In 1953, Bohr visited Israel and was made an Honorary Fellow of the Weizmann Institute.

Between 1913 and 1915, Bohr published his atomic theory, on which every new theory of the structure of matter would be based. From 1922 to 1927, Bohr managed to explain, on the basis of his theory, the structure of the periodic table, an explanation which was confirmed in 1922 with the discovery of a new element, hafnium, the properties of which Bohr had predicted on the basis of his theory. He spent much time contemplating the meaning of the philosophy of the development of quantum physics and atomic theory, as well as wave-particle duality.

Bohr's contribution to quantum theory is in no doubt. He was one of the greatest scientists of the twentieth century, though not on the same level as Isaac Newton, James Clerk Maxwell and Albert Einstein. They were the greatest scientists of all time.

CHAPTER THREE

God and the World: The Nature of Science

1. INTRODUCTION

MODERN MAN, WHO CONSIDERS HIMSELF TO BE AN intellectual, progressive, and liberal individuals, has to deal with a deep inner contradiction. On the one hand, he believes in "scientific" materialism, a view supported, in his opinion, by the extraordinary achievements of science. On the other hand, a person's rights and freedom are important to him and are an undisputable foundation of his social views. He believes in the totality of physical causality, which does not reconcile with a human being's free will. However, in the everyday life of the modern man, free will is the most crucial component. A person's basic freedoms cannot be protected without assuming he has the freedom to choose. Hence, free will should be a fundamental part of modern man's moral world view.

This issue is by no mean new. In 1785, Immanuel Kant in his *Groundwork of the Metaphysics of Morals* formulated this problem. It was clear to Kant that "To argue freedom [of will] away is as impossible for the most abstruse philosophy as it is for the most ordinary human reason" (123).

On the other hand, Kant believed that what happens in the world is inevitably determined by the laws of nature – the principle of causality. The contradiction is obvious. If everything in the world, including man, obeys the laws of nature, then man's behavior is also determined by the laws of nature and is not subject to free will.

Kant did not solve the issue of free will versus the causality of nature. In fact, he placed it in the category of problems which man is unable to solve and classified the problem as an antinomy – a conflict between laws and principles. How does modern man deal with the contradiction between free will and the causality of nature? I do not have a clear answer to this question. I can only hazard a guess. It is possible that many and perhaps most people do not think all that much about this problem. A significant proportion of religious people solve this problem by dissociating themselves from science and viewing it as a threat to their faith, which is predicated on the existence of free will. Amongst my colleagues, highly intelligent individuals, there are those who doubt the existence of free will. Not long ago I heard a lecture by an expert in the field of the brain, which ended with the sentence: "We must look for a bio-physical mechanism for the **illusion** of free will." However, on a practical level, these people care very much that their own free will not be adversely affected. With respect to his relationship to the causality–free will issue, modern man finds himself with a kind of split personality.

In this chapter, we will try to deal with this problem and offer a solution to it. As we will see below, the **causality–free will** problem is closely linked to the subject of this chapter, which is about the spiritual and material content of our world and its connection with God. As a preface to a comprehensive discussion of this topic, let us look at two phenomena with which we are fairly familiar, and which do not seem to contain any surprises.

The first phenomenon is the lawfulness of nature. We have become accustomed to the thought that there are laws in the inanimate world. Particles of matter – molecules, atoms, electrons, protons, and so on – move and behave according to certain laws. To recognize that which is extraordinary about this phenomenon, we must do our best to disregard for a moment our routine scholarly ways. When a person sees the same thing again and again, he becomes accustomed to it and is liable to lose his ability to recognize it. Thus a child – or an adult, for that matter – fails to see anything exceptional about a light bulb, for example. In fact, one needs to acquire a great amount of knowledge to understand the complexity and wonder of electricity and light and the laws that govern them, the laws of the electromagnetic field. But perhaps the true wonder lies in the fact that any laws exist at all. An explanation is required for the existence of laws, which we will discuss in later sections of this chapter.

The second phenomenon that I would like to mention here is the absence of lawfulness in the behavior of man. We are used to thinking that everything in the world moves, behaves and develops over time according to a certain order and in accordance with certain laws. Different bodies such as the planets, earth, artificial satellites and ballistic missiles all move in accordance with precise laws of physics, and their paths can be predicted with incredible accuracy. Physics can predict a solar eclipse and can calculate precisely when eclipses that occurred many years ago took place. However, when we look at the movements of animals, and particularly those of people, we are unable to identify any law that directs them. What characterizes objects that move according to particular laws is that their paths can be predicted in advance. However, in general we are unable to predict the paths of people. We might say that the laws of physics have absolutely no relevance to the task of predicting the behavior of people. This is not a philosophical, metaphysical claim, but rather a conclusion based on our accumulated experience. To put it another way, we know of no study that can provide us with a prediction of the paths of animals in general or of people in particular. I am aware of the argument to the contrary: if we take into account all the causes in the world, from creation to the present day, then it would be possible to make accurate predictions of the paths of all objects, including people. However, this claim cannot be tested with any experiment; it is a metaphysical claim which negates the existence of personal free will. Either way, we are still faced with the problem that we have already mentioned – free will versus general causality. In later sections, we will return to this discussion.

2. MATHEMATICS – THE LANGUAGE OF SCIENCE

When we study the structure of the laws of nature, something that really stands out is the tremendous part played by mathematics. We have no other way of formulating the laws of nature other than by mathematics. We can also say that the laws of nature are written in mathematical language – namely, they are expressed in symbols in a particular text and in a particular language, and that language is mathematics. This requires a more detailed explanation.

First, we will try to understand what mathematics is without looking at any particular mathematical theories. Initially, the development of mathematics was influenced by practical problems and by problems that arose from the observation of nature and was perhaps even conditioned on them. This is even reflected in the name of one of the first mathematical theories, geometry. In Greek this is *geometria*, from *geo*, meaning earth, and *metron*, meaning measure, as this science began with the measurement of Earth. The Greeks were the first to try to establish mathematics on foundations whose truth was guaranteed solely by human thought – namely, by logic. The entire structure of mathematical theory was based on basic assumptions, axioms, as self-evident eternal truths. Only in the nineteenth century, following the discovery of non-Euclidean geometries, did it become clear that the axioms of geometry were not universal truths but arbitrary conventions. The criteria for choosing the axioms and their relation to reality are not considered to be problems of pure mathematics. The mathematician must be concerned about the consistency and the absence of contradictions only within the framework of the axioms and their implications.

Actually, mathematics broke away from any experiments a long time ago. It deals with abstract thinking which completely ignores material reality. The motivation that set the development of mathematics in motion was the interest in the coordination and consistency of theoretical concepts and of theoretical constructions which constitute the essence of the mathematical theory. The distinguished scientist and philosopher, Alfred North Whitehead, wrote: "If many modern philosophers and men of science could have their way, they would have been dissuading Greeks, Jews, and Mohammedans from such useless studies, from such pure abstractions for which no foresight could divine the ghost of application. Luckily, they could not get at their ancestors."[1]

I should emphasize once again that many concepts that appeared as a result of the development of mathematics have no parallel in material reality. We are all familiar with one of the most ancient mathematical inventions: numbers. The invention of complex numbers was an important and logical stage in the theory of numbers, even though there has never been anything in reality resembling complex numbers or an imaginary unit which is the square root of minus one: $i = \sqrt{-1}$. Nothing in reality indicated a need for

---

1. *Adventures of Ideas*, 156.

complex numbers, and it was only centuries later that their application to theoretical physics was finally discovered.

While the development of physics (and other natural sciences) was constantly being tested by its links with reality and experience, mathematics developed in an apparently arbitrary way, without taking any external factors into account at all. Thus Eugene Wigner, one of the great physicists of the twentieth century, writes, "The great mathematician fully, almost ruthlessly, exploits the domain of permissible reasoning and skirts the impermissible. That his recklessness does not lead him into a morass of contradictions is a miracle in itself: certainly it is hard to believe that our reasoning power was brought, by Darwin's process of natural selection, to the perfection which it seems to possess."[2] Roger Penrose, another great scientist in the field of mathematical physics, was convinced that "[m]athematical truth is absolute, external, and eternal, and not based on man-made criteria; and that mathematical objects have a timeless existence of their own, not dependent on human society nor on particular physical objects."[3]

He also wrote, "There is something absolute and 'God-given' about mathematical truth."[4]

We can conclude by saying that mathematics is a spiritual entity that is objective, independent of material reality and human society, and was gradually revealed to man. We have said that mathematics is the language of the laws of nature – a claim attributed to Galileo. The incredible thing is that to a large degree, this language has developed and continues to do so independently of physics and the other natural sciences. It is worth mentioning that physics uses only a tiny fraction of the mathematical concepts that have developed, in most cases if not all, completely independently of physics. What does this remind us of? It reminds us of the development of human languages. Aside from the fact that the development of language is a necessary condition for communication between people, it is also a necessary condition for connecting with God, for divine revelation. Perhaps the

---

2. E. Wigner, "The Unreasonable Effectiveness of Mathematics in the Natural Sciences." *Communications on Pure and Applied Mathematics* 13/3.

3. R. Penrose, *The Emperor's New Mind,* 151.

4. *Ibid,* 146.

development of mathematics as the language of science is part of the divine plan – an early stage in the revelation of science to man.

We can also say that mathematics is not just similar to human language. It is actually part of it – or, to be more precise, mathematics is the fruit of its development and is its most advanced stage. This requires further explanation. Not everyone realizes that mathematics has actually already penetrated fairly deep into our language. Take numbers, for example. We are so used to using numbers that the force of habit camouflages the extent of abstraction of the discovery. We have no object in our lives, or in anything with which we are familiar, that can be called "five." There are five apples, five trees, five people, but there is no plain five. An enormous level of abstraction would be required to dissociate ourselves from our day-to-day experience and come to the concept of "fiveness." This is not a tangible concept; there is nothing that we can use to demonstrate the concept of "fiveness." Likewise, there is no object that is four, that expresses the concept of "fourness" or of "sevenness."

An even greater level of abstraction is needed to perform operations with these abstract concepts, such as the addition of two numbers: $5 + 7$, or division: $12 \div 3$. Mathematics is the most perfectly abstract skill that the human mind is capable of grasping. Many mathematical concepts have already entered our language, even if we are not always aware of this. There are primitive languages which only have the concepts of one, two and many. Clearly these languages cannot express complex relationships between particular groups of objects. So in these primitive languages it would be possible to say that in one flock there are many sheep, more than in the second flock, but it would not be possible to express the fact that in the first flock there are thirty-four sheep, three more than in the second flock. *In other words, mathematical symbols came into language in order to describe complex relations that cannot be described otherwise.* A language that includes arithmetic and natural numbers is richer than one that does not include these symbols.

In general, we can say that for a deeper understanding of reality, a richer language is required. Without a doubt, modern science has managed to achieve a very deep understanding of material reality. The theories of physics describe various aspects of reality in such a complex way that laymen are not capable of grasping them at all, just as people who speak a primitive language cannot grasp things that can only be described using a language that includes arithmetic. Likewise, a language that includes modern mathematics, the fruit of thousands of years of development, is capable of describing a far more complex and sophisticated reality than that which is perceived by people with a poor language that does not include modern mathematics.

And this is where the difference lies. For a long time, the language that we speak has included arithmetic and other mathematical concepts. We are so used to this that we pay no attention to it. On the other hand, modern mathematics has not entered our everyday, spoken language. It belongs to a select group of scientists and mathematicians. However, this does not change the fact that mathematics is part of human language in general, even if the majority of people still do not understand it.

How is it that the mathematical part of the language developed many years before its application to modern physics? The same question can be asked in relation to the development of the Hebrew language, the language of the Bible, before the People of Israel arrived at Mount Sinai. We can assume that a very long time was required for the spoken language, the alphabet and the written language to develop until Hebrew reached a level that would enable the people to receive and document the word of God. We can answer both of these questions, while exercising the necessary caution in interpreting God's intentions, by saying that the development of language prior to its application in understanding the world is part of God's great wisdom.

3. THE MYSTERY OF THE UNIFORMITY OF THE LAWS OF NATURE

Now let us turn to the natural sciences, first of all to physics. Here we come across some very interesting phenomena relating to the structure of science. For the time being we will ignore the question of how man discovers the laws of physics – Chapter Four deals with this subject. In any case, as we have already mentioned, physical theories are formulated and written in mathematical language. Even though we are used to this fact, it is actually an amazing thing that is difficult to comprehend. Wigner writes that "the enormous usefulness of mathematics in the natural sciences is something bordering on the mysterious and that there is no rational explanation for it."[5] Any physical theory must also be tested by experimentation. Here we encounter the fact that a physical theory that is formulated in mathematical

---

5. Wigner, ibid., 2.

language always gives a level of accuracy that is above that of any possible experiment. In other words, when we develop a particular theory in order to explain a certain experiment, the prediction that the theory will give will always be more precise than the results of the experiment. It is as if the mathematical formulation contains something that is not in the experiment.

And here is another strange thing that is difficult to comprehend. A scientist who tries to discover a new physical theory is limited to studying one particular phenomenon or a few phenomena only. Thus Galileo studied the behavior of different objects falling from a particular height, but in the end it was Newton who formulated the general law of gravity, which controls the movements of all the celestial bodies. Quantum mechanics, early in its development, focused on the study of the spectra of the emission and absorption of light by the hydrogen atom. However, the quantum mechanics that grew as a result of this study is capable of explaining many diverse phenomena that have no apparent connection to the hydrogen spectrum, such as superconductivity, a theory of solid bodies, wave-particle duality in experiments with elementary particles, and so on. Only habit and routine that prevent us from seeing the wonder that research of a small number of phenomena paves the way to understanding many other phenomena that are apparently unrelated.

Now let us look at the phenomenon that we presented in the title of this section. In order to understand it properly, we have to free ourselves from the shackles of routine. Let us assume that we want to study the laws of nature on a particular planet thousands or even millions of light-years away from Earth. This means that in order to reach this planet, we would need to travel for millions of years at the speed of light, which is clearly impossible. In principle, we could travel at a speed less than that of light, but the journey would take much longer. When the study of the laws of nature on the distant planet was completed, it would be possible to send the results back to Earth by a beam of light. However, the information that the researcher on Earth would receive would not be about the laws of nature on the planet in real time, but about the laws of nature that were in place millions of years previously. It is not possible to obtain information about the laws of nature in different places in the universe at the same time. In other words, there are many places in the world, almost in the whole universe, that cannot be reached in real time to study their laws of nature. Still, there is a fairly simple solution. It is sufficient to study the laws of nature on Earth. Then we will know the laws of nature of places far from us, too, since the same laws operate in both places.

The laws of nature are identical everywhere in the universe. The same laws apply on Earth and everywhere else. How do we know this? One might think that this is a scientific claim or a scientific conclusion, but one only needs to ponder it briefly to realize that this is not a scientific claim but rather a metaphysical claim about the structure of science. In this book, we can see the source of this metaphysical claim in the Jewish, biblical and Talmudic worldview – it comes from the unity of God. Without this metaphysical premise, modern science would not exist – all the accomplishments of cosmological science are based upon this premise. All the scientific information about the solar system, different galaxies and the early universe is based on the truth of this premise. In any case, it is worth pointing out that many experiments reinforce the supposition of the uniformity of the laws of nature. Thus, the observations confirm that the radiation spectrum of atoms in other galaxies is identical to the radiation spectrum of those atoms on Earth.

We – or, to be more precise, scientists – take the uniformity of the laws of nature for granted. It is in our consciousness as part of our routine way of thinking. We have already mentioned that the routine of life and everyday thinking prevent us from recognizing the wonders of the world and its facets. Although the concept of the uniformity of the laws of nature has become part of our mentality, this was not always the case. From a conceptual perspective, this was a new idea that Isaac Newton assimilated into the metaphysical foundation of modern science. Prior to Newton, the accepted wisdom in the intellectual world was that the celestial bodies, like every other body, had their own laws. Isaac Newton's belief in the unity of the world and the uniformity of the laws of nature derived from his religious world view. As we have mentioned (Chapter Two, section 9), Newton's religious view of the world was closely connected to Jewish thought. It is not an overstatement to say that there is a causal link between the genesis of modern science in Christian Europe and the element of Jewish heritage in Judeo-Christian civilization.

Since the premise of the uniformity of the laws of nature is so fundamental that without it there is no science, we can turn the tables and ask ourselves why the laws of physics, or the laws of nature in general, are identical everywhere in the universe. The claims of the universality, the generality and the uniformity of the laws of nature in space and time cannot be explained by science – they cannot be explained scientifically. Any scientific explanation is based on the laws of nature, which state that a certain thing is the cause of something else. In our case, a scientific explanation would exist if laws in a certain place (Earth, for example) were able to immediately determine the laws in distant places. However, such an imaginary possibility would complicate matters even more, since, according to Einstein's theory of relativity, the laws of nature prevent the instant propagation of information, namely at speeds greater than the speed of light. Karl Popper expresses it thus: ". . . the structural homogeneity of the world seems to resist any 'deeper' explanation: it remains a mystery."[6]

Here, when I cite Popper, I should point out another important aspect of the discussion of the laws of nature. Recently, there has been a lot of talk about the search for some kind of self-evident, necessary, logical principle from which it would be possible to derive the most fundamental laws of nature – The Theory of Everything (TOE). Popper wrote, regarding this kind of approach: "I do not think that thinking that the world is what it is by a kind of logical necessity can solve this mystery. The hope of reducing natural sciences to logic seems to me both absurd and repulsive."[7]

In the next section, I will present my understanding of all these "wonders and miracles." The solution to these mysteries is linked to the existence of the spiritual world as an inseparable part of our world. As we have already stated, the existence of the physical and spiritual parts of creation as a whole are anchored in the Jewish tradition. Here I would like to discuss the part of the spiritual reality that is connected with the natural sciences and mathematics, the place of science in the spiritual world.

4. THE LAWS OF NATURE AS PART OF THE SPIRITUAL WORLD

When [homo religiosus] confronts God's world, when he gazes at it . . . he is intrigued by the mystery of existence – the *mysterium tremendum* – and wants

---

6. K. Popper, *Realism and the Aim of Science,* 152.
7. Ibid., 152.

to emphasize that mystery . . . . For to him the concept of lawfulness is in itself the deepest of mysteries.   (Rabbi Soloveitchik, Halakhic Man, 6–7)

Let us return to the concept of "a spiritual thing." There are, *inter alia*, two essential elements of a spiritual entity: it cannot be physical, and it must have a certain message. Let me explain what I mean. Let us consider a particular text, such as a scientific article or a story about a particular event. This text is written or printed on paper using letters or symbols and with a particular type of ink. It is not difficult to appreciate that the kind of paper or ink used are secondary to the substance of the text. The same text could be expressed using electronic means, such as a computer screen or a television. It could also be read aloud and recorded. A person could learn the text by heart and recite it to others if required. It is clear that the various physical means of expressing the text are not part of the substance of the text itself. We must differentiate between the medium and the message. The content of the text, which is fixed and unchanging, is independent of the physical medium through which it is expressed.

Now we come to the second element that characterizes a spiritual entity. It is not just that this entity is not physical, but it also contains a particular message. We can imagine a random combination of words or letters. This can also be expressed using various different media, and it clearly is not a physical thing. Here is something that is not dependent on physical means. However, it has no message, content or meaning. Hence, we cannot say that this random collection of words or letters expresses any spiritual entity. From this perspective, it is clear that the laws of nature are a spiritual entity. They are denoted by a certain text (the equations of Newton, Einstein, Schrödinger, and so on), which is written in a particular language, the language of mathematics. This spiritual entity dictates the behavior of matter. It gives matter explicit instructions as to how it should "behave." Through various experiments, people can test, to a certain degree of accuracy, whether the material entity does indeed behave in accordance with these laws, according to the content of this text. It is important that we do not get caught up in the mistaken explanation that the spiritual world is a kind of super-entity that governs matter. As we explained above (Chapter One, section 12), God operates the connection between the spiritual world and the material world.

The difference between the extreme materialistic world view and the Jewish world view is in the way in which they understand the laws of nature. As far as the atheist is concerned, all that exists in the world is nature and its laws. Vitaly Ginzburg, one of the distinguished physicists of our time and a teacher of mine at the beginning of my scientific career, writes, "My atheist view is the intuitive claim that there is nothing but nature and the laws that govern it."[8] From the atheist's point of view, nature is the ultimate, final, absolute reality, and the laws of nature are an inseparable part of it. The laws of nature are an inherent part of nature. They are contained within it. They are immanent.

The source of this kind of view is Greek philosophy. According to the Greek view, a universe – a cosmos – which is a comprehensive collection of all things, exists and has a certain order. But what are the foundations of nature? For the Greeks, who took nature for granted, the answer was that the order in nature and the laws of nature themselves are the foundations of nature, and the source of the order lies in nature itself. We are accustomed to the idea that the source of the lawfulness in nature is found in nature itself. This is what we have been taught, even if our teachers did not explicitly explain the idea of the **immanence** of the laws of nature. Intellectual habit and routine do not permit us to see the peculiarity of the idea of lawfulness that is inherent in nature itself.

Let us look more deeply into the idea of **immanence** in the laws of nature. At first sight, it removes the mystery that keeps the mind of *homo religiosus* busy. Rabbi Soloveitchik says:

> [For homo religiosus] the revelation of the law and the comprehension of the order and interconnectedness of existence only intensifies and deepens the question and the problem. For while cognitive man discharges his obligation by establishing the reign of a causal structure of lawfulness in nature, homo religiosus is not satisfied with the perfection of the world under the dominion of the law. For to him the concept of lawfulness is in itself the deepest of mysteries. Cognition, according to the world view of the man of God, consists in the discovery of the wondrous and miraculous quality of the very laws of nature themselves.
> (Halakhic Man, 7)

---

8. Мои атеистические убеждения (это) интуитивное суждение о том, что существует лишь Природа и управляющие ею законы . . . В.Л. Гинзбург, О науке, о себе и о других, 486).

The idea of the **immanence** of the laws of nature also removes the question of the existence of reality in general from the agenda. It is clear that existential questions, such as the question of lawfulness in the world, must have an end – there must be an ultimate, definitive answer that involves an ultimate entity. This entity is nature and its laws. From a purely logical perspective, there is nothing wrong with this solution, but its meaning must be understood. This is nothing but a theological, deist solution. In this solution, nature is the ultimate entity, the source of all that exists, including man and all the creations in the world. In other words, nature is God. A philosophical stance that expresses this precise view actually exists – this is the philosophy of Baruch Spinoza, which we will discuss in the next section. Here it is important to understand that the atheist viewpoint is no different from the various pagan views, which viewed the forces of nature as expressions of different gods. In the words of Abraham J. Heschel,

> Some of us are inclined to deify the one supreme force or law that regulates all phenomena of nature, in the same manner in which primitive peoples once deified the stars. Yet, to refer to the supreme law of nature as God or to say that the world came into being by virtue of its own energy is to beg the question. For the cardinal solution is not what is the law that would explain the interaction of phenomena in the universe, but why there is a law, a universe at all. (Between God and Man, 100)

Conversely, biblical man has no natural foundations. The foundations of the physical world are not in the physical world itself. The land continues to exist according to the will of God: "It is He that sits upon the circle of the earth" (Isaiah 40:22). Biblical man is obviously aware that there is order in nature and that he can rely on it in his everyday life. But this order is inherent in nature as a result of God's will and remains dependent on Him at all times. It is not an immanent law, inherent in nature, but a *command, an order from God,* who controls everything – "When He gave to the sea its decree, that the waters should not pass His commandment: when He appointed the foundations of the earth" (Proverbs 8:29) – and continues to control from the outside. To a believing person, nature is an object of God's continuous supervision. The Jewish, biblical, view is correctly described by Alfred North Whitehead as the doctrine of the *imposed law,* as compared with the view of the law as *immanent* (inherent in nature itself) that was developed by the Greeks as part of their philosophy. Whitehead maintains that "[t]he history of Western thought consists in the attempted fusion of ideas which in their origin [are predominantly Hellenic, with ideas which in their origin] are predominantly Semitic."[9]

Biblical man sees nature as an entity connected with God. "In the beginning, God created the heaven and the earth" – these words express the dependence of all reality on the will of God. "To the Western man, [reality] is a thing in itself; to the Biblical Man, it is a thing through God. Looking at a thing his eyes see not so much form, color, force and motion as an act of God. The world is a gate, not a wall."[10]

It is not possible to prove, through logic, the truth of either of the two views presented here. These are metaphysical claims that can neither be proved nor disproved by logic or experiment. It is essentially a matter of belief, just as it is impossible to prove that our world really exists and is not just a dream. When we come to choose between different metaphysical views, when logic and experiments do not help us to decide which view is correct, it is the biblical and Talmudic view that determines it. However, after this has been determined, we can also look to common sense and our accumulated experience to help us. Thus, for example, when we arrive at a completely new place and see inscriptions written in a particular language, we are in no doubt that this is the result of an intelligent action and that intelligent beings exist or existed who wrote these inscriptions. And yet, when certain people come across texts from the laws of physics, such as

$$F = ma$$
$$E = mc^2$$
$$\operatorname{div} E = 4\pi\sigma$$
$$\operatorname{rot} E + \frac{1}{c}\frac{\partial H}{\partial t} = 0$$
$$\operatorname{div} H = 0$$
$$\operatorname{rot} H - \frac{1}{c}\frac{\partial E}{\partial t} = \frac{4\pi}{c} I$$

---

9. *Adventures of Ideas*, 121. (In the paperback edition of 1967, the words in the brackets are missing, while Heschel quotes a text including these missing words.)

10. A.J. Heschel, *Between God and Man*, 95.

they are unsure as to whether this is the result of an intellectual action of an intelligent being or merely something that is "inherent in nature itself." From the latter viewpoint, inscriptions written in ordinary languages as well as all human creations, including human beings themselves – all these are ultimately the product of nature. This is the Hellenistic view, which verges on the absurd.

I will now summarize my view, which is a product of the general Jewish approach. Our world has two sides, a material side and a spiritual side. Another way of saying this is that there are two worlds: a physical world and a spiritual world. The spiritual world contains our souls, our spiritual creations and human emotions: love, devotion, hatred, desires, and so on. However, here in this section, it is important to me to point out that the laws of nature are a part of the spiritual world. The laws of nature and their language, mathematics, are definitely a spiritual entity. They are not material and they have certain properties. According to the alternate view that originates in Greek philosophy, the laws of nature are something immanent, inherent in nature and part of it. This view has been adopted, knowingly or otherwise, by people looking to justify their atheistic views. My view, which takes its lead from Jewish philosophy, is that both **the laws of nature and mathematics are spiritual entities that are connected with and dependent on God.** Just as the material world is an objective reality which is independent of people, the same is true for the spiritual world. The operation of the accessible spiritual world (Popper's world three) is dependent on people, while God operates the spiritual world in general. Generally, human beings do not have direct access to this spiritual world. The revelation of certain parts and layers – some deeper, some less deep – of the spiritual world is a creative process carried out by a select group of individuals, and is dependent on the will of God. In Chapter Four of this book, we will discuss the process of understanding the laws of nature.

The spiritual world (including science and mathematics) – the real entity that exists objectively – existed even before human beings started to become involved in mathematics and science. Herein lies the difference between my views and the views of science held by Kant and Popper. According to Kant, it is human understanding that creates the laws of nature. Likewise, Popper's world three, a world of objective science, was made by man. World three would be destroyed if we were to destroy all books, other repositories of data and the knowledge that exists in people's memories. According to this view, it is impossible to talk about this spiritual reality without human beings. In fact, this kind of view is idealistic in essence, since according to it the laws of nature, the theories of physics and mathematics are the fruits of human creation.

According to our view, the spiritual world, which is just as real as the material world, is a divine creation that exists and develops under God's supervision. Every discovery of the spiritual world by human beings is also connected to providence. From our perspective, Popper's world three is just an account of part of the entire spiritual reality. We could say that world three is the accessible spiritual world, which can be accessed through books, journals, electronic means and so on. Losing these resources could certainly reduce its accessibility, but it would not change the essence of the spiritual world one bit. **This world exists objectively and is not dependent on our accessibility to it.**

Now we can analyze the strange attributes of science that we discussed in the previous section. One feature, which we can call its **multi-field nature**, may be described as follows: scientific research is designed to solve a particular problem in a particular field, but it also brings with it solutions to problems in many other fields. For example, a study of the emission and absorption of light by a hydrogen atom leads to a theory of numerous physical properties in other fields such as superconductivity and the theory of lasers, to name only two. We can understand the **multi-field** quality as a result of the connection with the spiritual world. The scientist succeeds in developing a new theory of physics, such as quantum theory, not as a logical inference from experimental data but as flash of inspiration, as a divine revelation. Through this kind of revelation, the scientist comes into contact with the spiritual world. Suddenly a spiritual world, a spiritual dimension, is opened up to the scientist – a dimension that is not only relevant to the particular problem that he had set out to research, but to an entire section of the spiritual world. Thus, the new theory reveals and explains numerous phenomena in various fields.

Another characteristic of science that we discussed in the previous section can be called **multi-spatiality**. A study done at a particular location in space can testify to the laws of nature in a different place in the universe – in fact, in every place in the universe. These two places may be so far away from each other that no physical influence can connect them. This gives rise to the question: how can we explain the fact that the laws of nature are identical in places that are millions of light years distant from one another? How do they "know" each other?

My solution to the mystery of the uniformity of the laws of nature is as follows: In addition to the material world, which exists in space, there exists another dimension, a spiritual one, which is not dependent on space or location. In other words, the spiritual dimension is identical in every place. To what is this similar? To the new space dimension, which, being independent, is not contingent on the "old" dimensions. Let us picture imaginary two-dimensional creatures that live in a two-dimensional world, such as a flat plane. Suddenly, one of these creatures discovers that space also includes a third dimension. This property, or phenomenon of the third dimension, has absolutely no relevance to the plane's two dimensions. The third dimension, called height, is not dependent on the dimensions of the plane or a particular location in it. In the same way, we can imagine that the spiritual world is another dimension of the world, which is not dependent on space. This "explains" why the laws of nature are identical everywhere in the universe.

There may well be many people who remain unconvinced by the above analogy. I will try to give some further explanation. Let us understand where the problem arises. The source of the problem is in the premise of "immanent law" that the ancient Greeks developed. Many atheist thinkers also support this view, according to which the laws of nature are actually part of nature itself – they are derived from nature. Now let us look at different places around the world. When we adopt the view that the law is a derivative of nature, there is no necessity for the same laws to apply in different places. For if nature "creates" its laws, then the question of how nature in one place can "know" which laws are operated by nature in another place light years from the first one is completely legitimate. Hence, the identical nature of the laws in different places is a mystery, a riddle that the immanent law leaves unexplained. On the other hand, there is no mystery in the identity of the laws everywhere in the universe when the source of the law is external and supernatural, when the law is a command of God. Such a command is not contingent on one place or another. Thus, according to our view, the laws of nature are a part of the divine spiritual world, and therefore there is no problem regarding the connection between the laws of nature and their location in the universe. The laws of nature belong to the spiritual world, **and are therefore not dependent on location** – or, in other words, **therefore they are identical everywhere in the universe.** Thus, in Jewish philosophy we have a solution for an issue for which there is no solution in the works of the naturalist philosophy of the deification, or to be more precise, the idolization of nature.

5. GOD, A SPIRITUAL WORLD AND A PHYSICAL WORLD. THE PHILOSOPHY OF BARUCH SPINOZA AND THE JEWISH APPROACH

Our understanding of the world in which we live is dependent on our understanding of the status of our world and our status within it vis-à-vis God. Theoretically, there are several possibilities.

First, let us look at the view that claims that the laws of nature that are at the basis of the spiritual world determine everything that happens in the world and pre-determine the world's future developments precisely. This is a *deterministic* view of a *deterministic* world. The spiritual world, **which is identical to the laws of nature**, unequivocally determines the development of matter. In this case, the two statements **that the laws of nature are inherent (immanent) in nature** and that **the laws of nature compel the development of nature** are equivalent. There is no way to choose between them.

It is easy to see that in a world like this, God's role is rather odd. He does not direct but is Himself directed; He does not control but is Himself controlled by the laws of nature. In fact, He is superfluous. We can call nature "God," or, alternatively, we can call God "nature."

This is an option of secular belief or of pantheism. The word *God* can be waived without affecting the substance of this view, expressed in the philosophy of Baruch Spinoza.[11]

According to Spinoza (1634–1677), all of reality, everything, is God. There is nothing other than God. God is the necessary cause for all things, not in His existence, which is *external* to things, but in their being a part

---

11. 1634–1677. A brief summary of Spinoza's philosophy can be found in Ben-Shlomo's booklet, "Lectures on the Philosophy of Spinoza."

of Him, just as the whole is the cause of its parts – the whole does not exist separately from its parts. All things are different modes of God or parts of Him. God has infinite attributes, while we, human beings, grasp only two of them – the attribute of extension (the material world, in our terminology) and the attribute of thought (the spiritual world). Spinoza's philosophy can be translated into completely naturalistic language, leaving out the word *God* altogether. Everywhere that the term *God* appears, we could substitute it with the word *nature*. Still, we must bear in mind that Spinoza's nature is not identical to the material nature. The material universe is just one mode of nature, or of God.

Our world, according to Spinoza, is completely deterministic. Everything is foreseen and pre-determined, and the time element is actually superfluous. What we call "time" is nothing but our imaginary mode of thought. Spinoza maintains that the time element, which is necessary for us when we deal with physics and history, is actually not a real element at all. The flow of one thing from another is not in time, but is necessary and timeless, just as an inference flows from a premise by logic, or as a particular mathematical statement derives from a prior one. One person might need ten minutes to understand the proof of the logical connection between these two statements, while a second person needs only five minutes. This time is not included in the logical substance of the two statements.

Spinoza claims that this is just like the causal relationship between the objects in the world as a whole. A physical event also derives in a necessary and logical way from other events, and the time element is not real in this process. This is also true for events in historical time: if a person claims that event B occurred after event A in history, in time, that is only because the human intellect is limited and does not see how event B is already included in event A. All events, which for us occur in time, in fact already exist in eternity, in the timeless dimension of the inevitable causal lawfulness to which all things are subject.

According to Spinoza, there is no room for free will in this deterministic world. My position at this moment is not the result of my free will, but the inevitable result of a sequence of physiological, genetic, psychological, social and economic causes that have made me what I am and brought me to the point of writing this book.

Now let us present another theoretical possibility. Let us imagine another deterministic world, where God exists externally to it. Here, God does not interfere in worldly matters. He is a primary, initial cause of all causes. Since everything must have a cause, the cause itself must have its own cause, and so on and so forth until the initial cause, for which God is the cause. While God does not interfere in the world, even though He knows what is happening in the world, all the information in the world is at His disposal. This model is more or less that of the God of the Greeks, the God of Aristotle.

The Jewish view is in complete contrast to that of Spinoza or the Greeks. **First**, in the Jewish sources, starting with the Bible, God is a personal god. God has a will" and, makes demands on man and gives him commandments, and it is possible to worship and love Him in a personal way. **Second**, God is the creator of a world external to Himself. Judaism is very clear about the separation of the world and God, in contrast with the pantheist view. Man's soul is also not a part of God, but it can have a connection with Him. **Third**, according to Judaism, God is free to create the world or not to create it. The existence of the world is constantly dependent on God and hence the world is **contingent**. Human beings, who have free will, are even able to disobey God. The principle of free will is essential for the existence of the Jewish ethical system. **Fourth**, the dimension of time has special significance, which is in stark contrast to Spinoza's approach. In the Bible, the perception of history as a real dimension of reality is presented, in which the redemption of man and the world is realized. According to the Jewish approach, man can and must change the course of history towards redemption, taking part in the divine plan. Whether redemption occurs "at its proper time" or "earlier than its appointed time" is up to us, human beings.

In the context of understanding the time dimension, it is important to note human beings' limitations in understanding the essence of God. In Jewish thought, God is transcendent. He cannot be understood. His essence is not accessible to human beings, and we are only capable of grasping and understanding whatever He chooses to give to us. This is especially true when we are talking about whether God is temporal or not. When people say that God is outside time, this is difficult, and perhaps even impossible, to understand. There are those who say that since God is not limited by time, He "sees" the world "with one look" covering all times, including the distant future. It is not clear what they are trying to say here, except for stating that determinism rules our world completely, which is an absolute contradiction of the fundamentals of Judaism. To place God outside temporal experience means to deny that He is a personal God. If God is personal, then He must have temporal existence. He can know what is happening **now**. He can supervise, intervene and change the course of history in the **present**.

We have listed various options for the structure of the world and its connection with God. Now, let us ask ourselves: which of these possibilities (plus others that we have not enumerated here) is correct? Which one reflects how the world really is? It is clearly impossible to answer this question using only arguments based on logic and reasoning. We have already said (Chapter One, section 6) that we choose between different metaphysical assumptions by studying the Bible. Fundamentally, God's intervention, His revelation, is necessary for human beings to be able to distinguish between truth and falsehood, between the important and the incidental. The ancient Greeks, who came up with various philosophical approaches, were unable to choose the view that truly reflects reality. Divine revelation is what enables us to identify the option that truly reflects the structure of our world and its connection to God.

There was a particular period in history that was very significant, perhaps the most significant period in the history of mankind, during which God revealed Himself to the People of Israel. This period is documented in the Bible. The uniqueness of the Bible lies in its detailed documentation of the connection between man and his creator. Hence, studying the Bible, which is recognized even by the nations of the world as the "book of books," enables us to choose and identify metaphysical principles that reflect reality and its connection with God.

6. "SCIENTIFIC" DETERMINISM

In the previous section, we saw that the crucial difference between the Jewish view and the view that deifies nature is in the question of determinism versus non-determinism in the world. God's freedom of will and man's free will cannot be reconciled with a deterministic world in which everything is pre-determined from the first moment of creation, a world in which God Himself is subject to causal necessity. Hence, it is crucial to understand the arguments for the non-determinism of the world.

Intuitively, we can summarize the concept of determinism by comparing the world to a film. The picture that we are seeing right now in the film represents the present, the parts of the film that have already been screened represent the **past**, and all the parts of the film that have not yet been screened represent the **future**. In a film, the future exists together with the past. It is firmly fixed and its existence has the same significance as the existence of the past. The viewer may not know the events in the future, but in principle all future events, without exception, can be known with absolute certainty, exactly like the events in the past. In fact, the film's producer – the creator of that world – knows the future in full detail. As it happens, the origin of the concept of determinism is religious, though its source is not in Judaism. Religious determinism is connected to the concept of divine omnipotence – God's absolute control over the future – and divine omniscience, the idea that God knows the future now, and hence it is known and determined in advance.

Aside from religious determinism, there is another form of deterministic premise that can be called "scientific" determinism. We will focus here specifically on this form, since "scientific" determinism is the most commonly accepted type among those who regard themselves as intellectuals and who are convinced that the development of the world, including the creation of life, evolution and historical processes can be explained as the development of nature, with the laws of nature exclusively responsible for all that occurs in the world.

As we have already explained, from a historical perspective, one can view determinism as a result of the replacement of the concept of God with the concept of nature and the replacement of the concept of divine providence with the laws of nature. The laws of nature are now ascribed the omnipotence and omniscience that were previously ascribed to God. If we had all the information relevant to the current situation we could predict the future on the basis of our knowledge of the laws of nature. In contrast with the vague statement that every event has a cause, Pierre Simon Laplace (1749–1827) was the first to formulate the deterministic approach using the language of classical, Newtonian mechanics. According to Laplace, it is the laws of nature expressed in the equations of mechanics that determine the world's future and its past. In principle, it is sufficient to know the coordinates (the precise locations in space) and the speeds of all the particles in the world at a particular time in order to calculate everything that has occurred and everything that will occur using the equations of mechanics. I say "in principle," since human beings cannot actually perform this calculation. But this is not important. The information about the future and the past is included in these equations, and our future is already determined forever and ever.

Laplace's view, which derives the world's determinism from mechanics, failed. It failed together with the mechanistic world view – the view that assumes that everything in the world, without exception, behaves in accordance with the laws of classical, Newtonian mechanics. These days it is clear to all that this assumption is incorrect – everything cannot be explained by the laws of mechanics. However, for a long period of time, over two hundred years (from the seventeenth century until the nineteenth century) scientists and philosophers believed in the absolute truth and universality of Newtonian mechanics – in the fact that it describes everything that exists. In fact Immanuel Kant based many parts of his philosophy on the absolute truth of Newton's mechanics. However, at the end of the nineteenth century and in the twentieth century, the limitations of the mechanistic world view became clear and it was replaced by the physicalist world view: the laws of physics, the theory of the electromagnetic field, Einstein's general and special theories of relativity are what determine the development of everything in the world. As Albert Einstein says (see Chapter Two, section 11):

> The spatiotemporal laws are complete. This means, there is not a single law of nature that, in principle could not be reduced to a law within the domain of space-time concepts. This principle implies, for instance, the conviction that psychic (mental) entities and relations can be reduced, in the last analysis, to processes of a physical and chemical nature within the nervous system. According to this principle, there are no nonphysical elements in the causal system of the processes of nature. In this sense, there is no room for "free will."

Here we should note that Einstein "solved" the problem of **free will versus causality** by refuting the existence of free will. In contrast, Immanuel Kant was not prepared to forego the principle of free will, and included this among his antinomies – contradictions that could not be solved.

The failure of the mechanistic world view did not harm the deterministic belief – it simply changed its form to that of a physicalist belief. It is not the laws of mechanics but the laws of physics that govern the world – namely, the laws of electromagnetism and of the general and special theories of relativity. The positions of all the particles and all the physical fields in the world (electromagnetic and gravitational) at a particular time unequivocally determine the development of the world – everything that was and everything that will be.

Determinism, which is seemingly supported by scientific development, contradicts Judaism, which is based on the principle of free will. However, it also contradicts, in an extreme way, common sense and the possibility of giving human life any sort of meaning. Billions of years ago, according to the current scientific viewpoint, all the elementary particles in the world, such as electrons and protons, were in a state of chaos at extremely high temperatures, much higher than the temperature at the center of the sun. We are talking about the state of the world close to the Big Bang (see Chapter Five). At that time, not only were there no animals; there were also no solid bodies such as stones or metals. All that existed were particles colliding with one another at extremely high speeds. According to the determinist philosophy, billions of years ago, those particles "knew" everything that is happening in the world right now. It was determined back then that I would be writing this sentence at this very moment. Also you, the reader, did not decide freely to read this book – it was something decreed for you billions of years ago. None of your emotions – love, jealousy, resentment, friendship, anger, devotion, self-sacrifice – is real. They are nothing but the results of the movements of particles at the time of the Big Bang.

What about great achievements in science and the arts? They have no independent status either. They are not *new* things, but they were predetermined at the moment of the creation of the world. Whether we are talking about ordinary human beings or about the great minds that have produced masterpieces throughout history, they are simply robots whose behavior was determined billions of years before they were born. Clearly in this world of "science," the meaning of life becomes non-existent. None of our actions has meaning. Our actions do not even belong to us – they belong to the particles of the Big Bang.

According to the view presented here, the world is purely a physical system. As we saw in Chapter Two (section 2), the development of a physical system is determined by two factors: the laws of physics and the initial position. In a sense, the details of the initial position have much greater significance than the laws themselves. All the information included in the deterministic system is found in the details of its initial position; the laws themselves add nothing new. We could say that the laws only carry out a transformation: they change the form of the information that is inherent in the system from the start and transfer this information from one time to another. In a world like this, the concept of time has no relevance, as we explained in the previous section when we spoke about the philosophy of Baruch Spinoza.

When people say that everything can be explained "naturally," they mean that it can be explained by deterministic development according to the laws of nature. Furthermore, they assume that there is no need to explain where these laws came from. The laws of nature are part of nature; they are a property of nature. The laws of nature are inherent in nature, included in it, immanent (see section 4). Nature and its laws are the source of everything and explain everything, including the souls of human beings and human culture. However, as we have seen above, in the world of "scientific" determinism, the main information is inherent in the *details of the initial position*. We may now ask: where does the enormous mass of knowledge come from that includes the great works of art – the compositions of Bach, Mozart and Beethoven, the works of Homer and Shakespeare, the Bible, Einstein's theory of relativity, modern technology, and so on? To say that nature is the source of everything means that even in a deterministic world, one must endow nature with human and superhuman qualities. In such a world, the laws of nature have a completely secondary role. One can imagine that a great, supernatural intellect infused the world with infinite knowledge – an impressive image, but probably far from reality.

7. THE SCIENTIFIC NON-DETERMINISM OF THE QUANTUM WORLD

We will continue studying the "scientific" world – a world whose development is determined solely by the laws of physics. Until now, we have assumed that these laws were deterministic, that they determined the development of the world. Based on these laws, it is possible to make an accurate prediction of the future and to compute the past if we know the position of the world at a given time. However, as we know from our study of science (see Chapter Two, section 6), not every development of the world is dictated by deterministic laws. The development of the physical world is not completely deterministic, but only partially so. Here we must differentiate between the development of a macrocosm and that of a microcosm. What is a macrocosm? It is the world as a whole, everything that we see around us. In this world, laws that determine the world's development – deterministic laws – prevail. In contrast, the microcosm is a world of tiny particles, including atomic and subatomic particles. The macrocosm is composed of these particles. The microcosm therefore exists within the macrocosm. The laws of the microcosm, which are quantum laws – the laws described by quantum theory – are non-deterministic. While in the macrocosm, the laws unequivocally determine a connection between two events – the cause and the effect – the laws of quantum theory determine probabilities, likelihoods of **possible** events. There is a loose connection between the cause and the effect.

We can illustrate the situation using the case of radiation from a radioactive substance such as radium or uranium. Radioactivity can last for a long time – in the case of uranium, for millions of years – and over time its power fades away. By doing a fairly simple scientific calculation, we can predict the weakening of the radioactivity in the very distant future, millions of years from now. Radioactive matter, such as one gram of uranium, is made up of a huge number (around 10^{24}) of uranium atoms. Not all these atoms radiate, but the number of active, radiating atoms is also very large. The radiation of the radioactive material is made up of the radiation of the atoms within it. We have already said that we can accurately predict the strength of the radiation from the matter at any given moment over a very long period of time, and that it decreases gradually. This is not the case with each and every individual atom within a macroscopic block of atoms.

In order to describe the radiation of a single atom, we must use quantum theory. The quantum behavior of the radioactive atom is quite strange. In order to radiate, the atom must be in an excited state, with an energy level higher than that of a non-radiating atom. The atom can be in an excited state and not radiate for an extended period of time, but at a certain moment it goes into a non-excited state, with lower energy, and emits a photon. A photon, which is a quant – the smallest possible unit of radiation – is discrete and non-continuous. Unlike the continuous macroscopic radiation, the quantum radiation of a single atom occurs with the emission of the photon and the atom's switching to a non-excited state at a particular moment. This process is completely random. *There is no law that determines when the photon will be emitted.* Quantum theory only determines the probability of the emission of the photon. Knowledge of this probability makes it possible to calculate the radiation process for a system that contains a very large number of atoms – for example, one gram of uranium.

We discussed another example of a quantum process in Chapter Two – the double-slit experiment. There, we saw that no law exists that determines where on the screen the single electron will land. Quantum theory gives only the probability of its ending up in one place or another.

Generally, in the physical system, **not all developments have laws that precisely determine them.** Even though the quantum laws act on the **micro** level, in principle they can also affect processes on the **macro** level, as a source of certain inaccuracies in the predictions of macro processes. If we return to the description of the deterministic development of the world that we described at the end of the previous section, we need to add to it a certain degree of uncertainty in the process of transferring the information latent in the initial position. The quantum processes, in general, affect the reliability of the transfer of information from one time to another. In other words, the quantum processes introduce a certain degree of uncertainty into the development of the world. It is worth pointing out that quantum uncertainty, as well as the non-determinism that derives from it, has no connection with our knowledge or lack of knowledge. Even if we obtain the maximum information about an initial position, we cannot produce a precise prediction of the future development of any quantum system.

It is worth emphasizing that quantum uncertainty, and, as a result, the world's non-determinism, do not contribute directly to our understanding of free will. There is a substantial difference between the uncertainty that derives from free will and that of quantum phenomena. Quantum laws relate to the probabilities of different random processes. Quantum uncertainty deals with the randomness of quantum processes. People's choices direct them towards a particular goal. The behavior of human beings is teleological and purposeful – namely, it is directed by the aspiration towards a goal that a person defines for himself. There is an enormous difference between purposefulness and randomness.

Let us consider further the concept of determinism. I am not aware of a Hebrew word for this concept, but the word comes from *to determine* in

English or *determinare* in Latin. While the linguistic analysis of the word is not particularly important, the way in which it is used is. A study of dictionaries and encyclopedias shows that the common denominator in all the definitions of determinism is the contrast between determinism and human free will. Determinism means that human behavior is determined not by our choices or our wills, but by externals factors. From this perspective, there is no difference between classical determinism and quantum non-determinism. In both cases, everything is determined by material elements in the world, by the *materia* in the world and the movements of particles from which everything is composed. In a sense, the issue of the existence or non-existence of advance knowledge of the development of matter is secondary. In the classic case, in principle, it is possible to know in advance and to predict the future at every stage of development, while in the quantum scenario, the future cannot be accurately predicted. However, in both cases, the movement of *materia* determines everything in the world and a person's choice plays no part. Hence, the word *determinism* can be applied to an equal degree to every development that is exclusively determined by the laws of nature.

8. INTERACTION BETWEEN SPIRIT AND MATTER – THE OPENNESS OF THE PHYSICAL WORLD TO DIVINE AND HUMAN WILL[12]

We have already reached the conclusion (Chapter One, sections 11 and 12) that our world can be presented as being comprised of a spiritual world and a material world, with God controlling the connection between these two worlds. This structure is shown in the diagram below. The spiritual world includes, among other things, the laws of nature, which God imposes on the material world. According to the Jewish view, which is based on the Bible, God is the Creator of the world and the law and order within in, and He supervises it. God created the world consisting of two parts, or two worlds – the spiritual and the material. In fact, the vast majority of the Bible

---

12. Certain parts of this section may seem slightly (or very) complex. However, I have not placed it in shaded text as it is an important subject. Even if it appears difficult, it is worth at least skimming this section.

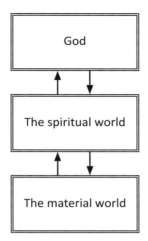

is dedicated to the spiritual world. The spiritual world could be considered the divine operating system of the material world.

However, when we talk about the spiritual world and the physical world, we must remember, as we have already mentioned (Chapter One, section 11), that they are not equal. The existence of the material world is constantly dependent on the spiritual world. Later on, I will attempt to clarify the nature of this dependence. In Chapter Four, section 8, which summarizes the part on the laws of nature, we will see in more detail how this dependence can be understood using scientific concepts.

In sections 6 and 7, we looked at the materialistic world view, which derives from the metaphysical assumption that nature is the source of everything in the world, including ourselves. According to this view, the laws of nature are an integral part of nature, and everything can be explained by nature and its laws. There is a certain difficulty in accepting a view according to which matter itself is the source of the laws that govern it. After all, the laws of nature are a list of directives that indicate the structure of matter and how it must change over time. This applies both to isolated material systems and about the world as a whole. As hard as it is to accept the view that the system commands itself as to how to change, this is not the main problem.

Ultimately, the current or future state of the physical world is determined by the world's original initial position. To a certain extent, the laws of nature play the secondary role of transferring the information inherent at the start to all the other points in time. The fidelity of the transfer depends on the relationship between the deterministic part of the laws of nature and the non-deterministic part (namely, quantum phenomena). In order to explain everything by the "forces of nature," nature must be endowed not only with the ability to make the laws, but also to program itself. The software, namely the content of the initial position, must include a huge – actually, an infinite – amount of information in order to adapt itself to the world.

One cannot logically prove that the "scientific" world, which we outlined here and in sections 6 and 7, is not the world in which we live. In this imaginary world, in which the laws of nature are the exclusive cause of all development, all our actions and all our behavior are determined at the beginning of time. Although there is no place in this world for free will or creativity, there is no formal logical contradiction here. Quantum non-determinism is not responsible for free will. However, there are many absurd things that do not contradict logic. For example, the solipsist's claim that the world is not real, that it is just a figment of the imagination, does not actually contradict formal logic. The reason that we are devoting so much attention to the "scientific" version of the structure of the world and its development is because this view is so widely held among the general public.

The prevalence of this view is largely bound up with the popularity of science. Anything connected with science appears to have the credibility of science. According to this view, everything in the world behaves in accordance with scientific laws. Likewise, every development in the world can be described scientifically, including the stages of the evolution of life and the history of mankind. If we do not yet know all the details, it is just a matter of time before we will be able to have the full picture. But it is not the credibility of science that is under scrutiny here. One cannot conclude from the fact that science describes physical processes with the utmost reliability that the entire world behaves according to the laws of nature – in other words, the laws of physics. Another more significant metaphysical assumption lies at the basis of determinism (or semi-determinism – quantum non-determinism). From a historical perspective, the "scientific" deterministic world view came about as a result of the integration of Newton's physics and the metaphysics of John Locke (1632–1704). Locke made a metaphysical assumption that everything in the world behaves in accordance with the laws of physics. Ever since then, implicitly or explicitly, this premise has been at the basis of the discussion of the structure of the world and its development.

As we mentioned in the introduction to this chapter, Immanuel Kant identified an antinomy: the conflict between the principles of free will and causality. Kant could not give up on either of these principles. Laplace, a contemporary of Kant's, started from the assumption that Newton's equations described the entire world. In modern times, Albert Einstein set out the universality of the laws of physics and was hence prepared to give up the principle of free will. We quoted him in section 6 as saying: "[T]here are no nonphysical elements in the causal system of the processes of nature. In this sense, there is no room for 'free will'. . ."

We should emphasize that the metaphysical assumption regarding the universality of the laws of nature is actually fairly arbitrary. The belief that everything in the world, as well as the world itself, obeys the laws of physics is not based on our accumulated day-to-day experience. Furthermore, one might say that it actually contradicts our experience. All we have to do is look at the movements of almost everything that we see in order to understand that they cannot be described solely according to the laws of physics. Consider animals, for example – dogs, cats, and so on. The equations of physics cannot predict their paths or account for them. This is surely all the more so in the case of human behavior, which cannot be accounted for or predicted with scientific accuracy. However, reliance on everyday experience is not necessarily the most sensible approach. In fact, many phenomena of modem physics, particularly quantum physics, do not sit well with our experience. Yet to start with, we do rely on our everyday experience and common sense, and will consider other possibilities only in light of facts and the results of experiments that contradict them.

This is not the case here. The insistence on the universality of science, on the fact that science must explain everything, does not derive from any facts or experiments that verify the universality of science. This is not pressure from newly discovered facts, but rather a point of view. There is an element of breaking away from God as well as a tendency to deify nature – a desire to prove the omnipotence of nature, to prove that nature can replace God. This is an atheistic perspective. In the opposing viewpoint, from Jewish thought, God is the Creator of everything. He intervenes in all things and oversees them. He also created the laws that govern nature – the laws of nature. These laws are not inherent in nature itself. They are not included in it. They are not immanent. According to the biblical perspective, it is God who imposes the laws of nature upon nature. But the important point here is that the laws of nature are only one element of divine management. God is not restricted by the laws of nature. He has the ability to intervene in the world, using both the laws of nature and other tools that are outside the laws of nature.

While we cannot understand how God operates, we can consider the ways in which human beings, who were created in God's image, operate. In the analysis of Karl Popper's three worlds (Chapter One, section 10), we came to the conclusion that our world is open to God, and that world one, the physical world, is also open to mankind. Man was created in God's image, and just as the entire world is open to God, the physical world is also open to man's soul, to his free will. This openness is the real cause of the non-determinism in the world.

As we have said, we, human beings, are not capable of grasping how the world is open to God. However, we see and feel the openness of the physical world, world one, to mankind almost constantly. Whenever I feel myself I feel the involvement of my *Self* in the material world. This does not mean that I truly understand how the *Self* operates the body and causes it to turn left, right, walk straight or stop moving. The interaction between the body and the mind is part of the psycho-physical problem that has plagued philosophers for many years. I do not presume to get to the bottom of it here. I am not sure that it can ever be solved using scientific tools. While modern science has come a long way in its scientific understanding of the structure of matter, my Self is not a subject of science. Much is shared in the mental world of human beings, and this shared element is psychology. But what is special about my Self, its uniqueness, is what determines my destiny in the world, and something that is unique cannot be the object of any science. Therefore, in the body-mind pair, one part – the mind – cannot be described scientifically. Whatever we learn from this is that the interaction between the body and the mind is not subject solely to scientific laws.

Nevertheless, it is difficult to be satisfied with a complete surrender to circumstances. The analogy can help us answer the questions that arise about the interaction between the body and the mind. The important question that we keep coming back to is whether the openness of the physical world to the human mind contradicts modern physics. Some people think that an entirely new physics needs to be discovered now, one that we are not yet aware of. I disagree, and I would like to show that interaction between the body and mind can occur without contravening the physical laws. It is compatible with science. The circumstantial evidence for this is in the fact that human beings have existed for thousands of years, while modern science has only been around for a few centuries, and up to now there have been no signs of a new physics that deals with the interaction between human beings and their environment.

We have not been able to go into great detail about the mechanism of the interaction between the mind and the body, but we can show that God created the laws of physics in such a way that they are compatible with the realization of our will and that of God, which does not involve any violation of these laws. I will attempt to show this below.

First, it should be made clear that in a system of completely deterministic laws, where all movements of a physical object are pre-determined, there is no spiritual entity that is capable of affecting an object's path. In other words, in a case such as this, interaction between matter and spirit is impossible. The explanation for this is simple. When the position of an object at a particular moment is known, then its movements are determined for all time by deterministic laws, and therefore no spiritual entity can change its path. In this case, there is absolute separation between matter and spirit. The physical world, world one, is a deterministic world that is closed to the involvement of the spirit. It may seem that quantum non-determinism does not help us understand the openness of the physical world to the involvement of the spirit. We know that macroscopic objects obey deterministic physical laws. It is true that these objects, such as a ballistic missile or a human body, are made up of molecules, atoms, electrons, protons and other particles. Even though their atoms and molecules move according to the laws of quantum physics, the macroscopic bodies themselves move in accordance with the laws of classical deterministic physics with an impressive degree of accuracy. Nevertheless, as we shall see below, quantum non-determinism changes the situation.

In order to be convinced that mind-body interaction is possible and can happen without violating the laws of physics, we will consider four thought experiments, four models. I have chosen to look at the movements of spaceships in outer space because, in a sense, they are the simplest examples.

A. **A spaceship with a timer.** Let us consider the movement of a spaceship in outer space. We'll assume that we know the spaceship's mass and its speed at a particular time and place, as well as the gravitational field at every point along its path. Thus, according to the laws of mechanics, we can predict the spaceship's trajectory with great accuracy. If we enter all the data, including the laws of mechanics, into a computer, we can obtain the data of the spaceship's path. The observation of the spaceship's movement will confirm our prediction. Suddenly, something happens and the spaceship starts to move in an unexpected manner. How can this be? Are the laws of mechanics wrong? This is impossible. After all, innumerable experiments have been performed that confirm the laws of mechanics! These laws are still valid and the computer calculation was correct. Apparently, we did not take into account that inside the spaceship is a timer, a device by which we can perform certain operations at pre-determined times (like a time-switch). At specific moments, the timer operates devices that fire gases or liquids from the spaceship. Every time this happens, the spaceship deviates from its path. This is easy to explain. The emission of matter from the spaceship causes it to move in the opposite direction to the emission. Ballistic missiles operate according to this principle – an emission of gases or liquids causes the missile to accelerate or decelerate. The energy required for this action is taken from a source within the spaceship. This means that there is no violation of the laws of physics. All the movements of the spaceship – even the "deviations" from its expected trajectory – can be predicted in advance once all the data of the initial position are taken into account. These data also include the initial position of the timer, which over time operates devices that emit gasses or liquids from the spaceship. A description of this kind of initial position includes a great deal of information about the internal structure of the spaceship.

B. **A remotely-controlled spaceship.** We can imagine a spaceship that contains a device that controls the emission of materials. However, this time the emissions are not fixed in advance by a timer, but are controlled by a person who sends electromagnetic signals, such as radio waves, from Earth.

We should point out that the energy of electromagnetic signals is so low that it can be ignored relative to the total amount of energy.[13] It can be in the realm of the energy of a single quantum particle, or individual photons. There are highly sensitive instruments that react to energies in the quantum realm, and it is well known that the human eye is capable of reacting even to very dim light made up of just a few lone photons. This means that objects with the minutest amount of energy can have a significant effect.

C. **A spaceship navigated by a person inside it.** We know how to treat the two examples A and B above using scientific tools, at least in principle. All the elements of the thought experiments are physical. This is not so in this example. It is the man inside the spaceship who determines its movements. The spaceship contains highly sophisticated instruments and tools. The person operates them using his own brain. The human brain is, without a doubt, the most sophisticated instrument in the world. However, ultimately, it is the person's self that makes the decisions and determines the path of the spaceship. Hence, it is impossible to calculate the spaceship's path using scientific tools. It is determined by a sequence of decisions made by the human being at the helm.

D. **A spaceship with a Geiger counter.** Let us now imagine that on top of the spaceship is a Geiger counter – a device that reacts to lone particles that attack any object in outer space in a completely random way. Let us assume that every time a cosmic particle hits the Geiger counter, the spaceship changes its direction by a particular angle. Let us also assume that the direction of ship's deviation and the increase in its speed are determined by the energy and speed (or momentum) of the particle that hits the Geiger counter. As a result, an external observer would see that the spaceship weaves in a seemingly drunken fashion, randomly changing direction. In this example, the path of the spaceship cannot be scientifically predicted even though the spaceship is moving in accordance with the laws of physics. How is this possible? Surely macroscopic objects have to comply with the

---

13. The energy of a photon from radio waves is equal to $\hbar\omega = \varepsilon \sim {}^{-27}\ 10 \times 108\ {}^{-19}$ erg ~ 10. This means that the ratio of the energy of one radio photon to the energy of a macroscopic object (such as a spaceship) is in the order of magnitude of 10^{-19}, and maybe even less.

deterministic laws of classical physics. The difference is that in this example, quantum processes affect the movements of the macroscopic object. If there were quantum processes in our brains affecting our behavior, we would all move as though we were drunk. In this model, the spaceship is not a closed system, but is affected by cosmic particles external to it. However, it would not be difficult to come up with a model of a closed spaceship that can be affected by random quantum processes. In order to do this, one would need to place the source of the particle and Geiger counter inside the spaceship. Then the spaceship would make the same movements, but it would be a completely closed physical system.

We have already mentioned that the movements of animals and people, and of objects that are managed and controlled by human beings, are fairly complex and seemingly incompatible with the laws of physics. Their paths do not resemble the relatively simple paths dictated by the laws of physics. The examples above are intended to explain how a physical system closed to the effect of external physical forces can move in an arbitrary way, not according to the laws of classical macroscopic physics. It is well known that macroscopic objects such as spaceships, ballistic missiles and heavenly bodies must obey the laws of classical physics.

From the first example, that of a spaceship with a timer, we learn that even in a completely deterministic world, the spaceship can move entirely arbitrarily, but all its movements can be predicted in advance if we know the details of the timer. Example A actually represents the scientific world, which operates like a precise clock. In this world, everything is pre-determined. The animals and the human beings are robots even though they appear to have free will.

In example B, the remotely-controlled spaceship, the spaceship is also able to move arbitrarily and according to the person's will. However, unlike in example A, the spaceship receives electromagnetic signals sent by a person on Earth. These signals can contain only a limited number of radio photons, such that their total energy is in the quantum order of magnitude. Nevertheless, the spaceship is not a closed physical system. Hence, example B does not provide us with an answer to the question of how a physical system that is closed to external physical forces can move in arbitrary paths.

Example C, **the spaceship controlled by a person inside it**, represents the fact that is well known to us from many other examples: a person can move physical systems at will. A skeptic would claim that this is not a matter of free will, but rather just an illusion. What seems to us to be free will is actually an inevitable action, just as in example A.

We have stressed on numerous occasions that we do not have the tools needed to explain the interaction between matter and spirit. Here we come to the critical point: Even though we are unable to analyze the interaction between matter and spirit, **we are able to determine whether the laws of physics are compatible with free will**. It is important to understand that not every system of physical laws is compatible with the existence of free will. Thus, the laws of classical physics, including the theory of relativity, do not allow for free will. We have seen that in a system of completely deterministic laws, in which every movement of a physical object is pre-determined, no spiritual entity whatsoever is capable of affecting its path.

In contrast, modern physics, which also includes quantum theory, is compatible with the existence of free will. Therefore the following criterion of compatibility of the laws of physics with free will could be proposed: *A closed physical system can move arbitrarily, not in accordance with any particular laws, and without violating the laws of physics*. It is clear that when all the movements of a system are dictated solely by the laws of physics there is no room for free will. And we have already mentioned that movements of lone quantum particles are not determined by any law at all and do not violate the laws of physics. But we cannot compare human body or spaceship with quantum particle.

Now, let us look at example D – **a spaceship with a Geiger counter**. What is new about this example is that it shows that **a macroscopic system like the human body is also capable of moving arbitrarily without obeying the classical deterministic laws and without violating the laws of physics**. We must emphasize that we have not proved that the existence of free will can be derived from modern physics. We have shown that modern physics is compatible with man's free will; it does not contradict it. Conversely, classical physics is not compatible with free will. This is how Immanuel Kant arrived at his antinomy – the contradiction between causality (in classical physics) and the principle of free will.

We have actually shown that a necessary (but not sufficient) condition that the physical laws have to fulfill in order not to contradict man's free will is their non-determinism: **The initial position and the laws of physics do not unequivocally determine the development of the physical system over time.** It is worth clarifying this point employing example D. Let us place a radioactive atom in an excited state inside the spaceship. At a particular moment, which is impossible to predict, the atom will emit a photon. This photon will activate a device within the spaceship that ultimately causes the spaceship to deviate from its path. The moment that the spaceship deviates from its path is not determined by any law or initial position. It is random. The physical system – the spaceship – is able to deviate from its path in a way that is not pre-determined by the laws of physics. Let us compare this event – the random deviation of the spaceship – to another event, the deviation of the spaceship as a result of a person's free will as described in example C, **the spaceship controlled by a person inside it.** It is interesting that the outside observer would not be able to distinguish between these two events, neither of which is pre-determined by the laws of physics. Clearly, a necessary condition for the existence of free will is the **possibility of events occurring that are not pre-determined by the laws of physics.**

We have looked at different examples of spaceships controlled in different ways. We chose a spaceship because of the relative simplicity of the example. In actual fact, in our lives we constantly see examples of physical systems that are operated by spiritual entities. Each of us human beings is a physical system operated by the mind. The most elaborate apparatus in the world, the human body, is under the control of the mind. The conclusion that we have reached here is that there is no contradiction between the modern physical lawfulness and the existence of a spiritual entity that is capable of controlling a material entity in a way that is not subject to physical lawfulness.

9. THE IDEALIZATION OF SCIENCE

> Mind has erected the objective outside world of the natural philosopher out of its own stuff. Mind could not cope with this gigantic task otherwise than by the simplifying device of excluding itself – withdrawing from its conceptual creation. Hence the latter does not contain its creator. (Erwin Schrödinger, Mind and Matter, 42)

The title of the section requires some explanation. Until now, we have spoken about idealization in the context of various scientific approximations.

Idealization is simplification, making something simpler, while ignoring certain details that are considered either less important or of no importance at all. Simplification is important for us to understand things, but there is always a danger that along with the "unimportant" details, we may get rid of some crucial ones, too. In fact, there is no escape from using idealization in scientific research – we cannot take into account all the factors that are present in a particular study. Therefore, to a large degree, the history of physics is the history of the substitution of different idealizations.

Thus, modern physics began with the formulation of the law of inertia, which talks about an object moving at a fixed speed while there are no forces acting upon it. However, this is just an idealization. It can only be carried out in a very limited area of space and time. Another example is a fundamental premise of classical physics that one can always ignore the influence of the process of measuring on the measured object. But now there is quantum theory, according to which we cannot discount the impact of the investigation on the investigated object.

However, what is written in the title of the section and in the quotation at the start of this section is not another scientific idealization, but a claim that scientific description itself is an idealization, a simplification of reality. We cannot research and describe everything in the world with scientific tools, and I will attempt to show this now. Thus, a person who has a soul cannot be an object of a scientific study. Of course we cannot prove that a person possess a soul that has free will – the necessary property of a human mind. Such a premise belongs to the domain of metaphysics. But once we assume the premise that free will exists, the scientific description of the person is impossible. In this case, scientific laws are not the only source of the change. The person's decisions are additional sources of change, and purely scientific research of the person is impossible. The person, who has free will that characterizes his soul, his self, is not a suitable subject for a scientific study. The idealization of science has reached its limit. A spiritual entity such as a human soul is not a suitable subject for a scientific study. Therefore, the researcher must be convinced that the object of his research does not contain a human spirit.

But this is not enough to justify the idealization of science. This would have been the case if it had been proven that other than the human spirit there is no other spirit in the world. This is, in fact, an atheistic claim. We see that science is not able to verify any atheistic claim even though its very premise contains such a view. Even though experience teaches us that science is highly successful in studying different physical systems, this does not mean that it is possible to rely on science for entire, global systems such as the development of the entire universe or of life on Earth without taking divine providence into account. Perhaps partial success is possible in this area, but there is no logical or scientific proof.

10. CONCLUSION

In this chapter, we have largely dealt with the place of science in the order of the world, an issue on which different world views collide. One is the materialistic, atheistic, view; the other is the Jewish view, which develops from Jewish thought,

From the atheist's point of view, nature is the ultimate, final and absolute reality, and the laws of nature are an inseparable part of it. The laws of nature are immanent – inherent and contained within nature. Moreover, everything in the world progresses according to the laws of nature, which are the sole cause of all the movements in the world. In other words, according to this view, our world is a closed physical system. It is worth mentioning that in a world such as this, it is the information about the initial position of the world that determines what happens now and at all points in time, in the future and in the past. The laws of nature only transfer the information already inherent in nature from one time to another. The transfer of information can be very accurate, as the laws of nature are deterministic, like classical physics. However, the fidelity of the transfer can be affected by quantum phenomena that act upon the system.

Even if we assume that the laws of nature are inherent in nature and that they are derived from it, this is not enough to explain the richness and splendor of the world in which we live. Therefore, we must assume that from the start, nature was this splendid and that this splendor was inherent in it from the beginning of time. But this is no explanation, as we must assume the very thing that we are trying to explain. There is no reason at all to attribute such extreme properties to nature. But as we have mentioned several times, it is impossible to prove or refute a metaphysical assumption through logical means. On the other hand, there is no reason to adopt a philosophical approach that leads to such absurd conclusions. As Nobel Prize winner John Eccles remarks in *The Self and Its Brain* (written together with Karl Popper):

> I would like to add a comment about determinism. If physical determinism is true, then that is the end of all discussion or argument; everything is finished. There is no philosophy. All human persons are caught up in this inexorable web of circumstances and cannot break out of it. Everything that we think we are doing is an illusion and that is that. Will anybody live up to this situation? It even comes to this, that the laws of physics and all our understanding of physics is the result of the same inexorable web of circumstances. It isn't a matter any more of our struggling for truth to understand what this natural world is and how it came to be and what are the springs of its operation. All of this is illusion. If we want to have that purely deterministic physical world,[14] then we should remain silent.   (The Self and Its Brain, 546)

In short, this is a world of **robots**, whose movements are all pre-determined. They have no free will or freedom to choose. All their thinking is decreed in advance. There is no value in their actions or behavior. In fact, the very concept of "value" has no meaning – and the concept of "meaning" has no meaning, either. This is a world of the utterly absurd.

But this world has a positive side, too: it is simpler and easier to grasp than the real world in which we live. In the introduction to this chapter, we spoke about the split personality of modern man. He believes in "scientific" materialism and in physical causality, while at the same time, on a practical level, he worries that his own free will should not be harmed.

Jewish thought provides a way out of this impasse. From our point of view, the laws of nature are a part of the divine spiritual world. They are one of the many tools of providence. The physical world is not deterministic. It is not closed. It is open to the involvement and will of man's free will. We have tried to show that the structure of modern physics is compatible with the physical world's openness to the wills of God and man.

---

14. Of course everything that is written here also relates to a world that also contains quantum randomness.

CHAPTER FOUR

Knowledge of the World from a Jewish Perspective

1. INTRODUCTION

THE HUMAN KNOWLEDGE THAT HAS ACCUMULATED OVER time plays a crucial role in the life of man. Human development depends on the level of knowledge that human beings possess, and historical processes are influenced by the growth in human knowledge. The development of modern science over the past several centuries has changed our lives dramatically. Hence, the questions "What is the source of human knowledge?" and "How can man comprehend the laws of nature?" are of great importance. Although these questions do not seem particularly perplexing, the question of the source of scientific cognition is one of the most difficult and fundamental problems, both in general philosophy and in Jewish thought. Karl Popper, a pre-eminent philosopher of science, wrote: "The phenomenon of human knowledge is no doubt the greatest miracle in our universe."[1]

Albert Einstein expressed a similar idea: "The eternal mystery of the world is its comprehensibility .... The fact that it is comprehensible is a miracle."[2]

Popper and Einstein are joined by a great Jewish thinker, Rabbi Soloveit-

---

1. *Objective Knowledge*, VII.
2. *Ideas and Opinions*, 292.

chik: "The process of cognition [is] the problem of problems and enigma of enigmas of man."[3]

In this chapter we will try to understand the essence of the problem both in general philosophy and in Jewish thought.

2. A CRITIQUE OF THE PRINCIPLE OF INDUCTION

How is it possible to know the world? A central field in philosophy deals with this question: the theory of cognition, or epistemology. Many people, if not most, do not see anything particularly difficult about question of scientific cognition. They think that we can infer scientific theories and the laws of nature from experiment and observation. We get to know the world through our five senses. Experimental data and logical inference (rational thought) are enough to arrive at and formulate the laws of nature. This approach, **from the particular to the general**, from experiment to theory, is called **induction**. The opposite process, in which conclusions are drawn from the general to the particular, is called **deduction**. The basis of induction is the principle that it is possible to infer the general – in this case the laws of nature and scientific theories – from the particular – experimental results and observations.

Research scientists, who are not always experts in the theory of cognition, generally believe in induction. Moreover, Bertrand Russell, an important twentieth-century philosopher, claimed that science could not discover the laws of nature without the principle of induction. At first glance, the principle of induction fits our common-sense view of the world.

Yet in the eighteenth century, the Scottish philosopher David Hume proved that the principle of induction has no validity and is erroneous. In his book *Treatise of Human Nature*, he proves that it is impossible to infer laws of nature from experiments. In his opinion, induction has no substance, and no logical argument can prove that "the incidents about which we have no experience are similar to those for which we have experience." This means that "even observation of a regular or fixed combination of objects cannot infer anything about any object beyond our experience." **In other words, we cannot infer any theory from experience.** Of course, when we say that we

---

3. *Halakhic Man,* 8.

cannot infer theories from experience, we mean that we cannot construct theories in a rational way, using logical processes, based on observable data alone.

We can illustrate this with an analogy from mathematics. Let us take a particular numerical series. We will ask ourselves whether it is possible to infer any conclusion about it based on knowledge of part of it, even a large part. For instance, if we know that a small part of the series is 1, 2, 3, 4, what can we say about the whole series based on this partial knowledge? It is possible that this is a series of natural numbers: 1, 2, 3, 4, 5, 6, 7, 8, 9, 10 . . . ? However, it could also be part of a series of numbers such as 1, 2, 3, 4, 1, 2, 3, 4, 1, 2, 3, 4, 1, 2, 3, 4. Even more detailed knowledge, such as 1, 2, 3, 4, 1, 2, 3, 4, still does not necessarily indicate a specific known series. The series could be, for example, 1, 2, 3, 4, 1, 2, 3, 4, 4, 3, 2, 1, 4, 3, 2, 1, 1, 2, 3, 4, 1, 2, 3, 4 . . . . The possibilities are infinite. Based on the knowledge of a limited section, we cannot infer any conclusion about a particular sequence of numbers.

The law of induction contradicts simple logic. If this law were correct, then any theory (logically) based on a particular group of past experiments would determine the results of all experiments, past and future. As a result, limited knowledge, based on a group of past experiments, would determine the results of an infinite number of past and future experiments. In our example above of the infinite series of numbers, the principle of induction would determine the *entire* series on the basis of limited knowledge about certain numbers. It is important to note that the example of the series relies on the hidden assumption of a certain order in the numbers, and this is a simplified assumption that does not necessarily reflect reality. When we have the results of a limited number of experiments, not only are we unable to determine the results of all subsequent experiments, but we cannot even determine that there is a particular order in the future reality. In any case, such a conclusion does not stem from the results of our experiments and is not dependent on the number of experiments carried out. **On the basis of logical reasoning, we cannot rationally infer scientific theories from experiments.**

Nevertheless, I have the impression that many researchers in the field of the exact sciences are convinced that these are abstract philosophical conclusions that have no connection with the reality of scientific discovery. Therefore, it is worth looking into the history of scientific discoveries. Let us return to Newton's theory of motion (see Chapter Two, section 2). The first law of motion, the law of inertia, states that while there are no external forces acting upon an object, it will move in a straight line at a fixed speed. This law is not derived from any experiment, but from a **thought** experiment, from theoretical thinking. Of all the various types of motion in the world around us, fixed motion in a straight line was chosen as the simplest type of motion, though it is not self-evident that this is indeed the simplest type of motion. Aristotle, and subsequently Galileo, believed that the simplest type of motion was actually circular motion (Galileo thought that the circle was the circle around the globe). In Newton's second law, the situation is even more delicate. This law uses the terms **mass, acceleration** and **force**. The term **acceleration** had never been used before, while the terms **mass** and **force** were already in use. *Mass* was used to refer to the quantity of matter and *force* was used as a measure of exertion. But in Newtonian mechanics, mass is a quantitative property of motion – it is the degree of resistance to acceleration. In fact, mass is defined by Newton's second law of motion. This begs the question: what came first – the experiment or the theory? The claim that the theory derives from the experiment is essentially the principle of induction. According to this principle, in order to infer Newton's second law, one must measure three quantities – the force, acceleration and mass – of a particular object and examine the relationship between them. But neither the concept of (inertial) mass nor the concept of force existed prior to Newton's formulation of his second law:

$$\text{Force} = \text{Mass} \times \text{Acceleration}$$

In other words, a physical quantity is a result of a theory, and what an experiment can do is check the theory that existed before the experiment was carried out. If this is the case, then we are left with the following question: where does the theory come from? What is its source? We will discuss this later on. Right now, we can only say that Newton's mechanics is Isaac Newton's creature.

Likewise, the force of gravity, which is capable of acting between objects that are great distances apart, is an invention of Isaac Newton's. Nevertheless, when we talk about scientific theories that appeared at the dawn of modern science, one might be left with the *impression* that experiment has priority over theory. I stress the word *impression* because we have just seen that Newton's theory preceded experiment. But with the development of science, it becomes more and more difficult to justify the principle of induction and to claim that experiment precedes theory. It is hard to imagine how Maxwell's or Einstein's equations or the equations of quantum theory could be derived from experiment. And clearly, the idea that string theory, according to which there are eleven dimensions in spacetime, could have been produced logically from experience is simply ridiculous!

The denial of the law of induction brings up a serious problem for the theory of scientific cognition. How is it possible to arrive at the laws of nature if not by inferring them from the findings of our observations? Bertrand Russell expresses his opinion on this in a colorful way:

> He (Hume) arrives at the disastrous conclusion that from experience and observation nothing is to be learnt. There is no such thing as a rational belief .... The lunatic who believes that he is a poached egg is to be condemned solely on the ground that he is in a minority .... This is a desperate point of view, and it must be hoped that there is some way of escaping from it.[4]

Einstein writes the following in his autobiography about the general theory of relativity: "I have learned something else from the theory of gravitation: No ever so inclusive collection of empirical facts can ever lead to the setting up of such complicated equations. A theory can be tested by experience, *but there is no way from experience to the setting up of a theory.*"[5]

However, none of this manages to convince people, especially scientists. Usually, people give a simple example of repetitive events, such as the movement of a clock hand. All you have to do is to look at a clock face in order to come to the unequivocal conclusion that the second hand will change its position on the clock face every second, and to predict the positions of the hands for a long period of time. So, based on a short experiment – a quick look at a clock – we come to the theoretical conclusion – a theory of the movement of clock hands, a theory that seemingly enables us to predict the positions of the hands for an unlimited period of time. Let us look at another example – the transition between night and day that we witness

---

4. Bertrand Russell, *A History of Western Philosophy*, 672–673.

5. Autobiographical Notes in *Albert Einstein: Philosopher-Scientist*, Paul Arthur Schilpp, 89.

"Accidental" Discoveries

Sometimes people point to "accidental" discoveries as reinforcing induction – the drawing of general conclusions from a specific event. There are rare cases of completely accidental discoveries, such as the discovery of the vaccine against chicken cholera by Louis Pasteur, and in any case, this discovery is neither a law nor a theory. However, most seemingly accidental discoveries are not like this. As a rule, these discoveries are based on certain theoretical expectations. Thus, from 1800 until 1820, Hans Christian Oersted was busy carrying out experiments. He was looking for a way to turn electricity to magnetism and he found it. Likewise, Wilhelm Roentgen was looking for invisible rays and discovered X-rays (also known in some languages as Roentgen rays). Even Alexander Fleming's discovery of penicillin was not completely accidental, since it occurred while he was conducting experiments to find a bactericide.

on a daily basis. From our observations, we have no problem drawing the conclusion that this will continue in the future.

These and countless other examples do not contradict David Hume's conclusion that it is impossible to derive logically, with a formal proof, a theory that describes the behavior of an object over an unlimited period of time from a particular observation. In relatively simple cases, it is easy to guess, to assume that the future will not be different from the past. The claim that the cycle of night and day will continue for an unlimited time is not a conclusion that follows logically from the observation data, but is rather a guess, an assumption, a hypothesis that we postulate about the object's future behavior. Using further observations, we can reinforce or reject this assumption, but we can never verify it conclusively. To do so, we would need to carry out an infinite number of experiments, and even they would not confirm the assumption absolutely – they would only reinforce it. Incidentally, in the examples that we have used above, the assumption that repetitive behavior will continue for an unlimited period is simply not correct. The clock will stop working when its battery runs out. Even the cycle of night and day will stop when the sun's thermonuclear reactor eventually exhausts itself and dies.

In contrast to the simple examples above, the goal of the scientist is to discover the fundamental laws of nature. Here we realize that David Hume's discovery is not just an abstract philosophical claim with no connection to reality, but is actually quite practical. In general, there is no similarity between data from a particular experiment or from a series of experiments and the fundamental law of nature that the experiment is intended to comply with. When Albert Einstein finished formulating his general theory of relativity at the end of 1915, he defined three phenomena that derived from his theory. Among them was a prediction of the deflection of a beam of light passing through the sun. In 1919, an experiment was performed during a solar eclipse that supported his prediction – the deflection of the beam of light of 1."75 (1.75 seconds of an arc – less that one thousandth of a degree). This is the result of the experiment. However, there is not the slightest similarity between this result and Einstein's equations that describe the change in the curvature of spacetime over time.

There is another important point here. We made it clear (in Chapter Two, section 3) that a particular law of nature is expressed by a mathematical equation that describes an infinite number of paths. In other words, this equation has an infinite number of solutions according to the various initial positions. The law of nature is the common, fixed element for infinite movements, paths and solutions. Every solution changes with time and is a function of time, whereas a law of nature is fixed and not dependent on time. The most we can do with experiments is to reproduce them or find a particular part of the solution in a particular time interval. But we cannot derive the law from knowledge of fragments of solutions.

This situation is not at all similar to the examples of repetitive events that we cited above. While there it was fairly easy to make a guess at the future course of events, this is not the case when we know only fragments of the movements, paths and solutions. This knowledge does not really help us to build hypotheses about the possible form of a law. And here is another point that is important to understand. The planning and performance of physics experiments in the age of modern physics is carried out on the basis of an existing or suggested theory. We have already mentioned that Newton's second law was proposed prior to being tested empirically. This is all the more true for modern-day theories, such as quantum theory and the theory of relativity. The empirical testing of the general theory of relativity was carried out years after the theoretical work. Only then was it possible to formulate and suggest the experiments and a way to test them. Today, in order to design an experiment, scientists must first acquire a huge amount of theoretical knowledge. They must study for many years before they can even step into a science laboratory.

3. KNOWLEDGE OF THE WORLD ACCORDING TO THE PHILOSOPHY OF IMMANUEL KANT: A CRITIQUE OF THE CRITIQUE

Knowledge of the world, cognition theory, plays a central role in Kant's philosophy. Immanuel Kant was born in 1724 in Königsberg, Eastern Prussia. In 1781, at the age of fifty-seven, he published what was considered his most important work: *Critique of Pure Reason*. To a great extent, this book was seen as a response to David Hume's conclusion that it is impossible to derive laws of nature from experience. Kant himself wrote that it was Hume who woke him from his "dogmatic slumber," and it took him twelve years to put together his response to the challenge that Hume's work presented.

It is important that we appreciate the essence of Kant's philosophical method, which professes to give a secular answer, involving no deity, to the problem of knowledge of the world. In fact, Kant's philosophy is considered the basis for the view that places man at the center of the universe. According to this view, it is people who determine the laws of ethics. To this very day, there are philosophers who side with Kant's philosophical method. The article, "Immanuel Kant and Kantianism," published in the *Encyclopedia Britannica* (1997), states that despite the existing objections to Kant's philosophical method, Kant, together with Plato and Aristotle, are considered "the great triad of Western philosophical thought."

On the other hand, Bertrand Russell, in *A History of Western Philosophy*, denies that Kant was such a great thinker. Russell scorns him for his extreme dogmatism. As we have mentioned, Kant claimed that Hume aroused him from his dogmatic slumber, though Russell adds that ". . . the awakening was only temporary, and he soon invented a soporific which enabled him to sleep again."[6]

Either way, we have no choice but to consider Immanuel Kant's philosophical outlook. We have already said that to a certain extent, Kant's view

---

6. *A History of Western Philosophy*, 704.

constitutes the basis of the secular world view. If this is the case, then let us consider some of his fundamental premises. For most aspects of Kant's philosophy, Russell's comment about Kant's theory of space and time is relevant: "To explain Kant's theory of space and time clearly is not easy, because the theory itself is not clear."[7] Therefore, please bear with me while I describe several key elements of Kant's theory.

Over a period of twelve years, Kant tried to solve Hume's problem. If causality cannot be derived logically from experience, as Hume showed, how can it be determined at all? In more general terms, how do science and scientific laws exist when they cannot be derived from experience? Yet another thing: Kant was certain that scientific laws, namely Newtonian mechanics, are something proven, the absolute truth, and we just need to find a way to reach this truth. After twelve years, it took Kant only a few months to formulate a solution to the problem.

For Kant, one of the central things, if not the central thing, is the distinction between nature and phenomena. A phenomenon has a cause, but we can know nothing about that cause. It is a "thing in itself," *das Ding an sich* – the *noumen*. There is nothing to say about the *noumen* other than that it is the cause of the phenomenon. According to Kant, the external world is only the cause of sensations, while our intellectual system organizes the sensations in space and time and provides us with concepts through which we understand experience. The things in themselves, which are the causes of our perceptions, are not known and cannot be known. They do not exist in space and time. Space and time are subjective and personal. Since they are part of our intellectual system, everything that we look at is revealed to us by characteristics of space and time. If we put on blue-tinted glasses, then everything will look blue to us, as Kant himself illustrated. In the same way, just as we always wear spatial glasses in our minds, we always see everything in Euclidean space. Thus, geometry is *a priori*, in the sense that it must be correct with respect to everything that we look at, with no connection to experience.

Kant's general idea is that it is the human intellect that creates its laws and imposes them on the raw material in the experiment. Mankind grasps these laws *a priori*, before the experiment and with no connection to it. "*The*

---

7. Ibid., 712.

understanding does not derive its laws (a priori) *from, but prescribes them, to nature.*[8] These laws, which are not the outcomes of experiment, organize the raw data of the experiment. These laws are claims – general, universal statements – that we assume about the world of the experiment. Euclidean space and time are *a priori* categories of this type. According to Kant, these categories are not derived from any experiment, but are functions and rules of the human intellect that enable us to organize and arrange the findings of our experience, and to use them.

This assumption about the geometry of space is not self-evident. In fact, the German mathematician Carl Gauss (1777–1855) noted that the Euclidean nature of space could be tested experimentally, and even attempted to do this. With the birth of Einstein's theory of relativity, it became clear that the geometry of space is dependent on the matter that exists in space.

Kant was certain that he had solved the problem of scientific cognition once and for all. The solution was in "the search for the sources of given sciences [mathematics, natural sciences and metaphysics] in reason itself, so that its faculty of knowing something *a priori* may by its own deeds be investigated and measured."[9] This gives rise to the question: How does Kant investigate reason and arrive at the formulation of the sciences given above? How is it possible to achieve scientific accomplishments only through the study of reason? This question does not have a clear answer in Kant's philosophy. In fact, Kant does not come up with any new scientific findings through studying reason, though it was important to him to confirm the existing knowledge (in his time), which he saw as proven and eternal. When Solomon Maimon wrote in his private letter to Kant that both Newton's mechanics and Kant's theory were simply hypotheses, Kant replied saying that he was a "parasite, like all Jews."[10]

Immanuel Kant broadened the scope of his philosophy to include other areas, particularly ethics. According to Kant, just as the laws of physics can be learned from human reason, human reason can teach us the rules of ethics. Here, we come to the dogma of western humanism, which assumes that man determines the rules of ethics for himself – *an autonomous ethical system.*

---

8. Kant, *Prolegomena,* 67.
9. Ibid. 27.
10. Joseph Agassi, *The History of Modern Philosophy,* 278.

In this area, Kant came up with the concept of the categorical imperative, which exists in the mind of man. There are three categorical imperatives: (1) There is a moral requirement to carry out a duty for the sake of the duty. (2) There is a moral requirement to act (out of our own choice) in such a way that the action can be universalized. (3) It is ethical to treat oneself or another under the assumption that the person is an end in himself, and never merely as a means to an end.

How did Kant arrive at the conclusion that these specific imperatives and no others exist in man's intellect? There is no satisfactory answer to this question. Emil Fackenheim relates that during his trial in Jerusalem in 1961, Adolf Eichmann used Kant's categorical imperatives to justify his actions. Fackenheim showed that the categorical imperatives were not immune to being invoked for such an abominable purpose (*To Mend the World*, 270–273). This is also discussed in Israel Eldad's book, *Reflections on Israel*, in his article, "Thus Kant Begat Eichmann."

So far, we have seen a brief outline of Kant's philosophy. I would certainly agree with Russell (see note 6) that the difficulty in understanding Kant is an objective one – it is not that our intellect is flawed, but that there is a flaw in Kant's viewpoint. However, even nowadays Kant has many followers and successors.

It is worth noting here that most of the medieval Jewish philosophers had a problem reconciling Judaism and Jewish thought with the philosophies of Plato and Aristotle. "The most central concepts of medieval Jewish philosophy are rooted in ancient Greek and medieval Arabic thought and are not of Jewish origin at all. It is impossible to reconstruct a unique Jewish world perspective out of alien material."[11] Unfortunately, the situation today is not very different. Only now are many thinkers, both Jewish and non-Jewish, confronting Kant's philosophy and attempting to reconcile it with Judaism. Hence, we have good reason to clarify whether there is any basis at all to Kant's claims that philosophical problems can be solved by examining the human intellect.

We have mentioned several times that it is impossible to prove metaphysical statements (either through experiment or logic), and that it is equally impossible to refute them. The most important and profound things, the

---

11.   R. J.B. Soloveitchik, *The Halakhic Mind*, 100.

metaphysical foundations of the world, can be neither proved nor disproved. Human beings are helpless in the face of the problems of the foundation of the world. There are various philosophical schools that suggest their own answers for the structure and development of the world, but without assistance from a source external to human wisdom, there is no way to determine which of these views is the "correct" one. In this book, we will receive external, divine assistance, in the form of divine revelation, as documented in the Bible. *By human intellect alone, there is no way to choose between the various options.* There is no way to prove that our world is a deterministic one – that everything is predetermined – or that it is non-deterministic, that new things appear in the world. It is impossible to prove that we, human beings, have free will, just as it is impossible to prove that we do not.

Nevertheless, Kant claims unequivocally that he is providing an answer for all metaphysical problems, that he has the ability to solve them once and for all. In the preface to the first edition of his *Critique of Pure Reason,* he writes, "I venture to assert that there is not a single metaphysical problem which has not been solved, or for the solution of which the key at least has not been supplied."[12] After the *Critique* was published, Kant wrote a booklet that was intended to explain the *Critique* more clearly. He called the booklet *Prolegomena to Any Future Metaphysics That Will Be Able to Come Forward as Science.*

With the passage of time, the weakness and inconsistency of Kant's philosophy has become more and more apparent. We can look, for example, at Russell's critique in his *A History of Western Philosophy*, in his article about Kant; at Joseph Agassi's *A History of Modern Philosophy;* at the critique of Kant in Karl Popper's books and at the article *Immanuel Kant and Kantianism* in the *Encyclopedia Britannica*. In light of this extensive criticism, I will make do with only a few remarks.

Kant thought that he had invented a generic "recipe" for a solution to all philosophical problems. He announced that they could be solved by examination, by a study of human wisdom. However, this proclamation adds nothing to the solution of the problem because it does not include any direction for its solution. To say that the human intellect has a certain quality proves nothing, since (a) one cannot prove that the human intellect

---

12. English translation in *History of Western Philosophy*, B. Russell, 707.

has this quality, and (b) it is impossible to prove that the laws of nature, for example, are determined by the qualities of the intellect. As a counter-claim to point (b), Kant could say that the laws of nature, physics, determine a connection between phenomena, while it is the role of the intellect to order them. Again, Kant's argument contains no proof, and it is also impossible to say that it is a metaphysical claim. The point is that the entire development of physics points to the fact that physics deals not with phenomena but rather with the sources of the phenomena, with what Kant termed *das Ding an sich*, "the thing in itself," the *noumen*. Man grasps colors with his senses, whereas physics does not deal with colors in themselves, but with their source. Where we see the color green, physics speaks of an electromagnetic wave of a certain length. This electromagnetic wave causes us to sense green. We sense a stone, see it and touch it, while physics deals with electrons, protons, quarks and the like – with the thing itself, with the source of the perception of the stone.

Kant's successors, at least some of them, dispensed with the thing in itself, but not with the study of pure reason. Here we have some confusion. Kant does not distinguish between two types of *a priori* statements: scientific statements, which can be tested through experiment (for example, they can be refuted by experiment), and metaphysical statements that cannot be proved or disproved. Both of these, according to Kant, can be derived from human reason, by inquiry. I will cite several examples, but first I would like to remind the reader that according to Kant, "[T]he understanding is the origin of the universal order of nature, in that it comprehends all appearances under its own laws, and thereby produces, in an *a priori* manner, experience (as to its form), by means of which whatever is to be known only by experience is necessarily subjected to its laws."[13]

Now let us look at some examples – first at scientific statements. According to Kant, man, via his intellect, is only able to comprehend phenomena in the world in a spatial, Euclidean, three-dimensional way. According to Kant, this understanding is simply "an inevitable necessity of thought." In response, we might say: It is true that we cannot perceive or imagine non-Euclidean geometry, and clearly we are unable to perceive space with more than three dimensions. However, this does not prevent a physicist

---

13. *Prolegomena*, 69

from using concepts of non-Euclidean space, nor does he have to limit himself to only three spatial dimensions. Statements about the dimensions and Euclidean nature of space are not limited by pure reason. They are not limited by that which we are capable of imagining. They can be tested and refuted by experience. Kant's mistake was that he thought that something that could not be imagined was something that could not exist in reality. In mathematics and physics, it is often the case that what is possible today was impossible to imagine yesterday.

Here is another example. From Newton's general law of gravity comes the fact that the attraction between (any) two physical bodies diminishes at a rate that is inversely proportional to the square of the distance between them. Kant also claims here that it is the intellect that determines that the force of attraction decreases at a rate inversely proportional to the square of the distance.[14] It is almost superfluous to say that in the theory of relativity, the dependence on the distance could have been otherwise.

In these two examples, we have spoken about scientific statements. Surely it is now clear how absurd Kant's claim was that the intellect is what determines the laws of nature. However, Kant demanded even more: he found – or, rather, invented – proof for metaphysical statements. He offers the law of causality as an example. David Hume proved that it is impossible to derive (logically) causality from experiments, regardless of how many experiments are carried out. This means that the existence of causality is a metaphysical claim that cannot be proved or refuted through experiment. And here is where Kant created a "Copernican revolution," as he claimed. From now on, metaphysics is a new science, in which even metaphysical statements can be proved. "It is a perfectly new science, of which no one has ever even thought, the very idea of which was unknown . . . ."[15] Causality, Kant claimed, can be determined as an *a priori* principle, which derives from our way of thinking.

The critique of Kant's philosophy – the critique of the *Critique* – can be summarized as follows. Generally speaking, Kant tried to solve two completely different problems: (a) What is the source of science? How do human beings arrive at scientific theories, at laws of nature? and (b) What is the source of our metaphysical principles? Kant thought that the answers

14. Ibid., 68.
15. Ibid., 9.

to both of these questions could be provided by human reason. He believed that he had established a new science that solves these issues once and for all. It is here that he was mistaken.

This is an extremely harsh statement to make. Very rarely, if at all, is it possible to state that a particular philosophy is incorrect, that it can actually be refuted. For example, let us look at the philosophy of Baruch Spinoza. I do not believe in the deterministic metaphysical principles of his philosophy, and I am certain that they are incorrect, but I cannot prove it. The most that I can say is that Spinoza's philosophy is not compatible with Jewish thought. With regard to (a), Kant did not discover the source of science. Over time it became clear that his synthetic *a priori* statements, which belong to science, are not actually true. The scientific statements can be refuted. I will address this further below.

Kant's mistake was that he professed to have discovered and proved eternal truths. With regard to (b), his mistake was even more serious. He professed to prove the truth of certain metaphysical statements, such as the existence of causality in the world. But it is common knowledge that metaphysical claims cannot be proved or disproved. There is not even a shadow of proof for metaphysical statements in the claim that they are derived from human reason. It is true that, with his reason, man expresses and formulates metaphysical statements, but this is certainly not a hallmark of those statements' veracity. Baruch Spinoza invented deterministic metaphysics, and subsequent thinkers offered a non-deterministic picture of the world. There is no way of proving that one philosopher's intellect is greater than another's.

We can add to the discussion above Albert Einstein's attitude towards Kant's theory of knowledge. Below are two quotations in which Einstein comments on Kant's teachings. In one quotation, Einstein explains why the comprehensibility of the world is a mystery, and he criticizes Kant's "solution" to this mystery. In his *Letters to Solovine*, he writes:

> You find it remarkable that the comprehensibility of the world . . . seems to me a wonder or eternal secret. Now, a priori, one should, after all, expect a chaotic world that is in no way graspable through thinking. One could (even should) expect that the world turns out to be lawful only insofar as we make an ordering intervention. It would be a kind of ordering like putting into alphabetic order the words of a language [as Kant presents his theory of knowledge]. On the other hand, the kind of order which, for example, was created through [the

discovery] of Newton's theory of gravitation is of quite a different character. Even if the axioms of the theory are put forward by human agents, the success of such an enterprise does suppose a high degree of order in the objective world, which one had no justification whatever to expect a priori. Here lies the sense of "wonder" which increases even more with the development of our knowledge.   (Letters to Solovine, March 30, 1952)

Elsewhere, Einstein stresses that there is no basis to Kant's claim that man produces certain knowledge about the laws of nature from his intellect:

If, therefore, we have definitely assured knowledge, it must be grounded in reason itself. This is held to be the case, for example, in the propositions of geometry and in the principle of causality. These and certain other types of knowledge are, so to speak, a part of the implements of thinking and therefore do not previously have to be gained from sense data (i.e., they are *a priori* knowledge). *Today everyone knows, of course, that the mentioned concepts contain nothing of the certainty, of the inherent necessity, which Kant had attributed to them.*   (Ideas and Opinions, 22; emphasis mine)

It seems that Kant's overconfidence, together with his powers of persuasion and his authoritativeness, have hypnotized generations of thinkers, depriving them of the strength to shake off the dogmatic Kantian slumber. However, we must give Kant some credit. His zealous work in philosophy meant that he brought many philosophical problems to light and clarified them, even if he did not manage to solve them, leaving as antinomies. These include the problem of free will versus scientific causality, which we discussed above.

4. KNOWLEDGE OF THE WORLD ACCORDING TO POPPER

In *Creation Ex Nihilo*, I presented my understanding of the Jewish approach to the problem of cognition of the world. I would like to try to deepen our understanding of this problem, and I will do this in the next section. First, I will give an outline of Popper's theory of cognition. Karl Popper made a substantial contribution to solving the problem of scientific cognition. According to him, the main problem in the theory of cognition is the problem of induction.

Before I summarize the essence of Popper's theory of cognition, I will outline in general terms the structure of any physical scientific theory. In fact, mathematics provides a general model for the structure of physical theories. In the diagram below, I have shown an entirely schematic representation of the structure of a mathematical theory. The structure is similar to a tree, with the axioms – the fundamental premises – as the roots. From these axioms, one can infer, in accordance with the rules of logic, certain mathematical statements, from which other statements can then be derived, and so forth.

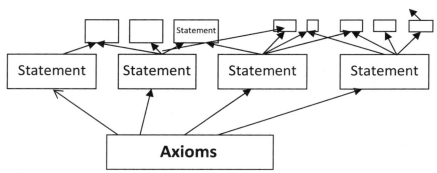

This model represents a deductive structure, both of a mathematical theory and of a physical theory. In this structure there is upward, but not downward, "movement." Statements are derived from the axioms, but not vice versa. Axioms cannot be derived from statements. In a physical theory, the basic laws and fundamental equations are equivalent to axioms. An infinite number of solutions can be inferred from the fundamental equations. While these solutions can describe particular experiments, one cannot infer the laws of nature, fundamental equations, from a particular solution or from a description of a particular experiment. The principle of induction does not hold. As David Hume was keen to stress, a law of nature cannot be inferred from experiment.

The question that Kant dealt with was: How is it possible to arrive at laws of nature if they cannot be inferred from experiments? From where can the laws of nature be derived if not from the material reality?

While Karl Popper offers a solution to the problem of induction in his monographs *Logik der Forschung, The Logic of Scientific Discovery, Conjectures and Refutations, Objective Knowledge* and *Unended Quest,* the essence of his theory of scientific cognition can be summarized in just a few sentences. Popper replaced the inductive methodology, which attempts to derive scientific laws from observations, from the specific to the general, with a deductive methodology, from the general to the specific. However, in order to move over to a deductive approach, we need to find axioms, fundamental premises that lie at the base of the structure. Where can we obtain these from? Popper's answer to this question appears to be fairly simple: we must view all scientific theories as hypotheses. These theories are human creations. They are nothing but fundamental premises that cannot be inferred from experience or from observations. Thus, the structure of science became deductive – from the general to the specific.

Both Kant and Popper agree that science is deductive. Both Kant and Popper agree that it is man that creates scientific theories. The difference between them is as follows. According to Kant, all of the theories are based on categories that are *a priori* (not produced from experience but are the necessary result of the human intellect – man is not capable of thinking any other way) and absolute. Conversely, Popper suggests that the theories are only hypotheses, guesses. The source of this difference is in the upheaval that rocked the world of physics with the publication of Einstein's theory of relativity. Immanuel Kant saw Newton's mechanics and his law of gravity as absolute truths. He therefore thought that he was committed to absolute, *a priori* concepts. After the appearance of Einstein's specific and general theories of relativity and quantum theory, it became evident that physical theories had ceased to be considered absolute, the ultimate truth. **Just as Newton's theory ceased to be absolute (and in fact never had been absolute) with the discovery of new theories that were more precise and that also applied to new phenomena, it is reasonable to think that in the future, quantum theory and the theory of relativity will be replaced by more accurate theories.**

New theories negate old ones, leaving them with a limited area of application. New physical theories, such as the special and general theories of relativity and quantum theory, are nothing but conjecture. This begs the question: are there any rational arguments or experiments that might lead us to favor one hypothesis over another? Karl Popper's answer is as follows: none of these hypotheses (namely of the scientific theories) can be *verified* by experiment. In order to verify a theory, an infinite number of experiments would need to be conducted, including future experiments, which is impossible in principle. While the majority of experiments can only **strengthen** or **corroborate** a scientific theory, they cannot **verify** it. They cannot **prove** that it is **true**. Many of the experiments that were done in the realm of Newton's mechanics and his law of gravity did not contradict these theories, but they did not verify them either. It is impossible to verify any theory, which is essentially a hypothesis, since no matter how many experiments may corroborate a theory, there is absolutely no guarantee that tomorrow a new experiment will not appear that will contradict it. According to Popper, **the only way to favor one hypothesis over another is to refute one of the hypotheses.** Refutation of a theory is possible either by contradiction or the theoretical or empirical refutation of the deductive implications of the theory (arrived at by logical inference). Hence, a few experiments, or even a single experiment, that contradicts a theory is enough to refute it. Until it is refuted, a scientific theory remains a hypothesis, a guess, but it is still preferable to a theory that has been refuted already.

Popper's solution to the problem of scientific cognition is based on the hypotheses, the guesses, of geniuses. These hypotheses (theories) are not necessarily correct. It is possible, and even very likely, that they will be replaced with new theories-hypotheses, which themselves will also will be no more than guesses.

However, Popper's theory, like Kant's, does not come close to the essence of the problem of scientific cognition, nor does it answer it. **From our point of view, the essence of the problem is in man's ability to discover the laws of nature.** Karl Popper does not even pretend to deal with this problem. Moreover, an analysis of the nature of scientific cognition brings him to the paradoxical conclusion that such cognition is impossible. "[E]ven on the assumption (which I share) that our quest for knowledge has been successful so far, and that we now know something of our universe, this success becomes miraculously improbable, and therefore inexplicable; for an appeal to an endless series of improbable accidents is not an explanation."[16] There is no theory that is capable of explaining why our search for the laws of nature is successful: "Successful explanation must retain . . . the probability zero, assuming that we measure this probability, approximately, by the ratio

---

16.   K.R. Popper, *Objective Knowledge*, 28.

of the 'successful' explanatory hypotheses to all hypotheses which might be designed by man."[17]

We can now understand the logic of scientific knowledge: *a priori* hypotheses, their refutation, new hypotheses and so on. However, the central problem of scientific cognition, the source of these hypotheses, lies outside this logic. The atheistic analysis, which ignores the interaction with an infinite intelligence, comes to the paradoxical conclusion that **man is not capable of producing a scientific discovery.** Or, to use scientific terminology, we can say that the probability of finding an appropriate hypothesis (that will explain many experiments, such as Newton's theory) is zero.

From a logical perspective, the creation of a new, fundamental theory is creation *ex nihilo*. Before Albert Einstein formulated his general theory of relativity, the theory simply did not exist. It was not derived from something else that already existed. It could not be inferred logically from a premise that existed before. In other words, new fundamental theories, such as Newton's mechanics, Einstein's general theory of relativity and quantum theory are **new creations.** They were created *ex nihilo*. However, not everything that man, with his limited understanding, sees as creation *ex nihilo* is necessarily so.

5. KNOWLEDGE OF THE WORLD FROM A JEWISH PERSPECTIVE

From a Jewish perspective, the concept *ex nihilo* expresses God's presence in the world. Without the divine dimension, the expression *ex nihilo* is understood as something mysterious and incomprehensible. In *Creation Ex Nihilo*, I mentioned the following parable:

> Basically, the entire physical world is comprised of matter and light. Now, let us imagine that we know nothing about the existence of light. Then we will "see" strange things take place in the world of matter: matter is not conserved, here and there matter is created out of nothing, and it sometimes disappears. The world is no longer strange when light is added to the picture. Light can create matter and matter can disappear when an atom goes to a higher energy

---

17.   K.R. Popper, *Conjectures and Refutations,* 96.

state with the emission of a photon. In this parable, matter represents our world and everything in it, including humanity and the human mind. Light is God. (Creation Ex Nihilo, 32)

Rabbi Soloveitchik expresses it thus:

> The most important issue in the Jewish outlook is the subject with which the book of Genesis begins: the creation of the world ex nihilo by the Creator .... We Jews believe that nothing in the world existed before Creation, other than God: "Master of the universe, Who reigned before any form was created" [from the Adon Olam prayer]. When we use the word "nothing" we have to remember that we only do so for the sake of convenience, since prior to creation there was in fact "something" – there was God Himself.[18]

However, it is crucial to understand that the Jewish view of the creation of the world *ex nihilo* is not that of a single creation that occurred only once in the past, after which God simply left the world alone and no longer interferes in it, as the Greek philosophers claimed. There is nothing further from Judaism than the idea that the creation of the world was God's only act. It is interesting that the Torah uses the name of God (*Elohim*), which is equal in numerical value to the Hebrew word for nature (*ha-teva*), for all things connected with the creation of the world itself, but when it talks about the relationship between the Creator and His creation in particular, man, – it starts to use the name connected with the verb "to be." "This name is used to symbolize the principle of 'was, is and will be,' namely the leadership of the world in practice. The world that was created needs to be led and supervised. Even though it has been created it also needs to continue to exist. The name means the continued existence and the constant creation of the world *ex nihilo*."[19]

The development of the world and of humanity occurs simultaneously in two different ways: by the fixed order, according to laws that were set at the beginning of time; and by providence, which is revealed to us in new creations – *ex nihilo*. (To be more precise, I should add that the fixed order is also one of the modes of providence.) Similarly a process of scientific discov-

---

18.   Rabbi J.B. Soloveitchik *Ha-adam ve-olamo*, 225–226.
19.   Ibid., 227.

ery also occurs in two ways: "(1) A process of logical operations, of rational thought. This process can be carried out by well-defined logical units of action such as algorithms. We can think about this process as though our personal computer, our brain, has performed it. (2) The second process has no connection to systematic logical thought. It is like a lightning flash in a very dark night sky. In contrast to the thought process, which is logical and consistent, a person does not control this second type of process. The "flash of lightning" comes to him; it is something that happens to him. It does not happen to every person. We must be ready for it, to be a worthy recipient."[20]

In Chapter Two of my book *Creation Ex Nihilo*, I summarized the Jewish view of scientific cognition.[21] A true scientific creation is one that is *ex nihilo*, a new creation, a gift from God, divine revelation. Following Maimonides, Solomon Maimon stated that man is capable of discovering a new creation, a synthetic a priori statement, only if his mind is connected with the infinite mind. In my article, *Comprehensibility of the World: a Jewish Outlook*, I indicated the divine source of scientific inspiration, and in my book, *Creation Ex Nihilo,* I formulated it as follows: *Science is divine revelation.* However, I should point out that this revelation is different from the revelations of the prophets. Often the scientist who reveals a new law of nature is unaware of the source of his flash of inspiration, whereas the prophets were always fully aware of the divine source of their revelations.

Now let us try to move forward and deepen our understanding of scientific cognition. First, I would like to state that the laws of nature are a vital part of the spiritual world. We have already emphasized (Chapter One, sections 11 and 12) the difference between Popper's world three and the spiritual world, part of which is connected with the laws of nature. Let us now return to that discussion and delve into it more deeply. Human beings reveal new theories and new laws, thereby filling world three, the world of accessible knowledge. As soon as a particular piece of new knowledge is revealed and documented, it becomes accessible to all humanity, and thus human knowledge is accumulated over time. However, the existence of the

---

20. *Creation Ex Nihilo*, 77–78.

21. I have referred to points in *Creation Ex Nihilo* just for the record. The ideas that I mention here stand alone. There is no need to refer to my first book in order to understand them.

spiritual world is not dependent on its revelations. Unlike Immanuel Kant, we are not of the opinion that human beings determine the laws of nature. Nature advances according to its own laws with absolutely no connection to the existence of man. According to the Jewish view, it is not man but God who determines the law and order in nature. Human beings only reveal these laws to a certain degree of accuracy, which improves over time. It is not only the accuracy that improves, our comprehension of these laws also improves. Einstein's theory of relativity broadens our understanding of nature compared with the understanding that we gained from Newton's mechanics and law of gravity. But we are in no doubt that man **only reveals** the lawfulness that exists in nature, a lawfulness that also exists in his absence.

This leads us to the conclusion that the spiritual world exists objectively and is not dependent on man. It is worth clarifying that our argument relates not to the whole spiritual world but only to the most crucial part of it: the laws of nature, the lawfulness in nature. Popper's world three is not a significant metaphysical dimension of our world. It is just an image, an approximate description, of certain parts of the spiritual world. Even before the scientists discover their theories, a spiritual reality exists that is not at all dependent upon them. Still, this does not mean that the human description of spiritual reality, of a spiritual world, has no human stamp or stamp of the scientist who discovers a particular law of nature. There can be different formulations of the same law, just as one thing can be expressed in several different languages. But ultimately, physical theories, formulated in one way or another, are tested using experiments, by action. The empirical implications have absolute, not relative, significance.

Now that we have determined the objective existence of the laws of nature in the spiritual world, an existence that is not contingent on human consciousness, we will return to the problem of knowledge of the world. Although Karl Popper professed to have solved this problem, he admitted that his solution was idealistic:

> "The epistemological idealist is right, in my view, in insisting that all knowledge, and the growth of knowledge . . . stem from ourselves, and that without these self-begotten ideas there would be no knowledge . . . . Kant was right that it is our intellect which imposes its laws – its ideas, its rules – upon the inarticulate mass of our 'sensations' and thereby brings order to them.

Where he was wrong is that he did not see that we rarely succeed with our imposition . . ."[22]

According to Immanuel Kant there is no objective knowledge; the source of every scientific idea is within us, in our minds. In contrast, according to Popper, there is no certain knowledge, and all of our ideas are nothing but guesses. Amongst an infinite number of possible guesses, only a few, such as Newton's mechanics, Einstein's theory of relativity and quantum theory, accord with experiments, with reality. To date, for around a century, there has not been one experiment that has contradicted the theory of relativity or quantum theory. The problem is that a "correct" guess is like a miracle.

The probability of making a "correct" guess, of coming up with a scientific theory that will be compatible with an infinite number of experiments, is zero. In other words, a correct guess is impossible. Man is not capable of knowing the world in which he lives. This is Popper's conclusion, although he did not use these exact words: The correct guess can happen only through a miracle. Albert Einstein agrees: "The eternal mystery of the world is its comprehensibility . . . . The fact that it is comprehensible is a miracle."

In order to understand the Jewish view of knowledge of the world, I have included here the three-part model that we looked at in Chapter One, section 12, which shows, at the top, man's soul, which operates the connection between the spiritual entity and the physical entity and supervises the continued existence of this connection.

We also came to the conclusion that our world can be presented as being comprised of a spiritual world and a physical world, with God operating the connection between these worlds and supervising them.

I should point out that the idea of God, who uses a spiritual entity as an operating system for the world, appears more than once in our sources. For example, it is written in the Zohar that when God wanted to create the world, he looked at each word in the Torah and produced his works of art (all his creation) accordingly, since everything that exists in all the worlds is in the Torah. Hence God looked at it, and thus He created the world.[23]

---

22. *Objective Knowledge*, 68.
23. Zohar, *Teruma*, 161a.

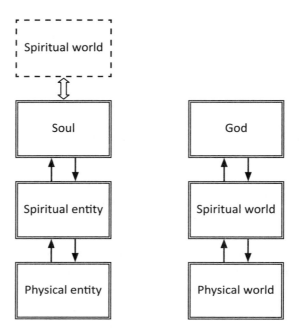

The two models above draw a parallel between God and the human soul. This parallel is deeply rooted in our tradition. In Chapter One, section 12, we cited the Babylonian Talmud (*Berachot* 10a), which relates five similarities between man's soul in his body and the power of God in the world.

God created the universe comprised of two worlds: a spiritual world and a material, physical world. The spiritual world, which is a kind of divine system for operating the world, is rich, plentiful and diverse. In contrast to the world of Plato, which is a world of static forms, the divine spiritual world is an ever-changing and constantly developing world. It is revealed to us, human beings, gradually, and it is reasonable to assume that up to this point we have only been exposed to a small fraction of it. We have already seen a quote from Albert Einstein, who reached this conclusion during the course of his work: "His [the scientist's] religious feeling takes the form of a rapturous amazement at the harmony of natural law, which reveals an intelligence of such superiority that, compared with it, all the systematic thinking and acting of human beings is an utterly insignificant reflection."[24]

The spiritual world is a tool of divine providence. We can differentiate the parts of the spiritual world designated specifically to govern people and those that govern the world as a whole. The divine revelation at Mount Sinai, the revelation of the Torah to the Jewish people, and through them to humanity in general, greatly influenced and continues to influence human beings. We can assume that human art reflects a part of the spiritual world designated to influence the human soul. Everyone knows how strong an effect art can have. But it is not our goal to analyze all the channels of providence over human beings and humanity, and it is doubtful that this is even possible. We are focusing here on the subject of science and Judaism – science from the Jewish perspective.

In a certain sense, the "scientific" side of the spiritual world is simpler. We can ponder the question of whether a particular musical piece existed in the spiritual world before the composer "discovered" it, but it is blatantly clear that the laws of nature acted on nature, on the physical world, even before scientists discovered them. It is only according to the extreme anthropocentric view, such as Immanuel Kant's, that man imposes his laws on nature. I should remind you of our earlier conclusions (Chapter One, section 11) that the physical world and the spiritual world are not of equal status. The existence of the physical world is constantly dependent on the spiritual world: "the root of its existence is in spirituality." Later on, in section 8, we will try to clarify the nature of the physical world's dependence upon the spiritual world.

It is not man but God who created the laws of nature, and it is God who imposes them on nature. As we have already noted, the spiritual world is complex and varied, and it is constantly changing and developing. However, it also contains some fixed elements that are not subject to change. Equally, matter is in a state of constant motion dictated by the spiritual world, with the laws of nature as the fixed and relatively straightforward component.

Now we are drawing close to a very subtle point in our discussion of knowledge of the world. I will try to formulate the problem as clearly as

---

24. *Ideas and Opinions*, 40.

possible. Our world contains two worlds: a spiritual world and a physical world. We have unequivocally determined that we, human beings, cannot derive any theories from the physical world, that it is impossible to extract any laws of nature from experience or from observations of nature. On the other hand, the laws of nature are part of the spiritual world. If we had direct access to the spiritual world, we would be able to read the laws of nature, the scientific theories, from inside the spiritual world. Hence, acquiring knowledge of the world is dependent on our obtaining access to the spiritual world. We will now expand on this issue.

6. KNOWLEDGE OF THE WORLD AND ACCESS TO THE SPIRITUAL WORLD

Arthur Eddington, one of the great physicists who lived in the first half of the twentieth century, writes in the Introduction to his book, *The Nature of the Physical World,* about two tables. However, there are not just two tables. Everything around him is in duplicate: there are two chairs, two pens, and so on. We have known one of the tables all our lives from early childhood. This is the simplest object and, to a certain extent, symbolizes for us what we understand as our external world. How do we describe it? It has length, it is relatively permanent, it has a certain color, and most of all, it is real. It does not collapse when we lean on it. A table is an object. It is not space or time. If we want to give an example of matter, we say that it is something like a table.

The second table, a scientific table, is mostly vacuum. In this vacuum, minuscule particles – charges – move around at great speeds, the distances between them at least 100,000 times greater than the size of the particle itself.[25] The scientific table has no substance or materiality in the ordinary sense of the words. It is virtually empty. It is true that in the space between the particles, there is an electromagnetic field, but the layman does not ascribe material substance to physical fields.

There appears to be a great similarity to the picture described by Immanuel

---

25.   When we talk about the size of a particle, we mean the distance in which the interaction between the particle and another particle close to it is significant. However, in all modern physical theories, the particle is represented as a point or as a one-dimensional line – a string. Therefore, we can say that the volume of all the particles in a material object is equal to zero.

Kant – the world of phenomena and the world of "things in themselves" (*noumena*), which are the causes of the phenomena. But this is where the similarity ends. According to Kant, science deals with phenomena, but we can know nothing about the things in themselves, the causes of the phenomena. Yet in actual fact, science does deal with the causes of phenomena (with the scientific table), whereas the phenomenon (the first table) has absolutely no connection with the world of science. The sensations of color, hardness and permanence are actually closer to our spiritual world. Even though we only feel the phenomena through our senses, science manages to penetrate superbly into the mysteries of nature.

There is no straightforward route to the scientific spiritual world, to the permanent constituent of the spiritual world – the laws of nature. It reveals itself gradually. This revelation is not dependent on us, human beings; it happens to us. The revelation of the secrets of nature, meaning the revelation of the fixed element of the spiritual world, takes place under divine supervision. It is part of the divine plan, an example of God's wisdom. The revelation of the secrets of nature is one of the channels of providence. There is no free entry to the world of science. Having the skills and aptitude is a necessary, but not a sufficient, condition. Galileo's knowledge prior to his great discoveries was no greater than Aristotle's. But two thousand years passed until the start of the modern scientific age and the discoveries of Galileo and Newton.

The possibility of connecting with the spiritual world is of special importance. The essence of man that differentiates him from the rest of the animal kingdom, is his spirituality, his belonging to the spiritual world. When a baby is born, alongside his physical development, he gradually connects to the spiritual world. From his first smile to the broad range of emotions and intellectual achievements that he reaches by adulthood, the process of connecting to the spiritual world is continually developing.

This process should not be taken for granted. A kitten born on the same day as a baby will be more capable and well-suited for life than the baby a certain amount of time after birth. Although the kitten's body may be almost fully mature by that point, its ability to connect to the spiritual world is infinitely less than the baby's. The baby's absolute advantage will soon become evident.

We human beings are not equal in our spiritual skills and aptitudes. Some of us have a powerful affinity to particular realms of the spiritual world, such as music or art, while others have a stronger connection to religion or science. But ultimately, man's humanity is measured by his spirituality.

Knowledge of the world, or more specifically, knowledge of the laws of nature, is bound up with an association with the realm of the spiritual world that includes the laws of nature. We have already made it clear that this realm exists objectively. The laws of nature existed before they were discovered by human beings (and this discovery is always an approximation). After the knowledge was revealed to scientists, it became the spiritual property of humanity as a whole. Each person, to varying extents, can connect with this pool of knowledge in the spiritual world. We are already used to it, but it is not at all self-evident. A person looks, using the optical device installed in his body – his eyes – at black marks on white pieces of paper, and receives with his ears acoustic waves in the lecture hall at the university. As a result of these physical actions, he starts **to understand, to comprehend and even to feel highly complex concepts.** He understands ideas such as non-Euclidean space, space with more than three dimensions, or the most complex concepts of the theory of relativity and quantum theory. Immanuel Kant was convinced that people are incapable of understanding such concepts at all. I do not know what I find more surprising – the connection to a musical work by the reception of acoustic waves, or the enrichment of an inner spiritual world with lofty physical theories using purely material means. All these things were achieved by someone who started life as a baby and, at one point, was on an equal footing with a kitten.

It is difficult to grasp the connection to the accessible spiritual world, Popper's world three. The accessible world contains all the knowledge amassed for the benefit of humanity by masterminds in their chosen fields, such as religion, science and art. However, it is harder to grasp the act of discovering the secrets hidden in the spiritual world. We are talking here about the discovery of new laws, about the formation of science. Although the spiritual world is not fully open to us, from time to time new parts of it are revealed to a select few. Maimonides wrote that the processes of knowledge are similar in the divine sciences and the natural sciences.

> You should not think that these great secrets are fully and completely known to anyone among us. They are not. But sometimes truth flashes out to us so

that we think that it is day, and then matter and habit in their various forms conceal it so that we find ourselves again in an obscure night, almost as we were at first. We are like someone in a very dark night over whom lightning flashes time and time again.[26]

Although the spiritual world is not open to us in its entirety, but from time to time new parts of it are revealed to humanity by great prophets, scholars, philosophers, artists and scientists.

Let us continue with this metaphor: sometimes lightning flashes from within the darkness, illuminating the sky. The parts of the spiritual world that are still not open to human beings are steeped in darkness. On very rare occasions, to select individuals, great scientists, geniuses, a flash of brilliance comes, just like lightning in the night that illuminates the entire sky. But it is important to understand that man has to be ready to receive the flash of light. An ordinary person who is exposed to the revelations of the theory of relativity probably would not understand a thing. Only a person equipped with a great deal of knowledge is capable of catching the lightning flash, the flash of light. But as we have already noted, while it is necessary to have a great deal of knowledge, this is not sufficient. It is not man who determines how and when areas of the spiritual world that have remained in darkness will be revealed to him. This is a matter of divine providence.

A consequence of all this is that there are two ways to connect to the spiritual world – a direct, primary connection and an indirect, secondary connection. The divine spiritual world includes, among other things, the laws of nature, which constitute part of the divine operating system. God reveals the laws of nature to human beings gradually, and with a particular degree of accuracy, in accordance with the level of knowledge and the intellectual level at the time of the revelation. This revelation is given not to humanity as a whole, but to a particular individual, to a particular scientist. Many scientists are qualified, in terms of their level of knowledge, to receive the revelation, but only a few chosen ones actually receive it. It is thus that the laws of nature were revealed to Isaac Newton, James Clerk Maxwell and Albert Einstein. Their scientific discoveries are examples of a direct, primary

---

26. *Guide of the Perplexed,* Introduction, 7.

connection to the divine spiritual world. It is not a voluntary action on the scientist's part, but rather an example of divine providence.

After a new theory, such as the theory of relativity, is published, it becomes part of the spiritual world accessible to human beings (Popper's world three). Anyone with the requisite level of scientific knowledge can include the theory of relativity in his own spiritual world. This is an example of a secondary connection to the spiritual world. It should be noted that the ability to connect to the spiritual world, whether in a primary or secondary way, is what distinguishes man from all the other creatures on the planet. This quality is linked to man's ability to speak, to his understanding of languages and the documentation of spiritual messages. **Every human being has a part in the spiritual world, but people are separated from each other in their own spiritual world.**

After writing these words, I found a similarity between them and the words of Martin Buber, in his work *I and Thou*. I should point out that, by his own admission, Martin Buber's comments have a quality of divine revelation: "A vision which had come to me again and again since my youth, and which had been clouded over again and again, had now reached steady clarity. This clarity was so manifestly suprapersonal in its nature that I at once knew I had to bear witness to it" (*I and Thou*, 123). Buber writes that in the domain of spirit, "a division must be made between two fields . . . . It is the division between, on the one hand, what of spirit has already entered the world and can be perceived in it by means of our senses, and on the other hand what of spirit has not yet entered the world but is ready to do so, and become present to us" (ibid., 127). He goes on to say:

> Spirit becomes word, spirit becomes form – in some degree or other everyone who has been touched by the Spirit and did not shut himself to it, knows about the basic fact of the situation – that this does not germinate and grow in man's world without being sown, but arises from this world's meeting with the other. Not meetings with Platonic ideas – of which I have no direct knowledge at all and which I am not in a position to understand as what is in a course of being (Seiendes); but meetings with the Spirit which blows around us and in us. Again and again I am reminded of the strange confession of Nietzsche when he described the event of "inspiration" as taking but not asking who gives. Even if we do not ask we should thank. He who knows the

breath of the Spirit trespasses if he desires to get power over the Spirit or to ascertain its nature and qualities. But he is also disloyal when he ascribes the gift to himself. (Ibid., 129–130)

The last point – namely, who is giving – is very important. We mentioned in section 5 that science is the revelation of God. Jewish tradition emphasizes that God is the source of our knowledge. In our prayers, we recite, "You graciously endow man with wisdom and teach insight to frail mortals. Endow us graciously from Yourself with wisdom, insight and discernment."[27]

The Torah teaches us that new knowledge, as opposed to knowledge that already exists, comes to us from divine providence. In the Torah portion *Miketz*, which is in the book of Genesis, Pharaoh has a dream in which seven fat cows emerge from the Nile River, followed by seven haggard and lean cows, which proceed to eat the seven fat cows. He dreams a second time: Seven good, healthy ears of corn grow, followed by seven thin and bare ears of corn which then swallow the healthy ears.

The Egyptian scholars did not succeed in interpreting Pharaoh's dreams. His butler then remembered the young Hebrew man, Joseph, who had interpreted his dream correctly while they were together in prison. Pharaoh summons Joseph, who interprets the dreams correctly. Joseph's interpretation – that there would be seven years of plenty followed by seven years of famine – had important ramifications for the kingdom, for Joseph and for the Jewish nation as a whole. But we must understand that there was no way of arriving at that interpretation through simple logic. Joseph also understood this well. This was new knowledge, which only God bestows on a person and humanity. Joseph's words to Pharaoh actually express the essence of the Jewish theory of knowledge: "Joseph answered Pharaoh, saying: 'It is not in me. God will give Pharaoh an answer of peace'" (Genesis 41:16).

The meaning of this is clear: It is not I, Joseph the human being, who is creating this new knowledge, but rather, it is God who will answer. I would like to add to this: God is also the one who provides us with modern science, and humanity receives it. This is the theory of scientific cognition in a nutshell.

---

27. From the *Amida* prayer following the Sabbath.

7. SUMMARY: A GOD-CENTERED UNIVERSE VERSUS A MAN-CENTERED UNIVERSE

Throughout this book, a conflict has been developing between the Jewish world view and the materialistic world view, which places matter at the center of the world. This is on a philosophical-contemplative level, but on a level closer to human beings, the conflict is between the theocentric world view, a God-centered universe, and an anthropocentric world view, a man-centered universe.

Without going into the history of the various different opinions, we can safely say that Immanuel Kant was the one who planted the anthropocentric idea in the consciousness of western man. According to Kant, man is the sovereign law-maker both of the laws of nature and of the laws of ethics. Jewish philosophers were unable to accept the approach that man rather than God, is the source of morality. Yet paradoxically, not many Jewish philosophers objected to the idea that man is the legislator of the laws of nature. Rabbi Isaac Breuer, who is considered an expert in Kantian philosophy, wrote: "Within himself he [Kant] sensed the universal moral law just as he sensed within himself the universal theoretical law. He was indeed the discoverer of the latter . . . . But Kant did not discover the universal moral law, for **the moral universe is not what is, but what should be.**"[28]

Rabbi Soloveitchik seemed to hold a similar view:.

Man's transcendental consciousness . . . can therefore reveal even what the logos cannot. Kant's teaching, despite all the difficulties that it encountered, has not been undermined. Reason does not photograph the "given" but adapts it to its own needs. It sculpts the 'given' with the chisel of categorical concepts so as to prepare it for scientific understanding . . . . [Reason's] achievement is not, as realists have believed since the time of Aristotle, to describe the "given" as it is, but to create constructions and ideal symbols – and the fathers of modern physics agree with Kant that this is the case . . . .[29]

But we should look at this quote in the overall context of the essay "*U-vikashtem mi-sham*" (*And From There You Shall Seek*). Rabbi Soloveitchik clearly states that the true source of human creation is God. "True

---

28.   Quoted from *Confrontation*, by Zvi Kolitz, 153.
29.   *And From There You Shall Seek*, 13–14.

existence is the existence of God. **Creation is the issuing forth of something from the bosom of the Infinite."**[30] In contrast, from the point of view of the secular thinker, the phenomenon of creation is the greatest mystery in the world:

> I would even suggest that the greatest riddle of cosmology may well be neither the original big bang, nor the problem why there is something rather than nothing... but that the universe is, in a sense, creative: that it created life, and from it mind – our consciousness – which illuminates the universe, and which is creative in its turn.... Einstein said something like this: "If there were not this internal illumination, the universe would merely be a rubbish heap."[31]

In other words, the "creativity of nature" and the creativity of man are the greatest mysteries for the secular world view. However, the deep visionary skills of Popper and Einstein were needed to realize this, to appreciate the amazing aspect of reality amid routine. Indeed, in the anthropocentric world view, with man at its center, the phenomenon of creativity in general, and specifically the creativity of man, is the "greatest puzzle of cosmology." Let us try to understand this.

Let us look at the phenomenon of man from a purely secular perspective, and let us try to understand why the creativity of man is a mystery. When a baby is born, it has many qualities and inclinations. As it develops, it is capable of absorbing a great deal of knowledge from its surroundings, and thus its connection to the accessible spiritual world – to Popper's world three – becomes steadily stronger. We will ignore for a moment the problem of how the knowledge entered world three in the first place. When the baby is born, a fairly developed world of knowledge already exists. In the anthropocentric universe, other than man and his world of knowledge, there is no other spiritual entity that could provide the knowledge, above and beyond that which exists in man and in world three. It transpires from this that every collection of man's knowledge is made up of his own personal knowledge ("within his soul") plus the knowledge that he can extract from world three, from the accessible spiritual world. When a baby is born, he has almost no

---

30.   Ibid., 61.
31.   *The Self and Its Brain*, 61.

knowledge at all in his own personal collection of knowledge, but it fills up rather quickly.

If the child (or an adult, for that matter) has never learned or been taught French, for example, he will not know French. He cannot create the knowledge of the French language by himself. If this is so, then the question arises: If all the knowledge in the world is comprised of the personal knowledge of all human beings and the knowledge that has accumulated in human culture, where does **new knowledge** come from?

From the anthropocentric viewpoint, this question has no answer. The creation of new knowledge is a mystery. To clarify the issue, let us look at scientific creation. Scientific cognition, according to Popper and Einstein – two of the twentieth century's greatest thinkers – is without a doubt the greatest miracle in our universe. We start from the assumption that the external world, the world of nature, exists and develops in accordance with its own laws, which are independent of human beings. Nature existed and developed according to its laws prior to man's appearance in the world. How can man get to know the laws of nature? The simple, seemingly obvious answer is that he can learn the laws of nature from experiments that he carries out on nature. But this answer is incorrect. David Hume realized this. Other philosophers, including Kant, Popper and Einstein understood that there was a big problem here.

The solution that Kant suggested was "revolutionary," paradoxical and difficult to understand: it is man who makes the laws of nature. One might say that this is the height of the revolution that initiated the anthropocentric world view: not only does man determine the laws of ethics for himself, he also determines the laws of nature. In section 3, we discussed the unfeasibility of this claim. Nevertheless, we will stop for a moment to consider the claim that "reason does not photograph the "given" but adapts it to its own needs. It sculpts the 'given' with the chisel of categorical concepts so as to prepare it for scientific understanding."

A study of Newton's mechanics, which was the science with which Kant was familiar, appears to support Kant's claim. Let us consider the formula of Newton's second law:

F = ma: Force (F) = mass (m) times acceleration (a)

In fact, all the physical quantities that make up the formula – force, mass and acceleration – are not the result of an earlier experiment. They are human inventions, invented by Newton. Without these inventions, it would not be possible to carry out an experiment. But Newton not only invented new physical concepts – he also guessed the law that the new physical quantities comprised. Today, in the twenty-first century, one could say that this formula is almost self-evident. But we must not forget that Aristotle, who also grappled with this problem, did not reach the same conclusion as Newton. In fact, it took two thousand years, from Aristotle to Newton, for Newton to arrive at his guess.

If Newton's second law looks somewhat simple, the same cannot be said for Maxwell's equations:

$$\operatorname{div} \mathbf{E} = 4\pi\sigma$$

$$\operatorname{rot} \mathbf{E} + \frac{1}{c}\frac{\partial \mathbf{H}}{\partial t} = 0$$

$$\operatorname{div} \mathbf{H} = 0$$

$$\operatorname{rot} \mathbf{H} - \frac{1}{c}\frac{\partial \mathbf{E}}{\partial t} = \frac{4\pi}{c}\mathbf{I}$$

Einstein's equations certainly cannot be said to be "self-evident":

$$R_{\mu\nu} - \tfrac{1}{2}Rg_{\mu\nu} + \Lambda g_{\mu\nu} = -\kappa T_{\mu\nu}$$

I do not claim to shed any light on the essence of these equations. They are so complex that one would need to have studied for years just to understand what the symbols represent.

Now let us return to Kant's claim that **"the understanding does not derive its laws (a priori) from, but prescribes them, to nature"** (See section 3). We will try to understand this. The human intellect prescribes laws to nature; it imposes them on nature. In other words, man invents certain concepts and use them to formulate the laws of nature. However, after man has formulated a particular law, he has to test it through experiments. Scientific laws have empirical implications. If the law cannot be tested by experience, then it is not a scientific law. Various people can invent different concepts and laws, but they may not stand the test of experience. One might think that many different formulations of laws and theories could stand the test of experience, but it turns out that this is not the case. This is what Albert Einstein had to say on the matter:

> The supreme task of the physicist is to arrive at those universal elementary laws from which the cosmos can be built up by pure deduction. There is no logical path to these laws . . . . [O]ne might suppose that there were any number of possible systems of theoretical physics all equally well justified . . . . But the development of physics has shown that at any given moment, out of all conceivable constructions, a single one has always proved itself decidedly superior to all the rest.[32]

As far as we are concerned, the laws of nature exist objectively. They are part of the spiritual world. Man does not adapt the laws of nature to his needs; he looks for a correspondence between his guesses and reality. His guess must stand the test of experience. Immanuel Kant tried to match the universe to his reason, to his mechanistic view, as did many of his generation. Kant "sensed within himself the universal theoretical law," but over time it became clear that his mechanistic view did not correspond to the actual, independent reality, which is not dependent on man's understanding.

Man does not have any ordered or systematic access to the divine spiritual world. Primary access to the spiritual world has an element of divine revelation. It occurs only very rarely and to select individuals, to great minds. From a secular perspective, this is a complete mystery. The chance of coming up with a correct formulation of the laws of nature is equal to zero. When the reservoir of knowledge is located solely in man's mind and in his world three, **there is nowhere for new knowledge to appear from.** Every new scientific theory contains new knowledge that is not derived from something that already exists, from previous theories. In a world devoid of God, every appearance of new knowledge *ex nihilo*, every of a new scientific theory, is a miracle and a mystery.

But this is not the whole story. The secular world view is not consistent. The anthropocentric world view, the man-centered universe, contradicts the

---

32. *Ideas and Opinions*, 226.

secular, materialistic view. We mentioned in the introduction to Chapter Three that modern, secular man's world view is riddled with deep internal contradictions.

In the anthropocentric world, instead of God standing at the center of the world, man stands in His place. Man is not just a being that possess free will. he is also the lawmaker for the laws of ethics, he determines what is good and bad, and furthermore, he determines the laws of nature.

Alongside this trend, another trend is developing – the naturalistic revolution against God. Karl Popper describes the process:

> [T]he earlier, naturalistic revolution against God replaced the name 'God' by the name 'Nature'. Almost everything else was left unchanged. Theology, the Science of God, was replaced by the Science of Nature; God's laws by the laws of Nature; God's will and power by the will and power of Nature (the natural forces); and later God's design and God's judgement by Natural Selection. Theological determinism was replaced by a naturalistic determinism; that is, God's omnipotence and omniscience were replaced by the omnipotence of Nature and the omniscience of Science.[33]

What Kant saw as free and rational choice " was seen by Marx as the product of economic forces, or by Freud as deeply hidden sexual urges. According to Darwin, man literally evolved from the sub-human; more and more of what he was was understandable in terms of biology and biochemistry. The social sciences in this century have told us that man is product of his social and environmental conditioning and that human behavior, like animal behavior, operates according to certain deterministic laws . . . . Modern man now see that there is a continuum from the 'living slime,' as Nietzsche put it, all the way up to himself . . . . Man's superior dignity entitles him to the conquest of nature . . . . But modern natural science seems to demonstrate that there is no essential difference between man and nature, that man is simply a more organized and rational form of slime."[34]

Two contradictory trends lie at the foundation of today's secular world view. The deification of human beings, which is compatible with neither reason nor science, is also incompatible with another trend – the idolization

---

33. *Conjectures and Refutations,* 346.
34. Francis Fukuyama, *The End of History and the Last Man,* 297.

of nature – which gives human beings the status of robots entirely lacking in freedom or responsibility.

In the past, Jewish philosophers contended with Greek philosophers, primarily with Plato and Aristotle. In contrast, nowadays, many Jewish philosophers are contending with Kant, and are trying to reconcile their thoughts with his views. I believe that there is no justification for this trend. There is no reason to defer to other philosophical views – we have sources of our own.

8. CONCLUSION OF PART II: THE LAWS OF NATURE – THE SPIRITUAL WORLD AND THE MATERIAL WORLD IN THE LIGHT OF SCIENCE

This part of the book deals with the laws of nature and with science, which describes them. What we have learned here about the structure of science can help us reach a deeper understanding of the divine spiritual world. Knowledge of science has not only practical value. It also grants us a deeper understanding of the world and of creation, through which we can become closer to God.

Let us return to the three-part model that we saw in Chapter One.

The divine spiritual world is rich and diverse, and human beings cannot grasp it in its entirety. Over the past several centuries, our understanding of the laws of nature has deepened enormously. We have come to understand that the inanimate world, which in the past was always considered to be simplicity itself, is actually extremely complex and contains hidden messages. In fact, everything that we grasp with our senses as material, as physical, actually contains a deep spiritual element.

Let us consider the structure of matter as described by modern physics. At temperatures that man is accustomed to, all matter exists in the form of liquids, gases or solids. In all of these cases the matter is comprised of atoms or molecules. Electric and magnetic fields operate in between the atoms and molecules, and it is these that hold the matter in the state of solid, liquid or gas. The molecules are made up of atoms, and the atoms themselves are made up of electrons and atomic nuclei, between which electric and magnetic fields operate. The atoms' nuclei are comprised of protons and neutrons, which are all held together by nuclear force. Ultimately, all matter – even at extreme temperatures and pressures, such as the matter in the sun – is

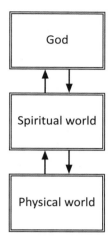

comprised of elementary and sub-elementary particles (such as quarks and strings) and physical fields (electromagnetic, nuclear).

From a physical perspective, all the volume of matter is taken up by physical fields, and the particles of matter do not take up any space at all, odd as it may sound. We would expect that the particles of matter – electrons, protons, neutrons, and so on – would take up, if not the majority of the volume of the matter, then at least a significant part of it. However, according to the principles of modern physics, the volume of all the particles in matter is equal to zero. Not a minuscule volume, but absolutely zero volume! This does not mean that the particles do not exist and are not real. They are real and exist in dimensions smaller than three-dimensional space – they are points, or one-dimensional lines: strings.

We have reached the conclusion that physical matter is a rather strange creature. It is made up of various entities – physical fields that take up all the volume of the matter, and particles that take up no volume at all. Now let us ask ourselves what characterizes these entities, what differentiates them from the spirit? We define a spiritual thing as something that is not physical. The answer is somewhat paradoxical: the spiritual entity – the laws of physics – is what defines the matter. What is the essence of a physical field, such as an electric field, if not the command of which force will act on a particular charge if it is placed at a certain spot in the space? Without these commands, the physical field does not exist. In other words, without the spiritual entity – the laws of physics – matter has no existence.

I would like to expand on the connection between the spiritual entity and the physical entity. We can distinguish different levels of matter's existence. In situations that are familiar to human beings, we see matter as solid objects (or liquids or gases), such as stones and machines, and objects such as the planets and other heavenly bodies. There is interaction between these objects. They are subject to the effect of the gravitational field, and they are actually a source of gravity. This is a rough, mechanistic view of the world. Newton was the first to discover and formulate the laws that govern the movements of physical objects, though Einstein discovered the more general laws in his general and special theories of relativity. Based on the picture emerging here, we can make an absolute distinction between material objects and the laws that determine their movements.

On this macroscopic level, there is a clear distinction between matter and spirit – material objects move in accordance with the laws of nature, which are spiritual commands or instructions. The split between the two worlds is unambiguous: the physical world – material objects; the spiritual world – the laws of nature. The laws of nature belong to the divine spiritual world, and the divine command is uniform across the entire universe. The uniformity of the laws of nature is impressive evidence for the claim that the laws of nature belong to the spiritual world (see Chapter Three, section 3).

However, the situation is more complicated when we look at the structure of the material objects themselves – on the microscopic level. I should point out that it is not possible to explain the existence of stable macroscopic objects, or of stable atoms and molecules, using pre-quantum modern physics. Only quantum physics can explain the stability of matter. Every material object has a structure. It is comprised of molecules and atoms, which themselves have their own structure – they are made up of electrons, protons and neutrons. Thus we come to the tiniest and, most fundamental particles. The existence of any physical object with its components and the components of its components up, to the most fundamental particles, is dependent on physical fields and forces that are an integral part of the system of physical particles. There is no clear separation between the spiritual and the physical. Both physical fields and fundamental particles are an outcome of the spiritual world. When we look deeply into matter, we see that without the laws of nature, without physical laws – the spiritual entity – matter has no existence at all.

I must clarify this point. It is not accurate to say that without the presence of a spiritual entity – the laws of physics – matter has no existence. It would be correct to say that *without the laws of physics acting on matter, the matter has no existence. Without God operating a spiritual entity – the laws of nature – on nature, nature has no existence.* This is what is meant by the statement that the world is contingent – at every moment the matter in the world is contingent on the operation of the divine spiritual world upon it. This spiritual world is the operating system, and it is not enough that it simply exists. If it is not operated, the material world does not exist.

As we have explained, it is God who operates and imposes the laws of nature on nature. We have already quoted Rabbi Dessler's remarks (in Chapter One, section 11) which precisely describe the situation: "The plan and purpose of creation is its spiritual content. Everything that exists in the physical world has a spiritual source."

What is this analogous to? Man was created in God's image, hence we can compare this with the operation of the laws of nature on the world through the action of man's soul. We have presented (Chapter One, section 12) the action of the soul using the diagram below.

The mind has in its possession a fairly sophisticated nervous system. This system is in fact primarily a spiritual entity. The main element of the nervous system is its spiritual content, just as the main part of computer software is its content, while the role of the physical elements – the CD or the magnetic strip – is purely to protect the content. We must make a distinction between the mind and its operating system. When I decide to raise my arm, I am generally not aware of the complex, sophisticated system that I am operating by this simple command. In order to build and operate a particular machine, such as a car, and to operate it, man may also use the accessible spiritual world (world three; see the upper part of the diagram). The man's mind controls both his body and the car. As soon as he turns off the car, it stops working, and its entire spiritual system, its operating system, ceases to function. The car is "dead." However, the man continues to function. His mind controls his actions. When his soul leaves his body, he too dies and ceases to function, but the physical matter remains, and as with all matter in the world, God presides over it. Clearly, the parallel here to the man's body and his machines is the world, and the parallel of the soul is God. Incidentally, here we can understand the essence of secular belief. According

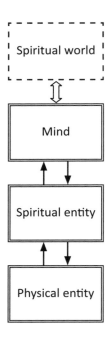

to the secular view, the human brain-computer operates without a soul: it is a spiritual entity without a soul, and the whole world with its laws operates without a soul – without God.

Modern science may be able to provide us with other analogies of the role of the divine spiritual world. Now let us bring an analogy for the spiritual world using a physical field – an electromagnetic field. In general, the field does not take up any space or specific volume. It is present everywhere in an area, but we neither see it nor feel it. An electromagnetic field can contain a large amount of information, but without taking special measures it is impossible to reveal its presence in a particular place, and it is also impossible to find the messages contained in it. Only a sufficiently complex and sophisticated device, such as a radio receiver or a television, together with a person, can discern the field and the messages that it carries with it. In the electromagnetic field's visual range, a sophisticated device such as the human eye connected to a nervous system (and to the human soul) is required in order to perceive the light and the messages contained in it.

The electromagnetic field and its messages are an analogy for the spiritual world. It, too, is present everywhere, and can neither be seen nor felt. Only a special kind of creature, such as a human being, is able, under special circumstances, to discern a small amount of the messages contained in the spiritual world and to reveal them. "Now man possesses as his proprium something in him that is very strange as it is not found in anything else that exists under sphere of the moon, namely, intellectual apprehension. In the exercise of this, no sense, no part of the body, none of extremities are used; and therefore this apprehension was likened unto the apprehension of the deity, which does not require an instrument, although in reality it is not like the latter apprehension, but only appears so to the first stirrings of opinion. It was because of this something, I mean **because of the divine intellect conjoined with man**, that it is said of the latter that he is *in the image of God and in His likeness* ....". (The Guide of the Perplexed, I, 1) Elsewhere, Maimonides writes about the divine spiritual world that influences man's soul: "... [I]ntellect which overflowed from Him, may He be exalted, toward us is the bond between us and Him. You have the choice: if you wish to strengthen and fortify this bond, you can do so; if, however, you wish gradually to make it weaker and feebler until you cut it, you can also do that." (Ibid., III, 51)

In the same way, divine providence, which acts on each and every detail, is in fact linked to the divine spiritual world that affects each and every one of us. The question now is how this influence can be reconciled with man's free will. Here is an analogy from quantum physics. The behavior and movement of a quantum particle are determined by wave function, which affects the particle. However, this influence is not absolute and does not unequivocally determine the behavior or movement of the particle, it leaves each particle with a fairly large amount of latitude: to a large degree, the movement of a single particle is not restricted by any physical law. However, the movement of a large number of particles is unequivocally determined by wave function. That is the analogy.

This may be likened to the fact that divine providence gives man free will, while the behavior of large numbers of people in the long-term is unequivocally determined: "Everything is foreseen," "There are many devices in a man's heart; but the counsel of the Lord, that shall stand" (Proverbs 19:21).

These analogies, which are taken from physics, illustrate the unity of the world – in the inanimate world, too, there are patterns that are similar, to a certain extent, to those in the upper worlds. But modern physics does not just provide us with analogies. Knowledge of the structure of the laws of physics helps us reach a deeper understanding of God's providence. What do I mean? The fact that God and man are able to intervene in what goes on in the world is at the core of Judaism. Divine providence and man's free will are fundamental precepts of Judaism, without which there would be no Jewish world view. Therefore a crucial issue is whether the structure of modern physics and the fundamental principles of divine providence and free will are compatible.

Our world, and indeed every one of us, contains matter that is governed by the laws of nature. This begs the question: How is it possible to reconcile the existence of the laws of physics, which determine the movement of matter, and the intervention of man and God in these movements? One example that we constantly encounter is our control over the movements of our own bodies. All the parts and particles in my body are material and they are all subject to the laws of physics. On the other hand, I, my mind, according to my own free will, determine my movements down to the tiniest details – when to raise my arm, when to walk, when to stand, when to sit, when to get up. If someone were to tell me that all my actions were pre-determined, I would ask him if according to his prediction I was about to turn to the right or the left. If he were to say, "Left," I could easily turn to the right, contradicting his prediction. Nevertheless, how can we reconcile the compliance of my body's particles with the laws of physics with my control over my own actions? This is precisely the essence of Immanuel Kant's antinomy, which I mentioned in the introduction to Chapter Three. On the one hand, Kant believed in free will, while he also believed that the movements of matter are subject to general causality. Hence he thought that there was a contradiction here that was impossible to solve, namely, an antinomy.

But there is a solution. The physical world, the world of matter, is not closed. It is open to the intervention of God and man. There is interaction between matter and spirit. The spirit can affect the movements of matter not only by the established spiritual system – the laws of nature – but also by constant providence over the movements and by the will of man. In Chapter Three, section 8, we discussed the interaction between spirit and matter and the openness of the physical world to the wills of God and man. It became clear that not every system of physical laws meets the condition of openness to the intervention of the spirit. The classic deterministic laws do not fulfill this condition. But what I showed there was that the laws of modern physics are compatible with the condition of openness of matter to spirit. However, we do not have to rely on the nature of the physical laws that we are aware of at this time. Immanuel Kant was unable to solve the problem because of his belief in the deterministic nature of the laws of classical mechanics. Our belief does not have to be subject to the state of our knowledge at any given time.

The material world's openness to the intervention of God and man is a metaphysical, religious principle that derives from the Torah, and it is a wonderful thing that science has reached the stage where it is compatible with this principle. However, we do not have "scientific" proof of the metaphysical principle that lies at the foundation of Judaism. I would say that the principle of openness of the material world is a metaphysical principle of all the sciences, and if classical physics does not comply with this principle, then this points to a flaw in classical physics. This flaw is in the description of the laws, not in the laws themselves, and it does not prevent us from using classical physics at a certain approximation and within certain limits.

There is another important aspect to understanding the nature of science and its connection with Judaism. From our point of view, the laws of nature are part of the divine spiritual world. God imposes them on matter, and as we have explained, matter would not exist at all without these laws. Nevertheless, the laws of nature are a separate spiritual entity that is not dependent on space. Understanding this enables us to solve one of the unsolvable mysteries in secular thought: the problem of the uniformity of the laws of nature – that both here on earth and in galaxies millions of light years away, there are exactly the same laws of nature. In Chapter Three, section 3, we mentioned the statement of Karl Popper: "... the structural homogeneity of the world seems to resist any 'deeper' explanation: it remains a mystery." It remains a mystery in secular thought, but from a Jewish perspective it has a natural explanation.

The process of scientific cognition also belongs to the unsolvable mysteries of the secular way of thinking. In section 1 above, we quoted Karl

Popper as saying, "The phenomenon of human knowledge is no doubt the greatest miracle in our universe." We also quoted Albert Einstein: "The eternal mystery of the world is its comprehensibility . . . . The fact that it is comprehensible is a miracle."

The problem is that a long time ago, it was proven by David Hume that it is impossible to infer knowledge about the laws of nature by the observation of nature, experiments and predictions. In the world of secular, materialist thought, there is no other source of scientific knowledge. The finding that the laws of nature belong to an objective spiritual world is a testament to the true source of scientific knowledge.

But this does not mean that we have found a way to make new scientific discoveries. Entry to the spiritual world, even to the part of it that contains the laws of nature, is not free. Every entry to the divine spiritual world is part of divine providence – divine revelation. What we have achieved is an understanding of the process of scientific cognition, something that remains a mystery to the secular viewpoint.

The idea of a spiritual world as part of our world is fairly natural in Jewish thought. A valuable concept, it enables us to understand things that would not be understood otherwise, and to solve mysteries that arise in a world view that lacks God.

Part 3

THE HISTORY OF THE WORLD

CHAPTER FIVE

The Creation of the World
and the Start of Its Development

1. CREATION OF THE WORLD *EX NIHILO*

THIS PART OF THE BOOK WILL BE DEVOTED TO THE account of the creation and development of the world from the very "first" moment to the present day. In a sense, the first four chapters were a preamble to this part of the book. The road to comprehending the history of the world is long. Even after everything that we learned in the preceding chapters, we have only a rough idea about the structure and development of the world, a faint shadow of the full picture.

Let us start from the beginning. The first event in our world was its own birth, the creation of the world, creation *ex nihilo*. We might ask ourselves: What was the *cause* of the beginning of the world? What or who triggered the creation of the world? We generally think that every thing, every event, must have a *cause*. It is not possible that an event as important as the inception of our world – an event that resulted in the development of everything, including ourselves, human beings – simply happened without any *cause* whatsoever.

When we talk about a single, unique event, such as the creation of the world, it is questionable whether it is even possible to use the concept of "cause" at all. David Hume answers this unequivocally, saying that one absolutely cannot talk about a cause in the case of a unique event: "It is only when two species of objects are found to be constantly conjoined that we can infer the one from the other; and were an effect presented, which is entirely singular, and could not be comprehended under any known species, I do not see that we could form conjecture or inference at all concerning its cause."[1]

Hence there are two kinds of causes: causes of events that recur on a regular basis, and causes of unique events, such as the creation of the world. Causes of regular events can be analyzed using scientific tools, using the assumption that the same cause always leads to the same result. This assumption can be tested by activating the same cause on various occasions, and as long as it leads to the same result, the assumption is not refuted. We cannot prove that the assumption is correct, but as long as it has not been refuted, we are able to talk about the scientific corroboration of the claim, the existence of the cause-effect connection.

However, there is another kind of cause-effect connection, one that we come across often, but cannot be analyzed using scientific tools. There is an infinite number of examples of "non-scientific" causes, the validity of which cannot be logically proven and that cannot be dealt with in a scientific way. A simple example: Yesterday I was in Israel. Today I am in London. The cause of my flight from Israel to London was the decision that I made two nights ago due to certain circumstances. Even though I know the cause of my flight to London with absolute certainty, we cannot provide any logical proof for the fact that my decision was in fact the cause. We also cannot analyze my decision using scientific tools. Of course, some philosophers deny the very possibility of making decisions, dismissing the very existence of human beings' free will. We have learned that the existence of free will is a metaphysical issue – it cannot be proved that man has free will, nor can it be proved that he does not. The metaphysical alternative is that everything was determined in advance at the moment of the creation of the world (absolute determinism), and my flight to London occurred due to a chain of causes that began at the moment of creation. We cannot prove that this is not true, just as we cannot prove that it is.

In fact, the existence of free will is a matter of belief. The existence of people other than ourselves – in fact, the existence of a world external to me – is also a matter of belief. Likewise, the existence of God is also a matter of belief. However, these three beliefs have something in common. The

---

1. *Enquiry Concerning the Human Understanding,* end of Section xi.

denial of each of these beliefs has practical implications for the lives of those who deny them.

If someone truly believes that he does not have free will, then he may be inclined to avoid any decision-making. The tendency to avoid making decisions is generally likely to lead to negative results. Moreover – and this is the key – the belief in free will is the foundation of responsible, ethical behavior. An ethical system has no meaning without the foundation of free will. A person who denies his own free will can claim that he is not responsible for his actions. The concept of morality does not exist for him.

The non-belief in the existence of a world external to human being can lead to the most terrible results. Even sworn adherents of solipsism[2] do not seem to take this belief seriously. In one of his books, Bertrand Russell writes about a letter that he received from a woman that presents her as a sworn solipsist. She wrote a book that included a decisive proof of solipsism, and vehemently complained that all the publishers to whom she had sent her manuscript had rejected it. She asked Russell to intervene on her behalf. The irony is that a solipsist should not be complaining about publishers, because as far as she is concerned, the publishers do not exist. She also does not need to request the involvement of the renowned philosopher, since, from her perspective, he does not exist either.

Finally, a lack of belief in God can also lead to moral decline and to horrific crimes. We only need mention the two atheistic regimes that existed in the twentieth century – Nazi Germany and Soviet Russia – which caused the deaths of tens of millions of innocent men, women and children.

So, there are two kinds of causality – scientific causality and spiritual causality. I use the term *scientific causality*, or simply *causality*, when two events, A and B, are connected by a particular law. The first event, A, is called the *cause*, and event B is its *effect*. When I throw a stone upward into the air, it always falls to the ground. The throwing of the stone (event A) is the cause of its falling to the ground (event B). The fall occurs in accordance with the law of gravity – the earth pulls every object that is above the ground down towards it.

Scientific causality describes repetitive events. Conversely, what I call spiritual causality is characterized by a one-off, unique pairing of events

---

2.   The philosophical idea that there is no reality other than myself.

– cause and effect. One-off events, by their very nature, do not belong to science. It is my decision, my choice, that causes a particular result. Clearly, the spiritual cause and its result are not connected to any physical law. In the example above, the flight to London itself is performed according to the laws of physics, but the cause of my flight to London is my decision to take the flight. The term *decision* belongs to the spiritual world (hence the term *spiritual cause*), and therefore it is impossible to describe it using material, physical – scientific – concepts.

Now let us return to the creation of the world. The concept of the creation of the world is one of the key messages of the Bible. The Torah starts with these two sentences:

> In the beginning God created the heaven and the earth.
> Now the earth was unformed and void, and darkness was upon the face of the deep; and the spirit of God hovered over the face of the waters.
>
> (Genesis 1:1–2)

The idea of the creation of the world is one of the most important foundations of the Bible.[3] It is the basis for the new world view that the Bible brought to the world. It is important to emphasize that just like the issue of the existence of God, the idea of the creation of the world also belongs to the metaphysical realm. It is not a scientific matter. Sometimes people mistakenly combine these two realms.

Thus, in the nineteenth century, people thought that the Bible's version of events contradicted scientific data, since according to the scientific view at the time, the world had always existed. By contrast, in the twentieth century a trend developed in which people sought to find support for the idea of creation in modern physics. Some people believe that the Big Bang theory confirms the act of creation. However, at best, the Big Bang theory can describe the expansion of the world after creation, but it can certainly not describe creation itself. The act of creation does not belong to the realm

---

3. From this point onward, I shall be aided somewhat by the chapter "The Creation of the World in the Bible" from the lectures of Joseph Ben Shlomo, *An Introduction to Jewish Philosophy*. These lectures were translated into Russian in 1994, and I edited them. Professor Ben Shlomo gave permission to publish his lectures in Russian but not in any other languages, including Hebrew.

of science. Once the world has been created, physics can investigate its laws. The creation of the world also includes the creation of its laws, as well as the creation of time and space. These concepts belong to a world that has already been created. The actual creation of the world must be considered on a metaphysical level.

How does something begin to exist? Before the Bible was received, numerous mythological ideas propagated from around the world which assumed that the world was formed out of some kind of primeval substance, namely that it was creation of something from something. Materialism, too, claims that the source of all things is *materia*, primeval matter, which is eternal and has always existed. Everything that exists in the world, including human beings, developed from *materia*. This view is not substantially different from the pantheist view proposed by Spinoza, who claimed that everything is God and there is nothing other than God. According to Spinoza, mankind has no special status, and one should relate to man's feelings as one does to other objects in nature. Man, too, is nothing but a part of nature.

The Bible's approach is completely different. The Bible sees the world and its very existence as the result of the will of God. The cause of the creation of the world is God's will. Here, I use the word cause in the sense of a spiritual cause.[4] The Torah's description of the creation of the world ignores two significant areas. It does not explain how creation occurred or why the world was created. These two issues – how the world was created and why – are beyond our understanding, beyond human comprehension. We are capable of understanding that our world is real, substantial, and that it is contingent – **its existence is contingent on the will of God**. The world is both real and contingent. The contingency of the world – in other word, the fact that its existence is not necessary – means that its existence has no cause or explanation within the world itself. There is an entity that created the world, and that entity is God.

Certain philosophical and religious doctrines, such as the idealist theories, claim that only the spiritual world is real. Eastern doctrines suggest that the world is an illusion. In contrast to these theories, the Bible claims that both the material world and the spiritual world truly exist, and that both are real. **The world is real because God created it.**

---

4. As I explained above, the term *spiritual cause* refers to a one-off, unique event.

The meaning of the **contingency** of the world is that the world cannot exist even for one moment without God's support. This is the concept of continuous and constantly renewing creation, as we recite in the daily morning prayer service: "[I]n His goodness [He] renews daily, perpetually, the work of creation." Rabbi Soloveitchik writes: "God created the world as a separate object, but He did not grant it independent existence. **The world exists because it is nurtured by some of the infinite being of God**" (*And From There You Shall Seek*, 104).

The existence of the world is dependent on the will and grace of its creator. This fact has a practical implication for mankind, and what is true for the world is also true for every person. The person of faith feels his dependence on God and an immediate connection with Him. He senses God's presence in every moment of his life.

2. THE CREATION OF THE WORLD – THE INITIAL PLAN

In general philosophy, there are many attempts to prove the existence of God. One of the most prominent of these proofs is the cosmological proof, which proves the existence of the Creator by looking at the world. We must credit Immanuel Kant with showing that it is impossible to **prove** the existence of God. It is equally impossible to prove that God does not exist. Rabbi Soloveitchik wrote: "[W]e have no right to use these categories, which result from our finite, contingent, temporal existence, to prove the truth of an infinite, absolute, eternal reality" (*And From There You Shall Seek*, 12). However, it seems that there is a great yearning for God in man's heart – he cannot stop himself from trying to prove the existence of God.

In modern times, these attempts have focused on the issue of reconciling the laws of nature with the formation of life on earth. The laws of nature were created alongside the creation of the world. From the physicalist perspective, the laws of nature were created at the moment of the Big Bang. We can suppose or imagine a wide variety of possible laws from which the laws of nature as we know them today were "chosen." We are able to imagine other worlds with other systems of laws. The laws of physics are expressed through mathematical equations that contain parameters or constants and set universal quantities, such as the charges and masses of electrons and protons, Planck's constant $\hbar$, the gravitational field constant G, the speed of light c, and others. The laws in the "other worlds" could differ from each other, say, by the values of these constants.

What results from an analysis of laws with parameters that differ from those of our laws? In worlds (real or imaginary; we will discuss this later on) with laws of nature that differ even slightly from those in our world, the existence of animals and people would be impossible. It is clear that our world was created, adjusted and fine-tuned to life on earth. We can say that the world was designed in the subtlest of ways for the creation of life in general, and for the creation of the life of man in particular. And if there is a **design**, then there must be a **designer**.

Scientists refer to the suitability of the laws of nature to life and to human beings as "**the anthropic principle**." This is, in fact, a modern version of a combination of **the Cosmological Argument and the Argument from Design** (it lies somewhere between these two traditional attempts to prove the existence of God). Many studies have been done and numerous papers written about the anthropic principle. Physicists John Barrow and Frank Tipler published a comprehensive 700-page book dedicated entirely to this issue, called *The Cosmological Anthropic Principle.*[5] In 2003, the book *God and Design*[6] was published, which contained a collection of articles on the subject, and many other works have been published on this topic.

It is clear that we must spend some time considering this idea because it is so close to our own subject. We might get the impression that researchers have managed to prove something that, in principle, cannot be proven: the existence of the **designer**. As we explained above, free will, an extremely important principle in Judaism, includes the freedom to decide whether to believe in the existence of God. If belief in God were forced upon us, then we would lack the freedom to choose between the responsibility that derives from the existence of a God who is involved in our affairs and a life in which no account is rendered to the supreme judge – a life without God.

When it became clear to scientists that the laws of nature were so precisely suited to the formation of life on earth, the question arose as to how this could be explained. The simplest explanation is to assume the existence of

---

5.   John D. Barrow and Frank J. Tipler, *The Anthropic Cosmological Principle*, 1996.

6.   *God and Design, the Teleological Argument and Modern Science,* Neil A. Manson, ed.

a designer. In fact, there really are people who think this way. However, scientists generally look for answers that are not connected to a factor outside the realm of science. In other words, he attempts to explain everything with scientific tools. But the question of the creation of the laws of nature, just like the question of why specifically these laws exist rather than others, does not belong to the realm of science. These questions are outside the scope of science – they are metaphysical questions. And what happened? The scientist, under the guise of a scientific theory, instead of recognizing the fact that he is dealing with a purely metaphysical issue and that he has ceased to act here as a scientist, comes up with an assumption, a metaphysical hypothesis, and thus attempts to "explain" the suitability of the laws of nature for the creation of life.

What are we talking about here? We are talking about the metaphysical hypothesis that, apart from our world, there is an infinite number of worlds with their own laws of nature. These laws of nature are distributed among the worlds on a completely random basis, from a series of different kinds of laws of nature with different universal physical constants. The "explanation" is as follows: Out of an infinite number of different worlds with different laws, there is also a world (or a number of worlds) whose laws are compatible with the formation of life. Clearly, it is in a world of this kind that we, human beings, live. In other worlds, the laws of nature are not suitable for the formation of life, and therefore creatures like us cannot be there. This is called the "Weak Anthropic Principle," which is in contrast to the "Strong Anthropic Principle," which states that the laws of nature were created for the purpose of the formation of man. But it is clear that the hypothesis regarding the existence of many worlds is a metaphysical hypothesis since there is no interaction, no reciprocal relationship, between our world and these other worlds. Hence, this explanation is not scientific but rather a metaphysical one, a matter of belief.

After the creation of the world, the world started to develop. In the story of creation, we can discern three distinct stages of the world's development: the development of the inanimate world, the creation of life together with evolution up to the creation of man, and the development of the society of human beings – human history. All of these stages are accompanied by divine providence: "The spirit of God hovered over the face of the waters."

3. THE DEVELOPMENT OF THE INANIMATE WORLD ACCORDING TO MODERN SCIENCE — A BRIEF OVERVIEW OF THE BIG BANG SCENARIO[7]

Let us ignore divine providence for the moment and describe the modern science's approach to the development of the inanimate world. We will use the word *universe* to denote the imaginary world that develops according to the laws of nature solely and distinguish it from the actual world, which exists and develops under divine providence. The current scientific theory of the creation of the world and its and development began in the wake of Einstein's general theory of relativity. Alexander Friedman was the first to find a solution to Einstein's equations, a solution known today as the "Big Bang Solution," according to which the world started to develop with an explosion from a state of infinite compression with infinite energy.

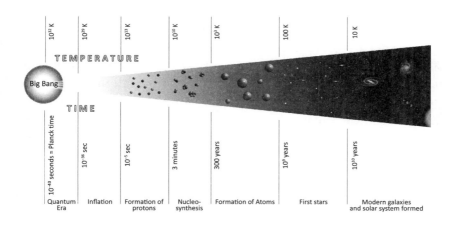

Figure 3.1: The development of the universe

We can summarize the modern theory of the world's creation and development with the help of Figure 3.1. Approximately fifteen billion years ago, the world erupted from one point with infinite energy. Note

---

7.   Any reader who finds this section too difficult may skip to the next section, which also includes a summary of this section.

that this point was not situated in any place within space. Rather, all space at that first moment was concentrated within it. Strange as it sounds, according to the general theory of relativity, all the places that exist in our world today were concentrated inside that point. However, in the very same breath we must say that as far as the first moment and the moments immediately after it are concerned, we cannot use the theory of relativity, from which it is derived that the whole world was inside that point. The point is that with such a high concentration of matter and energy – an infinite concentration at the first moment and an extremely high concentration immediately afterwards – one must take into account the quantum aspect of reality. The problem is that no theory has yet been devised that combines the theory of relativity with quantum theory – quantum gravity. The quantum age (for which it is vital to use quantum theory and the theory of relativity simultaneously) lasted for a period of time known at Planck time, t_p, which is equivalent to 10^{-43} seconds. This length of time is so minuscule that it is absolutely impossible to sense it. It is a tiny fraction of a second that is equal to one second divided by 1 followed by 43 zeros: 1/10,000,000,000,000,000,000,000,000,000,000,000,000,000,000.

At that time, the temperature of the universe must have been 10^{32}K (Kelvin), ten trillion times higher than the temperature deep inside the center of the sun (a trillion is a thousand billion). The universe contained elementary particles, sub-elementary particles and photons – quanta of light ("and there was light") – all colliding with one another. Over time, the universe expanded and cooled down. Somewhere between 10^{-36} seconds and 10^{-34} seconds after the explosion, the universe began to expand at an enormous rate, at least 10^{28} times the rate of its expansion prior to that. This means that in an extremely short timeframe, the size of the universe increased at a rate much higher than in the 15 billion years subsequently. This process, called *inflation*, is compatible with the general theory of relativity, but is not directly derived from it. Approximately one hundred-thousandth of a second (10^{-5} seconds) after the explosion, the universe cooled down enough (to 10 trillion Kelvin – 10^{13} K – approximately ten times the temperature at the center of the sun) to enable quarks (sub-elementary particles) to bind together in groups of three and allow for the formation of **protons and neutrons**. In the three minutes that followed, while the universe was cooling to nearly one billion degrees Kelvin, hydrogen and helium nuclei were formed, as well as tiny amounts of deuterium (a component of "heavy water") and lithium. This period is known as Primordial Nucleosynthesis – the primal synthesis of atom nuclei.

In the following three hundred thousand years, the universe continued to expand and cool down. Once the temperature dropped to several thousand degrees, the process of the formation of atoms began. Electrons that had moved around wildly slowed down and a situation was created in which the atomic nuclei, mostly hydrogen and helium atoms, were able to trap electrons and form the first atoms, which were electrically neutral. This was a turning point. From this point onward, the universe became transparent. Prior to the capture of the electrons, the universe was full of a dense plasma of positively charged particles, similar to nuclei, and negatively charged particles, similar to electrons. Photons, which react only to charges, were constantly scattered and moved around in the dense bath of charged particles, and they passed through almost no space before they collided with charged particles. The barrier that the charged particles created against the free movement of the photons caused the universe to seem almost completely opaque, like in thick fog or a raging, blinding blizzard. However, when the negatively charged electrons were brought into orbit around the positively charged nuclei, yielding neutral atoms, the charged obstacles disappeared and the screen of thick fog was lifted. From here onwards the photons from the Big Bang traveled without any obstacles in their way.

Around a billion years after this, in a universe that had calmed down significantly since its frenetic beginnings, galaxies, stars and eventually also planets started to appear as gravitationally connected lumps of the primeval elements.

Approximately ten billion years after the Big Bang, the solar system was formed, and within it, the earth. According to our current scientific understanding, the stars, including our sun, are actually thermonuclear reactors that have been operating for billions of years. The nuclear reactions that take place in these furnaces produce heavy elements, including the components of the human body and all materials that exist on earth. At a certain stage, life was created on earth, the evolution of life began and man was formed. Approximately ten thousand years ago, human history started to develop.

CORROBORATION OF THE BIG BANG SCENARIO

What are the facts and theoretical assumptions that corroborate the picture of the development of the universe that we have presented here? First of all, as we mentioned above, there is a "Big Bang solution" to Einstein's equations of the general theory of relativity that describes the "creation" of the universe from one point (as well as the creation of space and time). According to the Big Bang scenario, from the moment of its eruption, the universe has been continually expanding up to this day.

It transpires from Einstein's equations that the fabric of the universe is stretching, the distances between objects in space are growing, and the space between the galaxies is growing too.

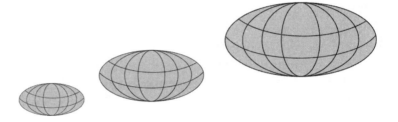

Figure 3.2 The expansion of an (imaginary) two-dimensional spherical universe

The image of the Big Bang as a cosmic explosion that emits the material contents of the universe like shrapnel from a bomb is rather graphic, but misleading. A bomb explodes at a particular location in space and at a particular moment in time, and the contents are emitted into the space around it. In contrast, in the Big Bang described by the general theory of relativity, space itself explodes. A balloon being blown up is a more accurate image for us to understand the expansion of the universe (the three-dimensional universe is illustrated here using a two-dimensional spherical universe). Objects that are on the surface of the balloon, such as galaxies, do not move at all. Rather, as the universe (the balloon) expands, the distance between them grows.

Is there empirical evidence that corroborates this theory? Yes. As early as the late 1920s and the early 1930s, Edwin Hubble's observations testified to the expansion of the universe. How did Hubble do this? How is it possible

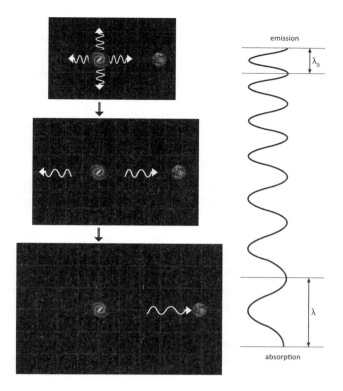

Figure 3.3 Increase in the photon's wavelength during
its journey in the expanding universe.

to ascertain whether the distance between the galaxies is increasing or, to be more precise, that the distance between the solar system and distant galaxies is increasing? It became clear from Edwin Hubble's astronomical observations that light that comes from distant galaxies has a red deviation ("red-shift") – the wavelength of the light that comes from a particular galaxy becomes longer during its journey in space. Now, if we assume that the universe is expanding, then we can show that as a result of the expansion of space the wavelength of a photon that travels within it is growing. Light with a longer wavelength is redder. In Figure 3.3 we can see how light from a distant galaxy (top) starts its journey with a wavelength of λ_o. At the end of its journey, the light reaches its destination with a wavelength of λ. ($\lambda > \lambda_o$, i.e. wavelength λ is larger than λ_o, the initial wavelength). Thus the light that reaches the telescope is redder.[8] This is precisely what Edwin Hubble observed: the more distant (and "older") the galaxy, the larger the red-shift will be.

Now let us turn to some further evidence that supports the Big Bang scenario. We have said that when the universe was approximately three hundred thousand years old, neutral atoms were formed and photons broke away from freely charged particles (which ceased to exist). From this point onward, the universe became transparent and photons were free to move around without any obstacles in the expanses of the universe. In the 1950s, physicist George Gamow and his students, Ralph Alpher and Robert Hermann, and Robert Dicke and Jim Peebles in the 1960s, understood that the modern-day universe should be permeated by an almost homogenous bath of these primordial photons, which cooled down over the last fifteen billion years of cosmic expansion to only a few degrees above absolute zero. In 1965, at the Bell Laboratories, Arno Penzias and Robert Wilson accidentally came across one of the most important discoveries of the twentieth century when they observed the afterglow of the Big Bang while they were working on an antenna intended for use in satellite communication. Further research led to improvements and reached its peak with measurements carried out by NATO's COBE satellite at the beginning of the 1990s. With the help of this data, scientists were able to corroborate with a high degree of accuracy that the universe is full of microwave radiation at a temperature of 2.7 degrees above absolute zero, which is completely in line with the predictions from the Big Bang theory.

The third piece of evidence that corroborates the Big Bang scenario is connected with the quantities of light elements in the universe. Using nuclear and thermodynamic theory, physicists came up with a prediction of the relative abundance of light elements that were formed during the primordial nucleosynthetic period, between one one-hundredth of a second and several minutes after the Big Bang. For example, according to the theory, around 23 percent of the universe should be comprised of helium. It has become clear that this prediction is fairly accurate. What is perhaps more impressive is the prediction and confirmation of the incidence of deuterium

---

8.   Clearly, we are talking here about a wavelength of a particular line in the spectrum of atoms in the stars in a distant galaxy (the spectral line).

in the universe, since no astrophysical process is known to scientists, other than the Big Bang, that can explain the small but definite presence of deuterium in the universe.

The essence of the Big Bang theory is that the universe is expanding and cooling. In fact, it does not tell us a thing about the explosion itself. The Big Bang theory describes the development of the universe but not its beginning. It is not a theory about the creation of the universe. No detailed theory exists for the formation of the stars and the galaxies, but it is clear that the forces of gravity have a decisive influence here.

4. A SCIENTIFIC DESCRIPTION OF THE DEVELOPMENT OF THE WORLD, AND ITS LIMITATIONS

In order to understand the essence of the "Big Bang" solution, let us examine how any matter behaves in extreme conditions of high energies and high temperatures. Let us perform the following thought experiment. We take a certain solid material – ice, for example, and we start to heat it. That is, we raise its temperature. At temperatures lower than zero degrees Celsius, the ice remains in a solid state, and when we reach temperatures above zero but below one hundred degrees Celsius, the ice becomes a liquid – water. At temperatures higher than one hundred degrees, the water turns to steam – a gas. Other materials, such as metals, also behave in this way. With an increase in temperature, metal also becomes first a liquid and then a gas. In a gas state the molecules of the substance move around at great speeds and collide with each other. The temperature of the gas is a measure of the average energy of its molecules.

What would happen if we were to increase the temperature of the gas to extremely high temperatures? The collisions between the molecules would become so violent that they would break the molecules apart into atoms, and the neutral atoms would then break up into electrons and charged nuclei. This is the **plasma** state. Plasma contains charges – electrons, and nuclei of atoms made up of protons and neutrons (as well as anti-protons, and positrons in cosmic plasma). What would happen at even higher temperatures, where the collisions between the charges became even more violent? The atom nuclei would break up into protons and neutrons, and these, together with the electrons, would break up into sub-elementary

231

particles – quarks. A further increase in the energies of the particles would bring us to the limit of modern physics, to an area that is unknown. In the **Big Bang scenario, everything happens in the opposite direction: from very high temperatures at the beginning of the universe, and the cooling, together with the expansion of the universe, up to the present state.**

We can summarize the Big Bang scenario as follows. At the beginning, around fifteen billion years ago, the universe was in an extremely dense state (according to the theory of relativity – in a single point), and from that time it began to expand and spread out. One billion years later, the first stars and galaxies began to form. Approximately ten billion years after the Big Bang, our solar system, containing Earth, was formed. At a certain stage, approximately three and a half billion years ago, life began on earth.

From the scientific description of the development of the universe, we learn a lesson about the literal meaning of the book of Genesis. There are people who think that the literal meaning of the word "day," which appears in Genesis 1, is 24 hours or $24 \times 60 \times 60 = 86,400$ seconds. However, the "reconciliation," or matching of the story of creation with modern science, leads us to an estimate that the length of the first three days (prior to the creation of the solar system) was more than ten billion years! However, we have already explained (Chapter One, section 5) that according to the Jewish tradition, we should not interpret the story of creation solely according to its literal meaning.

In section 1 of this chapter, we emphasized that there is no scientific theory, nor can there be, that describes the creation of the world. The story of creation does not belong to the scientific realm. Only after the world has been created can physics study its laws. The creation of the world also means the creation of its laws, as well as the creation of space and time, and these concepts belong to a world that has already been created. The creation of the world should be discussed on a metaphysical level. Some people think that the physical theory of the Big Bang corroborates the story of creation, but even in the best-case scenario, the Big Bang theory can only describe the expansion of the world subsequent to its creation, not the creation itself. It is true that the equations of the general theory of relativity, Einstein's equations, have a solution that describes the **model** of the development of the universe from a certain moment, when the whole universe was concentrated in one point. From that moment onward, the universe is extending and expanding. According to this, time and space begin from a particular moment, and the question "What was **before** that moment?" is meaningless because time itself began to exist at that moment.

I emphasized in the previous section that the theory of relativity could not be used in relation to the first moment and the moments immediately after it, since with such a high concentration of matter and energy, one must take the quantum aspect of reality into account. As we have said, we still do not have a consistent and well-established theory that combines the theory of relativity with quantum theory – a theory of **quantum gravity**, but theoretical attempts have been made to create models that take quantum physics into account. These attempts can be classified as scientific speculations. It is not our concern here to judge how well-grounded they are, but it is still interesting to note their conclusions: (a) At no moment in time was the universe in a state of one point – the universe always had a finite volume, not a volume of zero; (b) In the time prior to the first moment ("first" according to the model of the theory of relativity), the universe existed, or, according to a different theory, our universe is one of an infinite number of worlds that were created at various times, or are being created all the time.

There is no need for us to go into the details of these theoretical attempts, which in fact belong to the realm of metaphysics. They cannot be tested empirically. But one thing is clear: the idea of a universe concentrated inside a geometric point is the result of the idealization of the theory of relativity, which is not true for the first moment and the moments immediately after that. There is also no scientific proof for the existence or non-existence of the world or of other worlds prior to the "first moment." Again, there cannot be a scientific theory of the creation of the world since such a theory must describe the creation of the theory itself – i.e. the creation of scientific lawfulness.

In order to understand the limitations of science (and physics in particular) in the description of the world's development, it is worth looking at several principles of scientific study:

(a) By its nature, science deals with things that exist in large quantities, and not with unique things or events.

(b) The laws, and the mathematical equations that express them, constitute the foundation of science. But without the initial conditions, the law on its own does not describe reality.

(c) Science always deals with relatively simple systems, and ignores many factors that exist in reality.

(d) The scientist aspires to objectivity. He aspires to ignore the effects of the human spirit, and of the spirit at all, on the processes that he is studying. Scientific study ignores divine providence and does not take it into account.

Now we will discuss these principles, and their implications on the description of the development of the world, in more detail. Let us start with the first statement: Science is universal in nature. It deals with general things and events. Since the same laws operate in different places in the world and the universe, for example, a hydrogen atom in different laboratories, in different countries, or in a distant star or galaxy will have the same properties as described by the laws of physics. A description of a one-of-a-kind object or event does not belong to science. For example, today I felt a spiritual high while I was praying. Clearly, this event has no connection with science.[9] Since the creation of the world is a one-off, unique event, the question arises as to whether, in principle, science is capable of contributing something to the description of the process of the development of the world. In general, the answer to this question is in the negative, but there is a certain situation that makes a scientific description of a one-off event possible.

In order to understand this, let us return to the analysis in Chapter Two, section 3. There we determined that all the physical objects in the world (physical systems) obey the same law (or laws) of nature, and the law of nature does not change – it is fixed – during the development of the system. This means that the law of nature can describe the development of a single, unique physical system. But we must take into account that in general, the laws of nature are statistical. At the foundation of physics lies quantum

---

9. However, even though this claim seems to be self-evident, a person who sides with the determinist, materialist view could say that if we were to take into account all the causal connections since the beginning of the world, then a scientific explanation could also be found for this spiritual high. Nevertheless, we will return to our current topic, the problem of the development of the world.

theory, which is a statistical theory that describes non-deterministic processes and can provide us with statistical information.

Statistical Theory
The simplest example of a statistical process is a coin toss. We are not able to predict on which side the coin will land in a particular toss, for example, on the next toss. But when we throw the coin many times, the probability of landing on heads is equal to fifty percent, and the probability of it landing on tails is also fifty percent. In other words, the frequency of the coin landing on heads is one-half and the frequency of its landing on tails is fifty percent. The frequency of the event is a measure of the probability of the event. I should emphasize that knowing the probability does not tell us anything about a one-off event. Thus, knowing the probability of the coin's landing on heads gives us no knowledge or ability to predict on which side the coin will land on the next throw. In order to be convinced that the probability of an event has a particular value – in our case, fifty percent – we need to perform a large number of experiments (in our example, a large number of coin tosses).

A statistical theory, by its very nature, does not tell us anything about a lone physical system. It can provide statistical information only when there are many copies of that system, or when many experiments can be performed on the system. Therefore, when we have only one, unique system, as in the case of the development of the world, and there is only one world, the statistical law of nature cannot contribute anything to a description of the development of the world.

Nevertheless, one can suppose that at a certain stage, we can describe the development of the world with reasonable accuracy using a **deterministic** theory such as the general theory of relativity. If so, then it is possible in principle to study the development over time of a single system, the development of the world in our case, using scientific tools, **on the assumption that the development takes place deterministically** (not statistically). This is how it could be done (according to Popper's theory of cognition, see Chapter Four, section 4): We hypothesize that at the stage of the development of the world from the Big Bang up until the creation of life, we may describe the expansion and development of the world using the general theory of relativity (as well as other physical theories). If so, then every piece of information from astrophysics can corroborate or disprove the assumption. While the hypothesis is not disproved, it can be used as a scientific theory. If and when it is disproved by information from new experiments, we must look for a new hypothesis to replace the old one.

In fact, in the Big Bang scenario, we use the laws of physics to describe the development of our universe, which is one-of-a-kind, and make some progress in the description of the development of the world. In general, in the case of a statistical theory, there is not, and nor can there be, a scientific description of the development of a single object.

Now we will look at statement (b), which talks about initial conditions. It is worth mentioning that the laws of nature only contain a tiny fraction of our knowledge of the physical, inanimate world. All the laws of nature are conditional statements that enable us to predict the future on the basis of our knowledge of the situation at the initial time. We need to know everyrthing about the physical state of the universe at the start time – the time of the creation of the world (and, as we have said, the laws of nature do not include knowledge of the initial position). From here we see that a consistent and detailed scientific description of the development of the world is impossible in principle. This does not prevent us from attaining a certain level of partial, fragmented knowledge regarding certain aspects of the development of the world (assuming a particular simple, idealized set of initial conditions).

This raises the following question: If this is the situation, and if the laws of nature provide us with only partial, minute knowledge of reality, how are scientists able to deal with this situation and even accomplish significant achievements? Here we come to statement (c) above. Our world is a huge, perhaps even an infinite, mechanism (or organism, according to one view). There are both physical and non-physical connections between the various parts of the world, and it is apparently impossible to gain any knowledge of a particular part of the world without knowing everything about all its parts. Here we arrive at an assumption that stands at the foundation of every scientific study: it is often possible (and I am being careful not to say that it is always possible) to identify isolated physical systems, whose behavior is not affected by external factors. Thus the solar system – the sun and the planets that move around it – is considered to be an isolated system. According to this assumption, it is possible not to take into account, or to disregard, the influence of the rest of the heavenly bodies – the stars in other galaxies – on the solar system. Likewise, all sorts of physical devices are isolated systems (or a close enough approximation for the sake of scientific description). The achievements of science are possible due to the existence of isolated systems – or, to be more precise, because it is possible to find and to choose such systems. An atomic reactor, a radar, artificial satellites, various machines, including cars – these are all examples of systems that may be treated as if they were completely disconnected from the world.

Now we can return to the question of how scientific achievements are possible when science provides only a small part of the information – the laws of nature – without the initial conditions, with no description of the universe's position at a given time. The answer is that with small systems that are isolated from the rest of the world, we can measure the position at a given time. Measurement of the initial conditions – a study of the position at the beginning – fills in the gaps. This is not something that we can do in the case of our world as a whole.

In general, we can say that the art of science is expressed in the search for idealization, simplification – in the choice of simple, abstract, idealized systems that disregard other factors that exist in reality. For example, Isaac Newton introduced the concept of the inertial system into physics. In such a system, every object persists in a resting state or in fixed movement in a straight line (at a fixed speed), while it is not compelled to change this position by forces acting upon it. In nature there are no such systems, and in reality it is impossible to ignore all the forces that act upon an object. There is always friction, which causes the object to lose speed and eventually stop moving. It is also impossible to ignore the force of gravity. It may be ignored only for short time intervals and distances. Sooner or later, these forces will come into effect and affect the object's movement. Nevertheless, the idealization of the inertial system played a revolutionary role in the history of physics, and even today this concept is very important.

Idealization of the isolated system is extremely important. In fact, physics could not exist as a science without it. If we had to take into account the position of the whole world every time, it would not be possible to make any scientific predictions. It is worth mentioning that it is a property of the universe that there are approximately isolated systems. On the other hand, I must stress that the isolated system is an idealization, meaning that there are no such systems – it is always an abstraction. Even if we have a system that is isolated from all influences and is situated in the emptiness of cosmic space – even then it is not isolated from the gravitational field. Under certain conditions, the effect of gravity can be crucial, as in different galaxies. Even the formation of the stars and galaxies was affected first and foremost by the forces of gravity. Now we come to the fascinating question: Could there be, nevertheless, a closed and isolated system – our universe? After all, is it not the case that all the forces are inside the universe and not outside it?[10]

These questions bring us to statement (d): Is the physical world completely closed? Perhaps the closedness of the physical world is also an idealization, which is only valid to a certain approximation. We need only look around us to become convinced that this is indeed the case. Many objects around us, if not most of them, behave in a way that is not in accordance with the laws of physics. Cars that drive on the road and human beings themselves all behave in a way that is not in line with the laws of physics. I am not saying that the laws of physics are not valid for these objects. I am simply saying that something else acts together with the laws of physics – namely the human spirit, which affects the objects' behavior. The idealization that physics, and science in general, use is a consistent and constant attempt to ignore the human spirit. This is the price that science pays for objectivity – which actually means ignoring the human factor.

We saw in Chapter Three (section 9) that a scientific description in general, when all the physical factors are taken into account, is also limited. Science itself is an idealization. One can talk about the idealization of science. The achievements of science and its objectivity are linked to a great extent with the possibility of ignoring the effect of the human spirit. But thinkers who seek the truth must ask themselves the following: Is the spirit of man the only spirit that exists? As soon as we recognize the existence of the human

---

10.   From a purely physical perspective, there is a certain difficulty in defining the universe as an isolated system, since it is impossible to define the tensor of the energy-momentum of the gravitational field.

spirit and the free will that characterizes it,[11] it is almost inevitable that we will recognize the existence of a spirit other than that of human beings. Let us imagine the development of the world according to the naturalist, atheist, scenario that does not include God. In this scenario, before the appearance of man's spirit, no spirit existed at all. This begs the question: Where could a spiritual entity (such as man's soul) appear from development that was completely material? This question cannot be answered without recognition of the existence of the spirit from the very beginning.

Therefore, it is reasonable to assume the existence of a spiritual entity together with a material entity in the composition of the world. In Judaism, the existence of a spiritual entity in the world is a fundamental principle. The book of Genesis starts with God's spirit: "In the beginning God created the heaven and the earth. Now the earth was unformed and void, and darkness was upon the face of the deep; and the spirit of God hovered over the face of the waters" (Genesis 1:1–2). In fact, the entire Bible deals with God's spirit in the world and with human history. This is the cause of the problem of reconciling the Bible with science, which cast out the spiritual entity from within it or, to be more precise, did not permit it to enter.

In an analysis of partial, idealized systems in the world, we can ignore the spirit, and we even manage to do so. But we have no justification for doing so when we are dealing with the development of the world as a whole and the physical universe within it. There is no justification for the idealization of the world without a spiritual entity, without God.

5. THE PURPOSE OF CREATION AND THE NATURE OF THE DEVELOPMENT OF THE WORLD

I have no doubt that my behavior and the events of my life are determined not only by the laws of physics, but also by the choices that I make, by my self. If that is the case, then the world that I am a part of can also not behave solely according to the laws of physics. No, I do not have a superiority complex. I understand that the world's development is affected by other people, by other spiritual entities. Nor do I think that only human spiritual

---

11. Some people, including scientists, deny both free will and the existence of the soul, and exclude them from any substance. This decision is a metaphysical one.

entities affect the world. I believe that God manages the world, and I am convinced that just as all attempts to explain my behavior purely by the laws of physics are doomed, it will never be possible to explain the development of the world without the supervision of the supreme spiritual entity.

From this point onwards I will try, in my description of the development of the world, to bring evidence and signs of divine supervision. Clearly we are not talking here about scientific facts, since divine action is always creative and unique. The first divine act in our world was the creation of the world. The information about this act, just like the information about other divine actions, was received by human beings not from experiments or theories but from God himself, as divine revelation.

I said that scientific facts are not included in signs of divine activity in the world, but this is only true in a certain sense. In fact, the existence of order and lawfulness is a clear sign of divine activity in the world. The creation of a world that is so ordered – the creation of space and time and the laws of nature – is, without a doubt, evidence of intelligent, spiritual activity.

It is possible to reach certain conclusions from the act of the creation of the world itself. The creation of the world by a spiritual entity means that a world that develops as a result of creation must have meaning and purpose. Let us say that there is meaning in the process of the development of the world. From here, we can make an argument for the lack of determinism in the world, that everything is not pre-determined. In a deterministic world, where everything is pre-determined, there is no meaning to the **process of development**. Development does not lead to anything new. At time zero, the moment of creation, everything that will happen at all times was determined. Hence, the metaphysical hypothesis about the determinism of the world contradicts the claim that the world has meaning and purpose.

We human beings cannot know the meaning and purpose of the creation of the world, but from the biblical story of creation we see that man is connected to the purpose of creation. The biblical account of creation shows us certain stages in the world's development. First, the inanimate world was created, and then came the stage of the animate world and flora. Man was created at the end of creation, on the sixth day. It is worth mentioning at this point that these stages are identical to those accepted by modern science. Man is not only the last stage in the chain of creation, but it is said that he was created in the image of God. This corroborates the claim that man is connected with the purpose of creation.

Man was created as God's partner in the building and development of the world: "And God blessed them, and God said unto them: 'Be fruitful and multiply, replenish the earth and subdue it; and have dominion over the fish of the sea, and over the birds of the air, and over every living thing that moves on the earth'" (Genesis 1:28). Certain conditions and restrictions on the purpose of creation may be derived from this command. In the created world there must be law and order. In a situation of chaos, human beings would not be able to join with God in the act of creation. The structure of the world and the laws of its development must be clear and simple enough for this purpose. In order to use the laws of nature, human beings must be able to understand them. Moreover, the laws of nature must be sufficiently flexible to allow God's will and that of human beings to work together. We have seen above (Chapter Three, section 8) that the laws of modern physics possess this property.

The creation of the world is the creation of the world in its entirety – a spiritual world and a physical world together. "In the beginning God created the heaven and the earth" – we can interpret the word *heaven* as referring to the spiritual world, and the word *earth* as referring to the physical world.

The laws of nature that operate on matter belong to the spiritual world. However, according to the Jewish view, these laws are not the only factor that controls the world. They provide a kind of framework for the action of divine providence. What does this remind us of? Earlier, we used an analogy of a man driving a car. The man invents and designs the car and its operating system, and he starts the vehicle and operates it. A vehicle is a physical system. Its parts and its operating system are subject to the laws of physics. But its movements and its course are determined not only by the laws of physics, but also by the man. Ultimately, it is the man that determines the path of the vehicle. It is the man, his self, his mind, that determines the vehicle's path and his own movements.

From the behavior of man, who was created in God's image, we can also learn something about God's supervision in the world. The man's mind represents God – namely, the spiritual world is the world's operating system. The physical world is not a closed system that runs itself. This is what the materialists think. As far as they are concerned, matter is the source of everything and no external factor is necessary for its operation. From our point of view, the whole world, and man within it, is open to God's providence, and the physical world is also open to the intervention of man. Similarly, in the above analogy, the physical system – the car – is open to the man's supervision, to his mind.

In order to discern God's action in the world and his providence, we must look at our world and its development without being influenced by any preconceptions. Science may be able to help us to do so. I state here, unequivocally, that a person who is equipped with scientific knowledge is more capable than an uneducated person of understanding "your miracles that are with us every day.. your wonders and favors in every season – evening, morning and afternoon" (from the thanksgiving portion of the daily *Amida* prayer). In order to identify a unique, exceptional event, perhaps even a miracle, one must know what the norm is. As we have already mentioned, the purpose of science is to describe the regular situation, the events that happen many times or that repeat themselves over and over. In order to be able to recognize something that is not routine, we need to know what is routine. One needs to learn much and acquire a great deal of scientific knowledge in order to understand that my Self is something that is not in the realm of science. Likewise, your Self and the Selves of everyone else do not belong to the public domain.

We, in our world, identify new, unique things that appear to have come *ex nihilo*, as divine revelation. True development is accompanied by God's penetration into our world, while science is intended to describe only the fixed framework of the laws of nature. It never adds anything new, *ex nihilo*. The source of true development is in the Kingdom of Heaven.

Let us return to the first stage of the development of the world – the development of the inanimate world. We summarized the scientific knowledge about this stage in sections 3 and 4. This stage – the longest stage in the history of the world – lasted for more than ten billion years. In a way, this stage (without the creation of the world) is far less important than the other stages in the history of the world. Suffice it to say that a simple organism, such as a fly, is infinitely more complex and sophisticated than the entire universe prior to the creation of life. The most important event in this stage was the creation of the world – the creation of space, time and the laws of nature that are compatible with the formation of life and man on earth. This was the preparation period for the more important stages. The goal was to prepare all the materials and systems required for the formation of life, and it was necessary to do this using laws that were simple enough that man, who would be created in the future, would be able to grasp them. The simplicity of the laws may be the reason that the first stage took such a long time.

I said that it took a long time, but the concept of long or short is dependent on the scale. As we have said, the main purpose of the entire preparation era was to create the basic units for the next stage – the stage of life. According to modern scientific understanding, everything started from basic particles, such as quarks, electrons and photons, with very high energies. Only 10^{-5} seconds were required for the formation of protons and neutrons from quarks. By three minutes after the Big Bang, atomic nuclei were created, while the formation of the first atoms took only three hundred thousand years, followed by another ten billion years for the creation of modern stars and galaxies. The materials required for the creation of animals, people and their environment were formed inside the stars, which are huge thermonuclear furnaces.

We are talking here about completely different orders of magnitude – from one one-hundred-thousandth of a second to billions of years. The idea of length of time, long or short, is a human one. Human beings did not exist in that period, but from God's perspective: "For a thousand years in Thy sight are but as yesterday when it is past . . ." (Psalms 90:4).

Laymen are also highly impressed by the enormous distances that exist in the universe. One might get the impression that this is completely superfluous – why is the size of the observable universe[12] fifteen billion light-years?[13] For us, the solar system, the length of which is measured in a few light-minutes, is sufficient. The answer is that only when the universe expanded to its current size was life possible. It is possible that other laws of nature would have enabled life to exist in a much smaller universe. However, these laws might have been far more complex and intricate and unsuitable for the

---

12. The observable universe is the universe that can be observed using physical means.

13. This distance is equal to the distance through which light would take fifteen billion years to travel.

human intellect to grasp. But here we are treading on the somewhat shaky ground of metaphysical speculation.

In this prolonged preparatory period, it is hard for us to point convincingly at clear signs of divine providence other than the remarkable event of the creation of the world itself. What we do know from scientific theories is that the formation of the planets, stars and galaxies is compatible with the laws of physics. It is also compatible with providence even though it is impossible to say with absolute certainty that providence was required here, and perhaps the action of the laws of nature alone was sufficient. To be more exact, it could be that at this stage, the laws of nature were the only tool of providence. We seem to have reached a draw.

CHAPTER SIX

The Development of Life

1. INTRODUCTION – THE LAW OF EVOLUTION: SCIENCE OR MYTH?

WE HAVE ARRIVED AT A VERY IMPORTANT STAGE IN the history of the world. Something new has been created, something unlike anything that has preceded it. The era of life has begun.

Modern science estimates that life on earth began approximately three and a half billion years ago. Scientists believe that every living thing developed from one extremely simple, tiny creature. There are currently more than two million different species in the world. They differ enormously from each other in terms of size, shape and way of life. But it is remarkable that the entire animal kingdom – all animals, from the simplest organisms to human beings – as well as all plants – trees, bushes and flowers – are all formed in a uniform way.

We can say that living organisms are all highly complex and delicate "mechanisms" and that what unites them is the genetic material that is common to all living things. We find the same genetic material, DNA, in the simplest bacterium or plant and in human beings. DNA is a large, long molecule, a chain of units, and the only way in which human DNA differs from that of other living things is in its length (and, of course, the information that it contains).

Living beings have a wonderful quality that differentiates them from inanimate beings: they reproduce, replicate themselves and produce new living beings. The genetic material of the biological organism, which is "responsible" for the transfer of the organism's properties to its offspring, preserves its identity for future generations, but not in an absolute way. One can identify tiny changes from one generation to the next and between different individuals in the same species. A unit of genetic information is called a gene. Scientists estimate that 99.99 percent of the genes of all human beings are identical, and the difference between one person and the next is expressed in 0.01 percent of the genetic material, the DNA.

The outstanding achievement of biology in the last century is the realization that every living being is made up of uniform genetic material, information of which Darwin was unaware. Genetic material determines the majority of a living thing's physical characteristics of a living thing. A whole living organism develops from a seed ("Whence you came ? From a putrid drop . . ." *Ethics of the Fathers* 3:1), with all the instructions necessary for its development included in its genetic material. Clearly these instructions are written in letters, words and a particular language, like a computer language. Of course, there is no connection between the language of genetic material and human language or computer languages; this is simply an analogy that shows us that other languages exist in addition to human ones.

The genetic material located in the DNA in an organism's cells includes a complete series of instructions for its development. The genetic material determines the structure of the various kinds of proteins vital for the functioning of the living organisms. A particular combination of different molecules – different letters of the genetic text – is what determines a particular protein.

We have talked about molecule-letters. Now let us ponder how it is possible to write, express and preserve genetic text. Letters of this kind of text must be preserved for millions of years. The text itself changes gradually due to mutations, but the letters are preserved. All matter that we are familiar with from our everyday lives is matter that is destined eventually to wear away. Here we get to a crucial point: the letters of genetic material are made of molecules. They are not a product of human effort but "the finest masterpiece ever achieved along the lines of the Lord`s quantum mechanics."[1]

If we wished to transcribe or translate a human being's genetic information into ordinary letters, for example, the resulting text would fill approximately

---

1.   E. Schrödinger, *What is Life?*, 86.

two hundred volumes, each containing one thousand pages. All these books together would weigh about half a ton and would be one cubic meter in volume! In contrast, a human being's genetic information is concentrated in a cell nucleus that is 0.001 cubic millimeters in volume! (We must also take into account that not all the DNA is a source of genetic information.)

After the creation of the world, the formation of life on earth is the most notable incidence of new creation, *ex nihilo*. After the first living thing was created, it began to procreate and reproduce itself through its offspring. But as we have stated, even though the transfer of a creature's identity to the next generations is executed with a great degree of fidelity, minuscule "mistakes" occur during the transfer process.

As a result of the genetic changes that occur, there is the possibility of development, of the evolution of life. If the transfer of genetic instructions from one generation to the next were absolute, with no aberrations at all, then today, three and a half billion years after the creation of the very first creature, that same creature and only that creature would still exist, with numerous copies. The evolution of life is possible, at least in principle, only if genetic mutations exist.

In 1859, Charles Darwin proposed in his book, *On the Origin of Species*, the natural selection mechanism which, in his opinion, explains the process of the evolution of life. The idea of natural selection is fairly straightforward even though the way it works is highly complex and subtle. The essence of natural selection is as follows: In every population, some individuals produce more offspring than others. Those individuals whose genetic mutations are more advantageous will ultimately survive and reproduce, while those with less favorable genetics will either not reproduce at all or will reproduce at a slower rate than those with good genetics. With regard to the changes that pass to the next generation, there is a phenomenon of differential survival that accumulates through the generations. Thus, natural selection is constantly working to improve and preserve the adaptations of animals and plants to their environment and their way of life.

The basic mechanism called "*natural selection*" contains three elements: *heredity*, **mutation** and *natural selection*. Mutations are random changes caused by radioactive materials or cosmic particles. The mutations are responsible for genetic changes – namely, errors in the genetic mechanism. Biology has come a long way since Darwin's day, and we now know a great deal about the physics and chemistry of the genetic mechanism, and are able to decipher man's genetic code. However, the basic mechanism of *natural selection* is still considered the basis for understanding evolutionary change.

The mechanism of natural selection is a vital tool for understanding countless biological phenomena. For example, we can explain and understand the adaptation of bacteria to certain antibiotics such as penicillin through the mechanism of natural selection. Penicillin destroys the majority of bacteria. However, a tiny minority of bacteria, which came about as a result of mutations, are able to resist penicillin. These bacteria will pass on this quality to their offspring, and thus the penicillin-resistant bacteria will multiply. Another example of the natural selection mechanism at work is the protective mimicry of certain animals. There is no other way to describe, explain or comprehend these phenomena and many other biological phenomena other than through natural selection.

Many people, including intellectuals, scientists, philosophers and laymen, are convinced that the mechanism of natural selection explains the development of life on earth, from the creation of life up to the present day. Prior to Darwin's discoveries, it was commonly thought – or, I should say, believed – that the animal kingdom, with its myriad species, was the fruit of God's design. The British theologian William Paley, in his book *Natural Theology* (1802), used scientific data to support the claim of divine design. If we were to find a watch, even on a desert island, then the harmony among the parts of the watch would compel us, so Paley claimed, to conclude that it had been made by a skilled watchmaker. Paley goes on to argue that since the human eye is so much more complex and intricate than a watch, is there any way in which it could not have a creator? This argument made a great impression. It was clear to everyone that a complex and sophisticated plan was required to produce animals and plants. Here, Darwin suggested a "scientific," materialist explanation for the development of life on earth. The creation of plants and animals, including human beings, was accomplished by nature, as it developed.

Is this true? Did Darwin really suggest a scientific theory that explains the evolution of life? Is there a law of evolution that can provide a scientific prediction of all the stages of development of life? A scientific explanation means the ability to predict the creation of all the species that exist on earth. We will address these questions later on.

I would like to point out that the Darwinist explanation relates only to the period after the creation of life and has no bearing on the creation of life itself. Furthermore, there is no scientific explanation for the creation of the world, nor can there be. We have seen (Chapter Five, section 2) that from a purely materialist perspective, there is a problem explaining the suitability of the laws of nature to the creation of life. Of all the possible laws, only certain ones, within an extremely narrow range, are suited to the existence of life on earth. As well as the field of evolution, there are many other questions that the materialist view fails to answer, including the fundamental question of the existence of lawfulness and order in the inanimate world. Still, the materialist explanation of the evolution of life has helped to support and advance the world view that does not include God.

From a psychological perspective, this is understandable. If a scientific explanation has been presented for a particular era in the development of the world, one can hope that over time, scientific explanations will be found for all eras. However, an astute person will realize that the issue of lawfulness and order in the inanimate world has absolutely nothing to do with the realm of science, and therefore a scientific explanation for the existence of law and order in nature is, in principle, impossible.

2. DOES A SCIENTIFIC THEORY OF EVOLUTION EXIST?[2]

It is important to distinguish between two different concepts: the *theory of evolution*, which is based on the adaptation mechanism of natural selection, and the *fact of evolution* – the development of the profusion of life on earth, which began from primitive organisms and gradually developed over time into self-conscious beings. Confusing these two concepts can lead to serious misunderstandings. We must also distinguish between the adaptation mechanism of *natural selection* and the *theory of evolution*, since a successful explanation of any phenomenon of adaptation by the mechanism of natural selection is sometimes, mistakenly, understood as a corroboration of the theory of evolution.

The fact of evolution is based not on any particular theory, but on *paleon-*

---

2. Some parts of this section may be difficult to understand, so the reader may skip either to the next section, or to section 7, which concludes this chapter.

tological data, on the gamut of *fossilized* remains of living things from various periods. We should note that even up until the present day, scientists argue about the essence of the idea of gradual evolution as a cause of the formation of new species. Eldridge and Gould explain the absence of intermediate fossil sequences by asserting that development is not gradual. They suggest that new species developed over the course of a few thousand years (a minuscule moment in geological terms) after which there were no changes for millions of years. They termed this kind of development *"punctuated equilibrium."*

We may ask ourselves the following: what kind of certainty can we attribute to the possible explanation of the development of life on earth? Throughout this book, we have seen many times that we cannot logically prove anything that is truly meaningful. Therefore, we cannot expect an explanation of the development of life to be a logical proof. We can discuss the claim that a **scientific explanation and a scientific proof** exist, as it were, for the development of life as a purely materialist process, devoid of God. A scientific explanation means that a **scientific theory** exists regarding the evolution of life on earth.

The main thesis of the analysis presented below is that it is impossible to derive a scientific theory that describes evolution from paleontological data, from the fact of evolution – assuming that this is, indeed, a fact.

I will briefly reiterate the key points of Karl Popper's theory of scientific cognition (Chapter Four, section 4). According to Popper, a scientific theory is a hypothesis, an estimate, a guess, that must be tested by new experiments before it merits the status of a law of nature. It is impossible to discover any law of nature on the basis of a single experiment. The necessary condition that distinguishes a scientific theory from a metaphysical belief is that a scientific theory must be able to be disproved, refuted by future experiments. In contrast, by its very nature, a belief or metaphysical assumption cannot be disproved (nor can it be proved or verified). Scientific information develops through a series of competitions between different scientific hypotheses, between different scientific theories. A theory that has not yet been disproved is preferable to theories that have already been disproved. Experimental corroboration of a scientific theory is extremely important, but only the refutation of a scientific theory makes progress towards a new scientific theory possible.

What characterizes science – namely, scientific theory – is the possibility of being tested by experience. Conversely, one can never corroborate or disprove a metaphysical hypothesis by experience or logic. So far, we have discussed the problem of scientific cognition on a general level, without entering into the specifics. We will get to these later on.

On the basis of his theory of cognition, Karl Popper reached the general conclusion that Darwinism was not a scientific theory. This derives from the fact that the theory of evolution is a "singular historical statement." After all, it is about the development of life on earth in the past – that is, the history of a process that has already taken place. Of course, there is nothing wrong with speculation or conjecture about a possible explanation for this process, but a guess or hypothesis regarding the mechanism of the development of life on earth does not constitute a scientific theory. No conjecture about the development of life has the status of a scientific theory since it is impossible to test it with additional experiments.

Karl Popper concludes:

> The evolution of life on earth . . . is a unique historical process. Such a process, we may assume, proceeds in accordance with all kinds of causal laws, for example, the laws of mechanics, of chemistry, of heredity and segregation, natural selection, etc. Its description, however, is not a law, but only a singular historical statement.[3]

While I agree with Popper that Darwinism is not a scientific theory, I have a problem with his rationale. We have seen (Chapter Five, section 4) that one can use scientific tools even with regard to the development process of a single system. There we were talking about a particular stage in the development of the world. This is also a "singular historical statement." This does not prevent us from carrying out further experiments in astrophysics that can reveal new aspects of this development, but the difference is that we discussed the development of the world during its deterministic stage, while the evolution of life is a quintessentially non-deterministic process that we will discuss later on. We determined earlier (Chapter Five, section 4) that no scientific description exists for the non-deterministic development of a single system. This is a very general conclusion that relates both

---

3. *The Poverty of Historicism*, 108.

to the development of life on earth and to human development – to human history.

There is another aspect to the problem of describing the evolution of life using scientific tools. We cannot base the law of evolution on evolutionary data, but perhaps we can determine it using whatever metatheory is capable of describing all the events in the physical world. And there is indeed such a theory. In fact, physics presumes to describe and explain all physical events. So let us try to use physics, at least as a thought experiment, to determine the law of evolution. In order to use any physical theory we must identify an isolated, closed physical system that is not affected by external factors. This is a condition of the use of physical theories.

So what transpires from this? The system of life on earth, the biosphere, is not isolated from external influences. I am not talking about the effect of the sun or the forces of gravity – all of these can be taken into account in a physical scientific analysis. I am talking about the fact that the development of the biosphere is affected by random factors, such as cosmic particles. Moreover, the essence of the existence of development, of the evolution of life, is dependent on the effects of random changes. We mentioned that if the transfer of genetic instructions from one generation to the next were absolute, with no deviations whatsoever, then now, three and a half billion years after the creation of the first living organism, that same creature and only that creature would exist today, though in multiple copies. The evolution of life is possible, at least in principle, due to the occurrence of random genetic changes. Therefore, no physical theory is capable of explaining and predicting the development of life on earth since the biosphere is open to random influences, including chance factors.

What is this reminiscent of? Above, in Chapter Three, section 9, I cited example d, a spaceship fitted with a Geiger counter. This spaceship moves in full compliance with the laws of physics as long as there are no random disturbances such as those caused by cosmic particles. Each of these disturbances causes the spaceship to deviate from its path. Just as there are no deviations from the development path of the spaceship that is pre-determined by the laws of mechanics as long as there are no random disturbances, so too the development of life only becomes possible when random mutations – the result of chance factors such as cosmic particles – occur. Without them, there can be no change, development or evolution in the system of life on earth, in the biosphere. Nevertheless, we should note that physics is also capable of dealing with systems that are affected by random causes, and describes them using statistical theories. However, in the case of a lone, singular system such as the biosphere, a statistical theory that can describe only a group of biospheres is of no use.

We have come to two general conclusions:

1. It is impossible to build a scientific theory of evolution on the basis of paleontological data – the fossilized remains of living beings from various periods.
2. Not even physics can provide a scientific description of evolutionary processes, since the biosphere is an open system that is necessarily affected by random factors outside the system.

Until now, we have drawn conclusions from a general analysis that does not address the specific details of the development of life on earth. The main conclusion is that there is no scientific theory that describes how life on earth developed, nor can there be. The reader is welcome to make do with the discussion at this level and skip over the more detailed analysis in the rest of the section.

Now we will look in more detail at the Darwinist evolutionist hypothesis. The fundamental premise of Darwinism (or its modern version, which is known as Neo-Darwinism) is that the adaptation mechanism by means of natural selection explains the development of the living world from the formation of life to this day. We will look at two questions:

1. Can experiments that corroborate the Darwinist hypothesis be created?
2. Can the hypothesis be disproved?

The possibilities of corroboration and refutation are necessary conditions for the Darwinist explanation to have the status of a scientific theory.

In answer to the first question, we have already mentioned that the natural selection mechanism is an important tool in understanding biological phenomena such as the adaptation of bacteria to various antibiotics. There is no doubt that the natural selection mechanism is able, in a sense, to improve the functioning of individuals of a certain species. This kind of improvement is generally expressed in the better adaptation of an individual to its environment. But there is no experiment that can corroborate the formation of a new species as a result of natural selection. The claim that natural selection might be responsible for the formation of a new species is equivalent to claiming that development is controlled solely by the laws of nature and that the laws of physics and chemistry are capable of creating new things. This is actually a materialist, metaphysical belief that has no basis in our known reality. There is no indication in our reality that the laws of physics have the power to create.

It is important to note that from a purely logical perspective, a successful experiment in which something new is created solely as a result of the laws of physics would not prove that the law of evolution is a scientific theory. It would only add a certain degree of plausibility to the hypothesis that natural selection can cause the formation of a new species.

Now let us take a more detailed look at natural selection. A living creature passes on its characteristics and its structure through the genetic mechanism – all the genetic information encoded in the creature's DNA is passed on to the next generation with a high degree of fidelity. However, the transfer is not completely perfect, since random mutations are likely (or liable) to generate random changes that will be passed on to future generations.

It is important to realize that there is no directionality inherent in this mechanism – no development in a certain direction, such as that of progress. There is no evolutionary advancement from the simpler to the more complex. What we can expect from such a mechanism is that evolution will occur as a kind of "random walk" (in physics, the term "random walk" is used to describe the walk of a completely drunk person, or of a person who uses a roulette wheel to determine his every step.) One might argue against this comparison with a random walk, since the environment itself dictates that development be in the direction of better adaptation to the environment. While this is true, there is a difference between the adaptation of animals of a particular species to their environment and the tendency towards the creation of new, more complex species, on the assumption that the more complex species are also better suited to the environment.

Darwin attempted to explain "evolutionary ascent" – the formation of higher creatures from inferior creatures over a long period of time. At the start of evolution there were only primitive organisms, from which highly complex animals developed, with humans at the top. Darwin's explanation can be expressed as follows: Evolutionary ascent occurs because, of all life forms, only the fittest survive. But this can only be an explanation for evolutionary ascent if we add the assumption that the higher life forms are more suited to the environment than lower ones.

However, it is clear that this assumption is baseless. We know of certain lower life forms that have survived very long periods – from times predating the appearance of the higher life forms – and that still exist. We also know that many higher organisms, which appeared long after the life forms inferior to them, have become extinct, while the latter are still around. We do not know why these higher organisms disappeared. Perhaps they were killed by bacteria or viruses –lower life forms. In any event, these higher organisms were less suited to their environment than many primitive organisms. These facts indicate that there is no clear connection between the level or complexity of life forms and their suitability to the environment, and without such a connection we cannot take the Darwinist explanation for evolutionary ascent seriously. In general, we can say that there is no evidence that corroborates the Darwinist approach.

In answer to the second question, any scientific theory is characterized by the fact that it can theoretically be disproved. Every scientific theory is a hypothesis that can be refuted. If a particular assumption cannot, in principle, be disproved, then it cannot be the basis of any scientific theory, but can only be a metaphysical belief. As we have shown, a scientific hypothesis can never be verified; it can only be corroborated or disproved. Now we will see that the evolution hypothesis cannot be disproved in principle, just as we have seen that it cannot be corroborated either.

The theory of evolution professes to explain the development, abundance and diversity of life on earth. To explain it is to be able to predict in advance, from the formation of life up to the present day, the development of life from the simplest organisms to human beings. Can we refute it? Of course not. Let us imagine that a particular planet has similar conditions to those on earth. Let us say, too, that life was formed there, a simple living organism appeared, and as a result of the evolution of life on that planet, large quantities of new species did not develop, but that only two bacteria developed. Would this disprove the theory of evolution? Absolutely not. The theory of evolution can easily explain this. We could say that of all the mutants – the organisms that came about as a result of mutation – only two bacteria survived because only they were sufficiently suited to the environment. In this way, the theory of evolution can explain every possible discovery anywhere in the world.

Here is another theoretical example: In a laboratory, scientists manage to create conditions that will lead to the formation of life, and as a result, life forms develop that are entirely different from those that currently exist. Can this disprove the theory of evolution? Certainly not. It is always possible to claim that the environment in the experiment is not identical to that on earth. Even if it is identical, then there are simply different mutants in this experiment. Since the formation of mutants is a random process, no experiment would be able to disprove the theory of evolution.

The theory of evolution, if it exists, is incapable of predicting the abundance of species on earth, and therefore cannot explain it either. The general approach, based on logic, leads us to the inevitable conclusion that neither the theory of evolution nor the law of evolution exist.

It is important to emphasize that this was also the conclusion of several biological scientists in light of their research. Jacques Monod, who, together with André Lwoff and François Jacob, won the Nobel prize in 1965 for his contribution to genetic biology, writes in his book, *Chance and Necessity*: "The thesis I shall present in this book is that the biosphere does not contain a predictable class of objects or of events but constitutes a particular occurrence, compatible indeed with first principles, but not *deducible* from those principles and therefore essentially unpredictable."[4] In addition, he writes: "I believe that we can assert today that a universal theory, however completely successful in other domains, could never encompass the biosphere, its structure, and its evolution as phenomena *deducible* from first principles."[5]

If we were to tape the whole evolutionary process on film, every rerun would be a new film, showing a completely different history. With this vivid metaphor, Gould presents the idea that evolution is unpredictable. The key concept here is contingency, meaning the possibility of an event occurring. "A historical explanation does not rest on direct deduction from laws of nature, but on an unpredictable sequence of antecedent states, where any major change in any sequence would have altered the final result. This final

---

4. *Chance and Necessity*, 43.
5. Ibid., 42.

result is therefore dependent, or contingent, upon everything that came before – the unerasable and determining signature of history."[6]

Natural selection may well play an important role in understanding the process of evolution on earth. However, it is a great leap from this statement to the claim that the adaptation mechanism by natural selection **explains** the evolution of life on earth. Of course, this all depends on how we understand the word "explain." The prevailing opinion is that natural selection explains all evolution on earth, from the moment that life was created (I am intentionally ignoring here the problem of the creation of life on earth), and that it is apparently possible to predict the development of life on earth. But we have seen that it is actually impossible to make such predictions. Darwinism is not a scientific theory. All scientific theories can be corroborated, and more importantly, refuted by new experiments. If a particular hypothesis, such as Darwinism, does not fulfill both of these conditions, then it does not have the status of a scientific theory. All that we can say is that Darwinism has the status of a metaphysical assumption. This is, in fact, the belief that the laws of physics have creative power – a belief that is not based on any human experience or scientific experiment whatsoever.

After all that we have discussed above, it is worth pointing out that the theory of evolution still has one prediction that can be both corroborated and refuted. It transpires from the theory of evolution that the development of life must be evolutionary – in other words, gradual – in nature. The gradualness of the development of life on earth is the practical ramification of the law of evolution. However, we saw at the beginning of the previous section that this conclusion is also somewhat doubtful.

We can summarize the analysis in this section using the words of Karl Popper: "There exists no law of evolution, only the historical fact that plants and animals change, or more precisely, that they have changed. *The idea of a law which determines the direction and the character of evolution is a typical nineteenth-century mistake, arising out of the general tendency to ascribe to the 'Natural Law' the functions traditionally ascribed to God.*"[7]

---

6. *Wonderful Life*, 283.
7. *Conjectures and Refutations*, 340; emphasis mine.

3. THE LAWS OF NATURE DO NOT UNEQUIVOCALLY DETERMINE THE COURSE OF THE DEVELOPMENT OF LIFE

We have reached the conclusion that neither a scientific theory of evolution nor a law of evolution exists that can determine the development of life. This conclusion is not contingent on the validity of natural selection, or the lack of such validity, as a cause that determines the development of life. I personally do not believe that any physical mechanism can be the sole cause of the creation of new things, such as birds or human beings. But this is a matter of belief. Even if all the species on the planet were created by natural selection, there still would not be a law that determines a single course of the development of life. The reason for this is that the natural selection mechanism includes a random element – mutation. There are infinite possible courses that evolution might take, and there is no law that can determine or predict which course will be taken.

Let us look at this point in more detail. We know that the macroscopic system is controlled generally by the deterministic laws of physics, which entirely pre-determine its development. I say "generally" because there is an exception: microscopic, quantum events can affect the development of the macroscopic system. Quantum laws are not deterministic, and they do not unequivocally pre-determine the development of the system. They only determine the probabilities of possible events occurring. If quantum events can affect macroscopic systems, then the development of the macroscopic system is not deterministic. This is precisely the case with the development of life on earth. The development of life is affected by mutations that are generally quantum events. We saw another example of a macroscopic process that is affected by quantum events in example (d) in Chapter Three, section 8.

Let us try to understand what this is all about. Let us imagine that we have returned to the moment that life was first created on earth and ask ourselves: What can science tell us about the future development of life? Of course, this is based on the assumption that we can make all the necessary calculations and that we are completely familiar with all the laws of nature. In light of what we have discussed above, we would not be able to predict everything that would take place on Earth from the beginning of life. This kind of prediction would be possible in the case of deterministic laws of nature that unequivocally determine development, but that is not the case here. A random factor, mutation, operates throughout the development of life and determines its outcome. An infinite number of possible courses of development are compatible with the laws of nature. Thus, among all the possible courses of development, there could have been development without the creation of birds, or without people. There could also have been a course of life with only two bacteria, as well as one in which life was born and then immediately extinguished.

Science cannot provide even statistical information about the development of life.

Science can also describe non-deterministic processes – it can provide statistical information. What are we talking about here? Above, when we spoke about quantum theory, we emphasized that it is a statistical theory. The simplest example of a statistical process is a coin toss. We cannot predict which side the coin will land on in any particular throw. However, when we toss the coin a large number of times, then the probability it will land one-half, as is the probability that it will land tails. In other words, the frequency of the coin's landing on heads is equal to one-half, and the frequency of its landing on tails is also equal to one-half. The frequency of the event is a measure of its probability. We must understand that knowledge of the probability cannot tell us anything about a one-off event. Thus, knowledge of the probability that the coin will land on heads when we toss it gives us no information or prediction as to how the coin will land on the next toss. To prove that the probability of a particular event has a particular value (in our case, one-half), we need to carry out a very large number of coin tosses.

Apparently, science can, in principle, give probabilities for various possible paths of evolutionary development. But there is no value in this kind of information, since statistics only have meaning in an **ensemble**, or a group of many instances of the same system. In our case, this would be many instances of Earth, with the same initial position. But since we only have one Planet Earth, there is no value in having knowledge of the probabilities of various courses of the development of life upon it.

I would like to stress that even if we were to accept the metaphysical assumption that in the process of the development of life it is natural selection that determines the creation of new species (and there is absolutely no experimental evidence for this), then the conclusion that the laws of nature are incapable of predicting the development of life would still be valid. Nevertheless, it is crucial to emphasize that there is no scientific basis whatsoever to the claim that a physical (or chemical) mechanism could be responsible for creation, for the appearance of something new. Every creation is special and unique. Science does not deal with unique things, nor does it predict them.

Until now, we have analyzed the situation from a scientific perspective. It is very important to make a clear distinction between scientific analysis and a world view that utilizes science. While scientific statements can be tested through experiments, philosophical statements are metaphysical in nature, and these two qualities should not be confused. On the basis of the very same scientific theories, entirely different philosophies and outlooks can grow.

Nevertheless, we must stress that Judaism is also compatible with the picture that is based on the Darwinist metaphysical assumptions presented above. At the foundation of Judaism lies the principle that all development, including the evolution of life, is subject to divine providence, even when all the laws of nature (physics, chemistry, biology) apply, and this includes natural selection. This principle is also compatible with the standard explanation of the evolution of life. As we have seen, there is an infinite number of possible paths for the development of life. The deciding factor between the various evolutionary paths may be completely random or determined by divine providence. The choice between these two options is a metaphysical one, which lies outside the scope of scientific experimentation.

4. A NATURALISTIC, GOD-FREE WORLDVIEW THAT PROFESSES TO BE BASED ON THE THEORY OF EVOLUTION

Earlier, we mentioned the book *Chance and Necessity* by Jacques Monod, a well-known French scientist. In his book, Monod expresses a worldview based, in his opinion, on the modern theory of the world's development. As we pointed out above, Monod agrees that there is no law of evolution that can pre-determine the development of life. He also agrees that the creation of life on earth was not predictable prior to its occurrence. Monod draws a conclusion from this about the absolute randomness of the creation of life and man: "The universe was not pregnant with life nor the biosphere with man. Our number came up in the Monte Carlo game."[8]

It is also from here that the conclusion about the meaninglessness of our lives is derived: "The ancient covenant is in pieces; man knows at last that he is alone in the universe's unfeeling immensity, out of which he emerged only by chance. His destiny is nowhere spelled out, nor his duty."[9] We should remember that prior to Monod arriving at this worldview, apparently based on the achievements of modern science, he divorced himself from his idols, Marx and Engels, and especially from the idea of **progress**, Marx's and Hegel's idea that human history, together with the universe, comply with eternal laws of nature.

According to Monod, all development of life is a result of randomness, and hence we should rid ourselves of our Western, humanist legacy: "For their moral bases the 'liberal' societies of the West still teach – or pay lip-service to – a disgusting farrago of Judeo-Christian religiosity, scientific progressism, belief in the 'natural' rights of man . . . ."[10] Whenever a philosopher adheres to the belief that randomness is the source of the creation of life and its development, he cannot avoid the conclusion regarding the meaninglessness of our lives. But I stress once again that the view that evolution operates as a random process is not a scientific conclusion but a belief. In 1995, an argument took place at a meeting of the National Association of Biology Teachers (NABT) in the USA, where a vote was held on the Statement on the Teaching of Evolution that stated that "evolution is an unsupervised, impersonal, unpredictable and natural process." Following hours of arguments, the executive committee agreed to remove the words "unsupervised, impersonal." The executive director of the NABT, Wayne Carley, who insisted on the change, said that this change was in the spirit

---

8. *Chance and Necessity,* 146.
9. Ibid., 180.
10. Ibid., 171.

of good science and that "to say that evolution is unsupervised is to make a theological statement."[11]

In the end, the NABT executive committee agreed on the statement: "Evolution is an unpredictable and natural process." But this is not the opinion that is generally accepted among biologists, many of whom insist that evolution is indeed an unsupervised and impersonal process. Which group is larger I do not know, and it is not important, since this is not a case of majority rule. The important point is that it is impossible to determine, by either logic or science, which side is correct since this decision is within the realm of metaphysics, not science. The question of whether the process of evolution is controlled by divine providence or is unsupervised is a question of **belief**.

5. CHANCE OR CAUSALITY?

Let us summarize the position of the world starting from the creation of life. While most of the development of the world prior to the creation of life could be explained by the laws of physics, in the new state of affairs, systems were created whose development was not determined solely by the laws of physics. I will try to explain. The new life-bearing systems have a common characteristic: they can reproduce. They pass their traits on to their offspring with a high degree of fidelity. Inherent in the genetic material of the life systems, the DNA, is a detailed plan of the structure of the organism which is passed on to the offspring. I mentioned that the transfer of traits is with *a high degree of fidelity,* by which I mean that *almost* all – but not all – of the genetic information is passed to future generations. Since minuscule random changes take place in the genetic material with each generation, the genetic information is transferred with slight variations. These variations accumulate, eventually leading to significant changes in the offspring.

We can see that tiny changes in the genetic material at any stage of the transfer are a necessary condition for any change, as well as for the development of life systems. Without some alteration in the genetic material, there is no change, and there can be no evolution. We have learned that these

11.   *Scientific American,* September 1999.

changes, these mutations, are random. This means that random changes are a necessary factor for development. According to the Darwinist view, it is chance that determines development and the creation of new species. Without random mutations, the genetic mechanism would work without error, with complete fidelity. If the transfer from generation to generation occurred without random changes, if there was only regularity, then development would not bring about anything new. This is a good reason to think anew about the concepts **randomness** and **chance**.

We generally understand the concept of a random process as one that happens without rules, without any reason or purpose: chaos. In fact, we define randomness negatively. It does not stand alone as an independent entity, but is the absence of something else: the absence of law, the absence of planning and the absence of intention, just as darkness is the absence of light. It is difficult to determine whether a particular process or event is actually random. A meeting between two people on the street of a large city might appear to one of the parties to be a chance encounter, when in fact it was planned by the other. It is also hard to discern the absence of regularity in a particular process since an infinite number of connections between that process and other processes in the world exist. However, quantum theory gives us an example of absolute randomness, which is not connected with prior knowledge or with knowledge of the connections between one particular event and others. Science states that when an atom is in an excited state, it might emit a photon. However, science does not state when the photon will be emitted. It just gives the probability that the photon will be emitted at some time.

We can see that a process is random when two types of causes are missing from it: a scientific cause (the laws of nature) and a spiritual cause, such as human will. Let us return to the development of life on earth. We have seen that according to the modern scientific view, the development of life is determined by random (quantum) mutations. If this is the case, then scientific causality does not determine the development of life, and certain philosophers have concluded from this that we appeared here, on earth, randomly. From this perspective, there is no great difference between the creation of life, which is completely random, and the development of life, which is apparently a chain of random events. We arrive once again at the conclusion that the Darwinist "explanation" of the evolution of life is not scientific, but a (metaphysical) belief in the omnipotence of Her Majesty, Chance.[12]

One could look at the whole situation from a slightly different angle. **When there is a guiding hand,** the system of transferring the genetic information from one generation to the next together with the accumulating changes is the system best suited to improving the species or for the creation of new species. It has been many years since man first learned to nurture plants and animals by intervening in the process of transferring the genetic information, but despite this, it is not within man's the power to create new species. In my opinion, this is God's prerogative, as it is He who directs the development of life.

6. DIVINE PROVIDENCE AND THE EVOLUTION OF LIFE

We will now return to the description of the development of the world as a process that is managed and supervised by God. The stage of the creation of life stands out primarily in the changes in the spiritual world: a new system that sets the development of life in motion was created in the spiritual world, a system that is effectively cut off from the laws of physics. They continue to exist, but they do not determine the behavior and development of living organisms.

The concept of evolution applies to every slow, gradual modification of personality or of reality, physical or spiritual. There are two paradigms of development. Let us begin with the first. This kind of development, which is controlled by the laws of nature, is the developing system itself that is the activating factor in its own development. The Big Bang theory of cosmology describes development of this kind. The laws of physics in general, and specifically Einstein's equations of the general theory of relativity, describe the development of the universe. At the moment of creation, the universe

---

12.   The contrary claim is that there is also environmental influence, which directs development in a particular direction that suits it. But it is important to understand that the environment is also a product of evolution; it developed as life developed. The environment includes plants, an oxygen-rich atmosphere and many changes that were made by human beings.

was entirely concentrated in one minuscule point. Suddenly, an explosion took place, the universe spread out, and galaxies, stars and planets were formed, our earth among them. The laws of physics seemingly describe this process. I say "seemingly" since this description is actually nothing but a program of the research rather than a real physical description. Physics does not know how to describe a universe that is concentrated in one point. The laws of physics that we know are incapable of describing matter or energy concentrated in an extremely small space that contains a huge density of energy. In other words, the stage of the creation of the universe, "the first moment" – or, to be more precise, the time interval close to "time zero" – lies outside the field of the physics that we know. Nevertheless, we are able to imagine that a particular stage in the development of the world is controlled by the laws of physics. This stage includes neither the "first moment" (the creation of the world, as we clarified in an earlier chapter, does not belong to the realm of science at all) nor the present reality, in which man's choices influence development in addition to the laws of physics.

The stage of evolution of life cannot only be described as a derivative of the laws of nature. To aptly describe this stage in the development of the world, we can use human life as a paradigm. Over the course of his life man makes many decisions and choices according to his own will, while the laws of physics, chemistry and biology work alongside them. This paradigm assumes the concept of creation *ex nihilo*, or change due to the action of an external agent that supervises the development as a whole – namely, **divine providence**. A description using the paradigm of human life is just an analogy that can be understood in human terms. When we consider reality as a whole and its creative development, we come to the conclusion that there are not, in fact, two paradigms. There is one singular process of development of the world, and it takes place under divine providence. The closest analogy for us, human beings, is the life of man. The paradigm of development that is controlled solely by the laws of nature may be useful as an approximation to the development of the world at a certain stage and within a limited time-period. However, even as an approximation, this paradigm is not suitable to the stage of evolution of life, which cannot be described as happening **solely** via the laws of nature. Furthermore, we saw earlier that according to the modern scientific viewpoint, the development of life is not determined solely by the laws of nature, but is in the realm of randomness, the realm of the absence of physical lawfulness. From our point of view, it is not chance but divine providence that determines the development of life.

7. CONCLUSION: THE LAW OF EVOLUTION – AN IRRATIONAL BELIEF

In every discussion about the nature of the world and its development – whether there is a materialistic-atheist explanation for the creation of the world and its development, or whether the world was created and is managed by God – two issues arise: the age of the universe and the evolution of life. The first issue, which I do not consider to be of any great importance, has already been addressed in the Preface and Part I. The current chapter deals entirely with the second issue, with the various views of the development of life on earth.

When we consider the world around us, one attribute that stands out is the existence of numerous creations in the world. Only intellectual habit and routine prevent us from being astounded by the varied creations that we see all around us at every moment. There is no better proof for the existence of the creator than the existence of his creations. But this is not the commonly held view. Not long ago, I was in an elevator at the university with a student who was holding a sweet, smiling baby in her arms. I said to the student, "What a miracle!" to which she replied, "Yes, a miracle, but from nature."

This is precisely the point: people truly and honestly believe that there is a scientific explanation for the vast array of wondrous phenomena in the world, especially for the phenomenon of human beings and the human soul. They believe that nature produces all these phenomena, and science explains how nature does it. In this book, we have seen that we cannot logically prove anything meaningful. Therefore, we cannot expect that an explanation for the development of life would be a logical proof. **People claim that a scientific explanation and scientific proof exist** for the development of life as a purely materialist process, devoid of God. A scientific explanation means that there is a scientific theory of the evolution of life on earth. According to this, our appearance on earth and our creation also have a scientific explanation – the laws of nature determine the sequence of events, the chain of causes and effects, from the beginning of life on earth up until the present day. In this scenario, there is no explanation for the beginning of life. It is assumed that it was a random event whose chances of occurring were extremely small – in fact, negligible.

In Chapter Four, we learned about Karl Popper's theory of cognition. According to this theory, all scientific theories are estimates, guesses, hypotheses – though not every guess is a scientific theory. There are certain conditions that a hypothesis must fulfill in order to attain the status of a scientific theory. A scientific theory must be able to be tested by new experiments and must, in principle, be able to be disproved. We asked whether the Darwinist explanation of the evolution of life was a scientific explanation that meets these criteria, and **showed that Darwin's theory does not, in fact, have scientific status.** Had we wished to appeal to an expert in the field, what greater expert than the very person who came up with the theory of cognition, Karl Popper? As I already cited in section 2 of this chapter, Popper states the following:

> There exists no law of evolution, only the historical fact that plants and animals change, or more precisely, that they have changed. The idea of a law which determines the direction and the character of evolution is a typical nineteenth-century mistake, arising out of the general tendency to ascribe to the 'Natural Law' the functions traditionally ascribed to God.[13]

The mechanism of natural selection does not provide a scientific explanation for the evolution of life; this explanation is a metaphysical claim. There is no scientific explanation or logical proof for the development of life on earth. There is only the belief that natural selection is the exclusive cause of the development of life. This belief is based on neither life experience nor common sense. We have no experience of any act of creation by the forces of nature, and this is all the more true in the case of such complex and sophisticated creatures as human beings.

Thus, we are talking about a belief, a metaphysical supposition, that natural selection is the sole cause of the development of life on earth. While this is an irrational belief, Judaism actually provides us with a rational explanation *and sees in the Creator the cause of the existence of a creature.* I would emphasize that this is not a conflict between the scientific approach and

---

13. *Conjectures and Refutations*, 340.

267

An Analogy for the Development of Life

This can be made clearer by using the following analogy. In Chapter Three, section 8, I brought various examples of systems navigated by different agents. In example C, I presented a spaceship navigated by a person inside it. The person inside the spaceship determines its movements, and hence its path is determined by a series of decisions made by this man. In contrast, in example D, a spaceship fitted with a Geiger counter, the spaceship's maneuvers and its deviations from its path, which is determined by the laws of mechanics, are caused by random events, such as the actions of cosmic particles.

Now let us compare the paths of these two spaceships. Every disturbance by a single cosmic particle causes Spaceship D to deviate from its course. Likewise, each decision made by the person navigating Spaceship C, every action of his, causes a deviation of that spaceship from its course. If we were to observe a particular deviation of each of these two spaceships, we would not be able to distinguish which of the two was controlled by an intelligent creature. However, if we were to look at the totality of deviations of the two spaceships, we would easily be able to discern that the movements of Spaceship D are random, while Spaceship C behaves in a decisive manner and makes purposeful movements.

This is just an analogy. How can it help us understand the message of this chapter? Spaceship C represents the world managed by an intelligent entity, a world that is subject to divine providence. Spaceship D represents an imaginary world that exists without the supervision of any intelligent entity. What represents the theory of evolution, the belief in evolution controlled by natural selection? This is represented by the belief that if we place a sophisticated device inside the spaceship, a device that can reproduce and transmit its qualities to its offspring, and if we wait a long time, then, in the end, the spaceship will start to make purposeful movements. This is the belief that if we were to wait long enough, then the first primitive creature, whose appearance cannot be explained, would eventually be capable, as a result of purely random factors, to develop into man, with absolutely no involvement from any intelligent cause. In other words, a belief (an absurd one, in my opinion) that all the purposefulness that we see in the living world, our free wills, the great masterpieces of art — all these are the result of randomness.

religious belief. Rather, this is a conflict between two beliefs – belief versus belief, rational versus irrational belief.

But this is not the end of the story. Even within the metaphysical claim that the development of life is solely the result of natural selection, there is a problem explaining what can be called "evolutionary ascent" – namely, the formation of higher forms of living organisms from lower forms over a long period of time.

At the start of evolution, only primitive organisms existed, from which highly complex animals developed – the most complex, of course, being man himself. Darwin's explanation can be formulated as follows: Evolutionary ascent exists because, of all life forms, only the fittest survive. But this can only be an explanation for evolutionary ascent if we add the assumption that the higher life forms tend to be fitter than the lower ones. However, there is no justification for this assumption within the theory of evolution, as we have seen above. Ultimately, Darwin reached the conclusion that evolutionary ascent could not be explained by the theory of evolution. On December 4, 1872, he wrote to his friend, Alpheus Hyatt: "After long reflection, I cannot avoid the conviction that no innate tendency to progressive development exists."[14]

What are we talking about here? Darwin is trying to ascribe to nature the attribute of progress, and can find no reasoning to back this up. This is actually an attempt to ascribe a human or divine character to nature. The concept of progress, just like the concepts of planning and creation, belong to the divine spiritual world, and the idea of ascribing spiritual concepts to nature and its laws is odd. This is precisely what the theory of evolution does.

After all that has been said here, it is clear that only complete ignorance would cause someone to assert that any logical or scientific arguments support the claim that nature plans and brings about progressive development of life on earth, that nature produces new species, including man and his soul.

---

14. Quoted from *Wonderful Life*, 257.

CHAPTER SEVEN

Human History

1. THE CREATION OF MAN

O N THE SIXTH DAY OF CREATION MAN WAS CREATED AND a new and important stage in the history of the world began. In Chapter One, section 7, we quoted a *midrash* that likens the creation of man to a revolution. The ministering angels saw creation as a perfect composition that would be ruined by man's involvement. God, who had other ideas, saw creation as a work requiring perfection, as the verse states, "which God created to make," and the only being capable of perfecting it is man (according to Rabbi Kook, this is not an act of perfection but of completion).

Free will is the revolutionary attribute that characterizes man. Until this point, only God had a will, and now a creature has been created that, like God, possesses this quality. "And God created man in His own image, in the image of God He created him; male and female He created them" (Genesis 1:27). But free will is not the only similarity between man and God. In Chapter 1, section 12, we came to the conclusion that our world can be presented as being comprised of a spiritual world and a physical world, with God operating the connection between these worlds and supervising them. We described this structure using the following diagram.

Man's soul works similarly. Man, like God, uses the spiritual world as an operating system for a particular material entity. This material entity could be either external objects or man's own body.

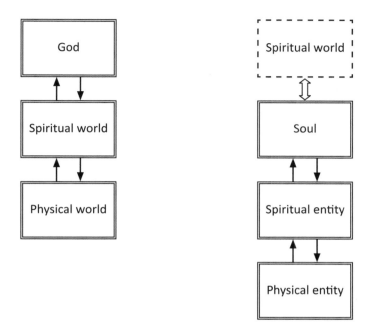

Man's uniqueness lies in the fact that **he is able to connect to places in the divine spiritual world** and make them a part of his own spiritual world. We have already discussed this (in Chapter Four, section 6), but it is such an important topic that it is worth reiterating.

Man's ability to connect to parts of the divine spiritual world is a wondrous phenomenon. The routine of our day-to-day lives prevents us from noticing how astonishing this is. There are two ways in which man connect to the spiritual world – a primary, direct connection and a secondary, indirect connection. The divine spiritual world includes, among other things, the laws of nature, which are part of God's operating system. God reveals the laws of nature to man gradually, to a certain approximation and in accordance with man's level of knowledge and intellectual ability at the time of the revelation. This revelation does not occur for humanity as a whole, but to a particular person, a particular scientist. This connection does not happen as a voluntary action by the scientist, but is an example of divine providence.

Once a new theory, such as the theory of relativity, is made public, it becomes part of the spiritual world that is accessible to human beings (Karl

Popper's world three). Now, every person with the requisite level of scientific knowledge is able to introduce the theory of relativity into his own spiritual world. This is an example of a secondary connection to the spiritual world. It is worth pointing out that the ability to connect to the spiritual world, either in a primary or in a secondary way, is what differentiates man from all other creatures on earth. *While every person has a part of the accessible spiritual world, people differ from one another in the quality and quantity of their own spiritual worlds.*

Man and his soul have a connection with God who created him, and this is where man's creativity, arguably man's most important quality that makes him similar to God, stems from. The meaning of man's life is chiefly expressed in his creations and innovations.

> When God created the world, He provided an opportunity for the work of his hands – man – to participate in His creation.
> (Rabbi Soloveitchik, Halakhic Man, 101)

> If a man wishes to attain the rank of holiness, he must become a creator of worlds. If a man never creates, never brings into being anything new, anything original, then he cannot be holy unto his God .... The most fundamental principle of all is that man must create himself. It is this idea that Judaism introduces into the world. (Ibid., 108–109)

Opportunities for creation in our lives are few and far between, but the desire for creation itself bestows meaning on the life of man.

2. DIVINE REVELATION AND FAITH

The most important event in human history happened many years ago in our part of the world, in the Middle East, specifically in the Land of Canaan. I am talking about the encounter between the People of Israel and God. The Bible documents this event – or, to be more precise, this series of events – in great detail. In his book, *God, Man and History*, Eliezer Berkovits examines the authenticity of this account. I do not intend to repeat all his arguments here, but I would like to add my thoughts on the subject.

Every encounter with God is a spiritual event, and leaves no material remnants in its wake. Every encounter with God is a one-off, unique event, the importance of which cannot be overstated, and each encounter brings with it its own unique message. However, the authenticity of the very fact of an encounter with God is strengthened with each additional encounter, and there have been a large number of them.

What were human beings supposed to do in order to immortalize these events for humanity? First, they had to document every encounter with God, and that is exactly what they did. The Bible documents each and every encounter. Clearly this was a necessary step, but it is not sufficient. There was absolutely no guarantee that the publication of the book alone would place God in people's consciousness for all future generations. To this end, other steps needed to be taken.

The Torah itself emphasizes that its message is not only for those who received it at that moment, but for all future generations.

> Neither with you only do I make this covenant and this oath; but with him that stands here with us this day before the Lord our God, and also with him that is not here with us this day. (Deuteronomy 29:13–14)

We can understand from this that inherent in the divine plan was the task of introducing the word of God to the spiritual world, not only of those who were present at Mount Sinai, but also to all future generations.

We have already mentioned that human beings possess a wondrous quality – the ability to connect to the divine spiritual world in two ways: a primary, direct connection and a secondary, indirect connection. Our ancestors, the prophets and anyone who was present at the revelation at Mount Sinai had a primary connection, while we are able to have a secondary connection. It is worth stressing that the connection to the spiritual world is not only a cognitive act, it also has a much deeper, conscious and emotional aspect to it. A person listening to a new piece of music has a conscious and emotional experience that enriches his spiritual world. He is able to feel and experience the piece, often to the same degree as the composer feels it, and sometimes at an even deeper level.

In addition to the divine message, any contact with God rocks the soul. The prophet Ezekiel describes an encounter with God thus: "... and I fell on my face. Then spirit entered into me, and set me upon my feet; and He spoke with me ..." (Ezekiel, 3:23–24). An encounter with God creates an intimate, direct and immediate feeling of deep faith. When the People of Israel felt God's presence at the parting of the Red Sea, they reacted in the following way: "Israel saw the great work which the Lord did in Egypt, and the people feared the Lord; and they believed in the Lord, and in His servant Moses" (Exodus 14:31). The shock of the encounter gave rise to an experience of faith. But what about those who were "not here with us this day"? Their faith is acquired through a secondary connection to the divine spiritual world. How?

Judaism provides the framework for connecting to the divine spiritual world. If we were to treat religious texts simply as reading material, then we would merely acquire new information and nothing else, in exactly the same way that studying historical documents enriches our wealth of knowledge. But this has nothing to do with feelings or religious experiences. It is nothing like the experience induced by a work of art, which might affect a person's soul beyond the moment that it was produced. How, and with what tools, does the Jewish tradition achieve this goal? The short answer to this question is the Jewish way of life. "Upon our retiring and arising, we will discuss Your decrees and we will rejoice with the words of Your Torah and with your commandments for all eternity. For they are our life and the length of our days, and about them we will meditate day and night . . ." (from the blessings before the recitation of the *Shema* in the daily evening prayer service). The Torah encompasses the believing Jew's life from childhood through old age. We learn from the first paragraph of the *Shema* that love of God is expressed first of all in the diligent and persistent education of one's children: "You shall love the Lord your God with all your heart, with all your soul and with all your might. Let these matters that I command you today be upon your heart. Teach them thoroughly to your children and speak of them while you sit in your home, while you walk on the way, when you retire and when you arise" (Deuteronomy 6:5–7).

Children born into observant Jewish families are immersed in an atmosphere that brings them closer to God. Torah study is both an act of learning and an extremely important religious commandment. In a sense, Jews are always part of a divine framework. When they get up in the morning, they recite the "Modeh Ani" prayer. They then wash their hands and make the appropriate blessing. They pray three times a day; eat and recite the grace after meals. Day in, day out, they are in God's company, and when the week comes to an end, Shabbat arrives. Even if they are not constantly feeling inspired and enlightened, fulfilling the commandments helps to keep them in a "state of preparedness."

This mechanism of passing down the original revelation to future generations is not a human invention, but is part of God's plan. At Mount Sinai this spiritual mechanism was already planned: "but with him that stands here with us this day before the Lord our God, and also with him that is not here with us this day." It is the mission of the Jewish people to pass on God's word for all the generations.

The story is told of the German Emperor Frederick who once asked, at a meeting of his generals, for proof of God's existence, but demanded that the answer be brief. His General of Cavalry promptly replied, "The Jews, Your Majesty!"

The subject of this part of the book is human history. To gain a deep understanding of the subject it is worth looking at it from various different perspectives. We will therefore devote the next two sections to a critique of secular approaches to history, after which we will return to the story of the development of humanity from the Jewish perspective.

3. HUMAN HISTORY FROM A SECULAR PERSPECTIVE — NO DIRECTIONALITY AND NO PURPOSE

The secular view of history is not uniform. We can identify two opposing tendencies. According to one fairly common view, one can attribute lawfulness and directionality to history. History has its own internal significance and internal, inherent laws, specific to it, and we can attribute the concept of progress to it. One can talk about the "law of history" meaning that "history will judge us." We learned in Chapter Three, section 4, about a similar view, the deification or idolization of nature, but these are in fact not different views at all since history is also a part of nature. The tendency to ascribe to history human or divine spiritual concepts is, as we have discussed, quite common. This view is very clearly expressed in the writings of Hegel, Marx, Engels and their successors, though it is not based on any logic or reason and has no scientific basis, as its supporters claim.

However, there is another secular viewpoint that denies any directionality, lawfulness or meaning in historical processes. Karl Popper, in his books

The Poverty of Historicism and *The Open Society and Its Enemies*, convincingly criticizes the first approach, the one that idolizes history. Without doubt, within the context of a secular approach, this critique is consistent and well-founded. Jacques Monod, too, in his book *Chance and Necessity*, reaches the conclusion that one cannot find meaning in human history. A world view that does not include God will consistently lead to conclusions of the meaninglessness of human history and the absurdity of life.

Since we have two opposing secular world views, let us look at them one by one. Marxism expresses the most developed secular notion of lawfulness in history. In 1859, Marx wrote: "The mode of production in material life determines the general character of the social, political, and intellectual processes of life. It is not the consciousness of men which determines their existence; it is, on the contrary, their social existence which determines their consciousness."[1]

This hypothesis, which rose to the level of the "Law of History," was later called Historical Materialism. Historical development is determined by economic conditions, and in particular by the development of means of production. We do not need to go into the nitty-gritty of historical materialism as it is formulated in the writings of Marx and his successors. What is important to us is the claim that there is a scientific theory that maintains that a law of history exists that determines all past historical development, as well as enabling us to predict future development.

This is where Karl Popper's critique comes into play. The very same arguments that led to the conclusion that there is no law of evolution (see the previous chapter) are also valid for the non-existence of the law of history. Any scientific theory must be tested by facts or experiments. In order to form a preference for one hypothesis over another, there must be a possibility of rejecting the incorrect hypothesis. However, with history, including the historical natural sciences such as geological history, the facts that are at our disposal are limited and we cannot repeat them at will. A hypothesis that cannot be tested by new facts is not a scientific theory. Therefore, it is impossible to establish a scientific historical theory that explains the past and can predict future development. We will return to Karl Popper's arguments in section 7, which discusses the Jewish analysis of historical processes.

---

1. Preface to Contribution to the *Critique of Political Economy*.

In the next section, we will look at the dialectical approach, which is very common in discussions about the nature of historical development. At the basis of the approach lies the premise that contradictions are the driving force, the source of developments both in history and in human thought, and as such are to be welcomed. I would not be fulfilling my duty properly if I did not touch on the dialectical approach, which comes to us from several sources such as Hegel, Marx and Engels.

4. THE DIALECTICAL THEORY OF DEVELOPMENT[2]

I mentioned that the development of the world is accompanied by an ongoing process of freedom from dependence on the laws of nature. At the stage of the evolution of life, there is no law that determines the development of the animate world. The historical development was determined by God, with the divine plan being implemented by human beings. Just as there is no law of evolution, there is also no law of history.

One cannot find anywhere in the writings of philosophers a formulation of the laws of history that is similar to the scientific formulation of the laws of nature. However, there is a great deal of discussion about the *dialectical* nature of the laws of history. Due to the prevalence of the use of dialectics, and because of the great appreciation that different thinkers have for dialectics, Jewish thinkers among them, we should also give some attention to this topic. The word *dialectics* expresses the art of argument through the use of logic. In the modern sense coined by Hegel, it is a view that proposes that the human intellect, nature and history develop in a dialectical triad: *thesis, antithesis, synthesis.*

First, there is a particular idea, theory or movement that can be called a *thesis.* This thesis may give rise to an objection, since, as with all things in our world, it also has limitations and weak points. The opposing idea, or the opposing movement, is called the *antithesis* because it is against the *thesis.* The conflict between the thesis and the antithesis continues until a solution

---

2. In this section we will be aided by Popper's analysis in his article "What Is Dialectic?" (in *Conjectures and Refutations,* 312). If the reader finds this section, or parts of it, difficult to understand, he/she may skip to the next section without losing the thread of the discussion.

is reached, which, in a sense, is supposed to be preferable to both the thesis and the antithesis while preserving the advantages of each and avoiding their pitfalls. This solution, the third stage, is called the *synthesis*. Once the synthesis is reached, it may then become the first stage of a new dialectical triad. This happens if the solution has weak points of its own. In such a case, opposition will arise once more, such that the synthesis can be described as a new thesis that gives rise to a new antithesis. Thus the dialectical triad reaches a new and higher level, with the production of a new synthesis.

The trial-and-error method is somewhat similar to the dialectical triad. In a way, the trial-and-error method rests on the foundation of scientific study. When a scientist looks into a particular problem he suggests a solution or theory. He accepts this theory as a temporary measure and tries, empirically or theoretically, to test his guess from all sides and to find out what its weak points are. As a result of this process the, scientist can refute his original guess and suggest a new one in its place, which will take into account all the drawbacks of the first guess, and so on and so forth.

The dialectical triad might be helpful in describing the various processes both in historical developments and intellectual developments, but we must be cautious about taking the images and metaphors of the dialecticians too seriously. For example, take the dialectical saying, "A thesis produces its own antithesis." In fact, it is our analytical stance that "produces" the antithesis, and when the analytical connection is missing, as happens from time to time, no antithesis is produced. Similarly, we should avoid saying that it is the "conflict" between the thesis and the antithesis that "produces" the synthesis. The conflict is in the realm of thoughts, and it is part of the intellectual process. The history of human thought contains many examples of conflicts that came to nothing. Even when a synthesis has been reached, it is not accurate to say that it preserves the good parts of the thesis and the antithesis. Such a description is undoubtedly wrong since in addition to the old ideas (the thesis and the antithesis) that the synthesis "preserves," it must also include a new idea – created from nothing – which that cannot be reduced to the earlier stages of the development. Without the innovative element, development is almost nonexistent. In other words, the synthesis, generally, must be much more than a structure built solely from the thesis and antithesis. If we take all of this into account, we can say that, even if it does fit, it is doubtful that a dialectical explanation can develop thought through the suggestion that the synthesis must be built from ideas contained in the thesis and the antithesis.

However, the key misunderstanding and confusion arises from the way the dialecticians talk about contradictions. It is true that contradictions fulfill an important role in the history of human thought, just like the critical method. This is because the essence of criticism is identifying a particular contradiction within the theory being reviewed or between the theory and an alternative theory that fits better with experience. However, there is a huge difference between the claim that we should search for contradictions in order to get rid of them, and the dialectician's claim that there is no need to avoid productive contradictions. They even claim that it is both impossible and unnecessary to avoid contradictions since they exist naturally throughout the world.

It should be clear that if we agree not to avoid contradictions but rather to leave them in a theory that is intended, as it were, to reflect a reality that contains such contradictions, then this kind of theory would contain everything, and hence would actually contain nothing. One can logically prove that if a theory has contradictory claims, then the conclusions that are derived from it will be completely arbitrary. For example, we can prove the following statements: *The temperature in the center of the sun is zero degrees Celsius, Dialectics is the law of the development of the world*, and *There are 133 dimensions in the world*. In short, anything can be derived from a theory that contains contradictions, and such a theory is utterly useless as a theory. The acceptance of contradictions means the end of the critical approach and the end of science.

A dialectician can argue that the proof above is based on formal logic, while dialectics is an important part of a new, different logic. However, in reality, there is no dialectical logic. Logic is a theory of deduction and there is no reason to believe that dialectics has anything in common with deduction. On the contrary, the things that dialecticians say are known for their obscurity and lack of clarity, and this is another of the hazards of dialectics. It is extremely easy to give a dialectical explanation for all kinds of developments in nature. For example, one of the processes for which dialecticians delight in providing a dialectical explanation is the growth of a plant. They identify the seed with the thesis, the plant that grows from the seed with the antithesis, and the seeds that the plant later produces as the synthesis.

Proof that if a theory contains contradictions, it contains everything

Here is the proof. The following statement is made up of two claims, A and B: A v B (claim A and/or claim B) is true if and only if at least one of its components is true. For example, let us consider the statement: **Today it is raining and/or today it is not raining.** This statement is true since one of the components is true. Now, let us suppose that our theory contains both the claim **p** and the claim **not-p** – in other words, it includes two claims that contradict each other. From the truth of claim **p**, it follows that the statement **p v q** is true, since one of the components is true, where claim **q** could be any arbitrary claim, such as one of those mentioned above. Therefore, the statement **p v q** is true. Now, from the truth of the claim **not-p** it follows that the sub-statement – or arbitrary claim – **q** is true. Therefore, it has been proven that when a theory contains the contradiction **p** and **not-p**, the arbitrary statement **q** must be true.

In arithmetic, from the statement 1 = 0, which contains an internal contradiction, an equation between two arbitrary numbers, a and b, follows. All we have to do is to multiply both sides of the equation by "a − b," to arrive at a − b = 0. Then (by adding b to both sides) we come to a = b.

Thus they say that all development that takes place in stages is dialectical development.

Dialecticians also like to use the word *negation* and the phrase *negation of the negation*. Accordingly, the germination of the plant is the negation of the seed, since the seed ceases to be a seed when the plant starts to grow, and the formation of a new seed is described as a negation of the negation – a new start at a higher level. But this is simply wordplay. Examples taken from the field of mathematics are even worse. Here is a famous example brought by Engels:

The law of the higher synthesis ... is commonly used in mathematics. The negative (−a) multiplied by itself becomes a^2, i.e. the negation of the negation has accomplished a new synthesis.[3]

---

3. F. Engels, *Anti-Dühring*.

One does not need to think particularly hard to realize the absurdity and arbitrariness of this example. If we assume that the letter **a** represents the thesis, and −**a** represents the antithesis, then we can expect that the negation of the negation is −(−**a**), which is **a**, which cannot be described as a "higher synthesis," but is identical to the original thesis, **a**. And anyway, why should the synthesis be calculated by multiplying the antithesis by itself, and not by adding the thesis to the antithesis (the result of which would be zero)? And in what sense is a^2 "higher" than a or −a? (Certainly not in the quantitative sense, since if $a = \frac{1}{2}$, then $a^2 = \frac{1}{4}$.) This example shows us the extreme arbitrariness of the implementation of dialectical ideas.

Hegel believed that he had discovered lawfulness in human history. He claimed that the forces that drive the development of history are the dialectical "contradictions," "negations" and "negations of negations." Marx and Engels adopted Hegel's approach. Engels wrote:

> What is therefore the negation of the negation? An extremely general . . . law of development of Nature, history and thought; a law, which . . . holds good in the animal and plant kingdom, in mathematics, in history, and in philosophy.[4]

Here we have an "extremely general law of development of Nature, history and thought"! The dialecticians claim that the world is full of contradictions, full of opposing facts. The world has a "polar" structure. As an example, they point to the existence of a positive electrical charge and a negative electrical charge. But there is no meaning at all in the claim that the positive charge and the negative charge contradict each other. A contradiction would be if the same object had both a positive and a negative charge simultaneously. Then it would both repel and attract negatively-charged objects.[5]

---

4. Ibid., Part I, "Dialectics: Negation of the Negation."

5. Apparently quantum mechanics provides us with an example of "dialectical" phenomena. An atom can be in a state of Energy E_1 or Energy E_2 as in the classical theory. But in quantum mechanics an atom can also be in two states simultaneously:

$$A\phi_1 + B\phi_2 = \Psi$$

But it is important to understand that the claim that an atom is in one state and another is only a figurative expression of the fact that other than the states described by wave functions ϕ_1 and ϕ_2 there are Ψ-type states that are not identical either to 1 or 2, these are other, superposition-type, states of states ϕ_1 and ϕ_2. It would be true to say that an atom can be in state ϕ_1, state ϕ_2, as well as in Ψ-type states.

In conclusion, one cannot say that nature, history or science develop according to the laws of dialectics. Just as there is no law of evolution of life, there is also no law of history. It is divine providence that determines the development of the world. The most that we can say about dialectics is that it can sometimes be used in order to describe, in an entirely qualitative way, a particular development. I can only note that, unfortunately, the dialectic concoction of Hegel, Marx and Engels has penetrated to some degree into Jewish thought. I have already mentioned the excessive influence of the philosophies of Plato and Aristotle on medieval Jewish thinkers and the influence of Immanuel Kant that is still felt today. The fact that these influences are greater than that of the Jewish sources is simply unbearable.

It is worth noting that adherence to dialectical materialism had a disastrous effect on science, an effect that can be compared with the persecution perpetrated by the church in the early stages of the development of science. For the sake of dialectics, Engels himself had to deny the second law of thermodynamics and the idea of natural selection. For the sake of these same principles, Zhdanov, one of the leaders of the Soviet Union, ordered Russian thinkers to denounce the Copenhagen School and quantum theory because they contradicted dialectical materialism. During the same period, Lysenko accused Soviet biologists who were studying genetics of deviating from the Marxist-Leninist theory. The Soviet regime cruelly persecuted these biologists, who were sent to concentration camps and executed.

5. THE NON-DETERMINISM OF THE WORLD THAT IS OPEN TO THE WILLS OF GOD AND MAN

The idea of the non-determinism of the world, that not everything is pre-determined, is fairly difficult to understand. People often simply pay lip-service to the fact of non-determinism, since if it were not the case, then how could there be free will? But deep in their consciousness, they believe in a deterministic world that is fixed in advance. These people paint the following picture: God, who is above time, looks down from the lofty heavens and sees everything that has happened and everything that will happen. This may be compared to being on top of a mountain or in an airplane, from which we can see many places at the same time. There is a hidden assumption here that the axis of time is similar to the axis of space.

From the theory of relativity we also tend to feel that the axis of time is the fourth coordinate in addition to the three spatial coordinates – length, width and height. Every event can be ascribed spatial and temporal coordinates. Put more simply, in order to pinpoint an event, we must state where it happened (spatial coordinates) and when it happened (temporal coordinates.) Hence, anyone who is beyond time and space – God – can see all the events in the world "simultaneously,"[6] the past and the future together.

Here I would like to stress that one who uses this kind of image is already starting from an assumption, consciously or not, that there is determinism in the world. Incidentally, the theory of relativity is an absolutely deterministic theory, so the use of this kind of picture with the theory of relativity is consistent. This is not so in the case of the real world. The image of God looking out over the world from a place beyond time and space is rather arbitrary. Anyone who uses this kind of argument proves nothing because in his picture – observation of the world from a standpoint external to it – there is already an inherent assumption regarding the determinism of the world.

I must state clearly that the claim that everything is pre-determined not only contradicts man's free will but also God's omnipotence and the freedom of His will: it is not just man who cannot change things that were pre-determined at the time of creation – God is also unable to do this. Here we come to an important point: the use of the word *future* may be misleading. When we talk about knowledge of the future by man or God, and when people say that it is impossible that God cannot know the future down to the smallest detail, they are assuming (perhaps unknowingly) that such a thing as the future really exists.

But this is not the case. In our world, open as it is to the wills of God and man, there is a significant difference between the **past** and the **future**. Everything that has **happened** is already fixed and cannot be changed. The possibility of changing the past contradicts logic. Let us imagine that a person uses a time machine to travel into the past, where he meets his mother and prevents her from marrying his father, thereby preventing his own birth. The logical contradiction lies in the fact that his interference has caused a situation in which he and his entire life history are impossible,

---

6.   The word *simultaneously* is written in quotation marks since it is meaningless when we are talking outside the scope of time.

in which his mother did not give birth to him, but he is alive. Our past and the world's past cannot be changed. This is in no way a restriction of God's omnipotence. There is no reason to attribute attributes to God that contradict logic. Likewise, we are not limiting God's omnipotence by saying that He cannot draw a triangle with four sides.

In contrast to the **past**, which is fixed by all the prior development, the future is open to the involvement of God and man. We tend to think that most future development has already been determined, that there is a fixed framework – the laws of physics, genetics etc. – and with this framework in the background, God's and man's involvement cause gradual, evolutionary changes. However, we have seen (see Chapter Five, section 1) that the world is contingent – it exists conditionally. The contingency of the world means that it cannot exist even for one moment without God's will. The world's existence and development are dependent on God; the laws of nature were created by God, and their existence is neither necessary nor self-evident. Earlier, we quoted Rabbi Soloveitchik saying that "**the world exists because it is nurtured by some of the infinite being of God.**" If the world is contingent, then our situation as human beings is all the more so.

Only if we assume that all development is pre-ordained by deterministic laws can we talk about a pre-determined future. But we can use this assumption (which is always just an approximation) in straightforward, simplified situations, such as the movements of the heavenly bodies in the solar system. In general, the concept of the future is not defined, and it does not derive causally and unequivocally from everything that has taken place in the past and the present. The development of the world is a sequence of new events that were not fixed at the creation of the world. "The Lord saw that the wickedness of man was great in the earth, and that every imagination of the thoughts of his heart was only evil continually. And it repented the Lord that He had made man on the earth, and it grieved Him at His heart" (Genesis 6:5–6). "The earth was corrupt before God, and the earth was filled with violence" (Ibid., 6:11). These verses clearly attest to the fact that this reality that came about was not latently hidden in creation, but was a result of human beings' actions and their free will.

"If you walk in My statutes and keep My commandments and do them; then I will give your rains in their season, and the land shall yield her produce and the trees of the field shall yield their fruit . . . . But if you will not hearken unto Me, and will not do all these commandments . . . . I also will do this unto you: I will appoint terror over you . . . . And your strength shall be spent in vain; for your land shall not yield her produce, neither shall the trees of the land yield their fruit" Leviticus 26:3–2). The Torah states, here and in many other places, that what happens in the **future** is dependent on the actions of human beings, and these actions are the results of their free will.

If this is the case, then we can conclude that the word *future* does not express any entity that exists in our world. There is only a changing reality. In principle, nothing is definite about what is going to happen in the next moment, neither on a personal nor a global level. On a personal level, we know that every moment in our lives could be our last. Both the existence of the world and the existence of time itself are constantly dependent on God's will. All that we can say is that the world, and human beings within it, are constantly changing and developing and that the result of this development is the future. But there is no certainty about what will happen in the world even at the very next moment – this is dependent on God's will, on man's choices, on this moment and on the moments preceding it. Therefore, any attempt to present the future as something that is defined and exists, as something that can be predicted, is doomed to failure. This does not contradict the fact of God's design or God's plan, as we will see in the next section.

6. EVERYTHING IS FORESEEN, YET THE FREEDOM OF CHOICE IS GIVEN

Now we will look at the issue of "Everything is foreseen, yet the freedom of choice is given," which is at the heart of human history. While human beings are the ones who carry out historical processes, it is God who designs and directs them. Divine providence is one of the key principles of Judaism. God interferes in human affairs and manages history. He is the God of history. The first of the Ten Commandments is "I am the Lord your God, who brought you out from the land of Egypt, out of the house of bondage" (Exodus 20:2). Another important principle is the fact that human beings were given free will. Human history is the story of how God deals with human beings who have been given free will and who are God's partners in the formation of history.

Philosophers have tried to solve the problem that, in their opinion, is inherent in the contradiction between the two parts of the saying: "**Everything is foreseen**" and "**freedom of choice is given.**" The first part seems to express absolute determinism, while the second part expresses the non-determinism related to man's free will. The first part apparently expresses the power, omnipotence and omniscience of divine providence. If God knows everything that is going to happen, if everything is foreseen, then where does man's free will fit in?

I believe that at least some of the above claims derive from foreign sources, as I have already mentioned (Chapter Four, section 3), and not from the Torah. The idea that God's omnipotence also includes omniscience does not come from the Torah at all. Furthermore, the Torah stresses in numerous places that its prophecy is always conditional upon human actions. In the previous section, we saw that all reality is contingent, conditional, dependent on God's will and human actions. From here, it becomes clear that the concept of the future is not defined as an entity that already exists at the present time, an entity that can be either known or not known. In contrast to the past, which has already been fixed by the development that occurred prior to the present, the future is open to both human and divine involvement. Put simply, I would say that it is impossible to know something that does not exist.

If this is the case, how can we understand the phrase "everything is foreseen"? In my opinion, this is talking about the divine plan. "Everything is foreseen" means that sooner or later, in one way or another, "the counsel of the Lord will stand," with the method and time of implementation being dependent on man's actions and choices. "Everything is foreseen" does not cancel out our free will. On the contrary: human beings are active partners with God in the building of the future. Whether the redemption comes "at the appointed time or sooner" depends on us, human beings. It is man who carries out historical processes, but under God's supervision. The real secret, which we cannot understand, is how God implements His plan despite all people's differing wills and desires.

Human history has meaning, a purpose and a goal – a view that is in stark contrast to the secular view, which asserts that human history is absurd and meaningless (see Chapter 6, section 4 and Chapter 7, section 3). Divine providence determines the direction of human development and its goal. In Judaism, God is the God of history, and His commandments have historical significance. Man is the partner of the Creator in the molding of humanity, and there is a reciprocal relationship between God and man in the process of human development. However, we still cannot explain how humanity is pointed in a particular direction towards the goal that has been pre-determined by God when human beings have absolute free will. Rabbi Akiva's paradox, "**Everything is foreseen yet the freedom of choice is given**," is not about God's knowledge of every detail of the future versus the individual's free will. As we have already stated, it is impossible to know something that does not exist. **The secret lies in the fact that history develops in a defined direction toward a goal set in advance by God, even though human beings have differing and sometimes even contradictory wills. The secret is how God manages to direct and manage historical processes.**

The story of Joseph and his brothers from the book of Genesis provides an example of pre-planned development despite the realization of contradictory human desires. Some commentators see the Israelites' exile from Canaan to the land of Goshen in Egypt as part of the divine plan. In Canaan, the Israelite minority faced the danger of assimilation into the idol-worshipping Canaanite culture, while in Goshen they could develop with only minimal contact with the local population. Individuals, each with his own desires and his own free will, carried out this plan. These desires were not always good. Joseph behaved arrogantly towards his brothers. Joseph's brothers wanted to kill him and in the end they sold him to Ishmaelites. Similarly, Potiphar's wife did not have good intentions either. The Bible is full of such examples. Nevertheless, men and women brought God's plan to fruition with their own hands.

To summarize: the future of the world and of humanity was not set at the beginning of days. The future of the world is constantly **dependent** on God's will and human action. **Freedom of choice is given** to human beings in their role as God's partners in the building of humanity's future, while the fulfillment of God's counsel, of the divine plan, is assured: **everything is foreseen.**

Although the explanation that I have given here contains no contradiction between *everything is foreseen* and the *freedom of choice is given*, a mystery remains: How does divine providence actually work behind the scenes? We can assume that this is where the boundary lies between that which we can understand and that which we cannot, the boundary of human understanding. I will state once more that my explanation of Rabbi Akiva's famous saying, "Everything is foreseen yet the freedom of choice is given," contains no contradiction. Why is it so important to emphasize the fact that there is no contradiction in this statement, which expresses the essence of historical development? This saying actually expresses the two fundamental principles of Judaism – divine providence and free will. Historical processes take place when these two principles exist, and a contradiction between then would raise doubts about our most important basic concepts. Therefore, it was crucial to explain the lack of contradiction in Rabbi Akiva's saying. Many Jewish philosophers have tackled this saying and tried to show that it contains no contradiction.[7]

As we discussed in the previous section, there is another way of thinking that welcomes the contradictions and sees them as the source of development both in history and in human thought. This thinking, which comes to us from foreign sources, is called dialectics, or the dialectical approach, and we have already shown the inconsistency inherent in it.

7. TWO APPROACHES TO THE HISTORY OF HUMANITY

A new reality came into being with the creation of man. Man's free will started to be a factor in the development of the world. To a certain extent, one can see the new reality as a continuation of the trend to "release the world from the tyranny of the laws of nature." Let me explain what I am talking about.

As we have mentioned numerous times, the principle of divine providence lies at the basis of Judaism. Divine providence has determined the development of the world since the moment of creation. God runs the world, and its development is carried out by an operating system that exists in the spiritual world. This system develops and changes, and at the various stages of the development of the world, it adapts itself, in a manner of speaking, to that particular stage.

In the first stage of the development of the world, a stage that lasted from the creation of the world up until but not including the creation of life, the laws of physics are the principal factor in the development. At least this is

---

7. See my review of these attempts in my book, *Creation Ex Nihilo*, Chapter Four.

what modern science seems to say. This means that the laws of physics are the main tool that God uses to supervise the world. I should point out here that just as with every stage in the world's development, the laws of nature are not the sole factor in its development. They are merely one of the tools at God's disposal.

The second stage of the world's development is from the creation of life up to, but not including, the creation of man. At this stage, the laws of physics have a purely preserving, conserving role. In the animal and plant kingdoms, a physical (and chemical) mechanism is responsible for the precise transfer of genetic information, located in the genetic code, from one generation to the next. However, an exact transfer of this information, without any deviations or changes, precludes the possibility of any development. Therefore, all developments in the animal kingdom happen outside the framework of the laws of physics and chemistry. However, not only is the **development** of the animal kingdom not tethered to the laws of physics, but the **behavior** of animals also does not comply solely with the laws of physics. Animals operate in a goal-oriented, teleological manner.

Alongside scientific causality, **purposefulness** comes to the world. I should mention that purposefulness – the behavior of animals according to a particular goal, a certain purpose – is outside the scope of science. Science deals with objects that move according to a particular cause, such as from a particular initial condition. A particular law (or laws) determines the outcome, the result. This is the scope of science. In contrast, a new phenomenon appeared in the animal kingdom – the purposeful behavior of animals. The materialist inclination of certain scientists and philosophers to reduce everything that happens in the world to the rigid system of scientific causality has failed. There is no scientific framework that can adequately describe animals' behavior scientifically. There is absolutely no possibility, at least at this point, of explaining a cat's behavior using scientific tools and predicting what the cat will do next.

Therefore, in the second stage of the world's development, from the creation of life until just before the creation of man, the laws of physics play a smaller role both in the behavior of animals and the evolution of life. At the risk of using unnecessary metaphysical speculation, we can still state cautiously that at this stage, God's involvement and divine providence were greater than in the previous stage – from the creation of the world until the creation of life. We can identify signs of God's involvement in the creation of new things, *ex nihilo*. In contrast to the first stage, in the second stage an enormous number of new things were created, including life itself and many new species.

In the third stage, from the creation of man until the present day, the laws of physics and the laws of nature play an even smaller role, both in the development of human society and the functioning of the individual, and a new factor appears on the scene: free will. The development of the world is determined not only by God's will, but also according to man's will, and man's will can even contradict God's will. It is at this point that the stage of **history** begins.

We see very clearly that the development of the world is accompanied by the expansion of the spiritual world – or, rather, by the expansion of its influence. If in the first stage the (active) spiritual world contained the laws of nature and the content of the initial position, then in the second stage it also includes the great accumulation of genetic information hidden in the genetic code. It is worth mentioning that the quantity of information in the genetic code is many times greater than that of the laws of physics. The historical stage also dramatically increases the world's spiritual wealth.

Divine providence works in a number of different ways and we, human beings, cannot comprehend God's actions. However, there is one channel that we can assume that providence uses. Human development, history, is dependent on the knowledge available to man. We mentioned (Chapter One, section 10) that if humankind were to lose its world of accessible knowledge, world three, then it would return to the position it was in thousands years ago. Knowledge in general, and particularly scientific knowledge, is cumulative in nature: earlier knowledge is vital to the acquisition of more advanced knowledge. Unless one has mastered classical mechanics and electromagnetism, one cannot understand the theory of relativity. Francis Fukuyama, in his book *The End of History*, searches for a mechanism that will explain the directionality in history. He reaches the conclusion that science is the "mechanism" concealed behind the directionality in history. Science is cumulative, and from this follows the possibility of its directional influence on history.

But it is not only scientific knowledge (in the sense of modern science) that affects historical developments. Knowledge in general also has an influence on history. Before modern science developed, humankind had come up with many inventions that dramatically affected its development. We need only mention a few examples such as the invention of the wheel, livestock farming and agriculture. But we must not think that only scientific and technological ideas affect humanity. No less influential, and arguably even more influential, are religious, social and artistic ideas.

It is interesting to see that there is a kind of agreement among various secular philosophers regarding the influence of the growth of knowledge on the course of history. Karl Popper writes: "The truth of this premise must be admitted even by those who see in our ideas, including our scientific ideas, merely by-products of material developments of some kinds or other."[8] For example, the appearance or invention of a new production tool first takes place on the spiritual level, as an idea, and only at a later stage is the idea made manifest as the physical tool.

We can illustrate the effect of scientific knowledge on humankind. The generation of scientific knowledge, together with greater technological know-how, led to an increase in the world population (see Y. Leibowitz, *Conversations on Science and Values*). In my book, *Creation Ex Nihilo*, I described this effect graphically. In the middle of the first century, according to a very rough estimate, the world population was approximately four hundred million people, and rose to seven hundred and fifty million by the middle of the eighteenth century. Over almost two thousand years, from the middle of the first century – sixty to eighty generations – the world population more or less doubled. This means that in each of these generations, the population barely grew, while over the course of ten to twelve generations, from the middle of the eighteenth century, the population grew by a factor of six to seven. Even though scientific thought existed prior to the eighteenth century, science only began to be applied to people's lives approximately two hundred years ago. Figure 7.1 shows the effect of the application of science on the growth of the global population.

So far, we have given a factual account of the effect of knowledge on historical development. Secular philosophers and religious individuals have drawn wildly differing conclusions from this account. Karl Popper draws the conclusion that there is no lawfulness, directionality or meaning in human

---

8. *The Poverty of Historicism,* vi.

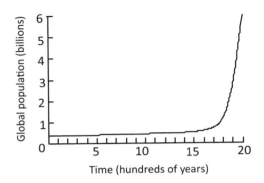

Figure 7.1 Global population growth over two thousand years

history. He argues his point in the foreword to his book, *The Poverty of Historicism*, thus:

1. The course of human history is strongly influenced by the growth of human knowledge.
2. We cannot predict, by rational or scientific methods, the future growth of our scientific knowledge. (This assertion can be proved logically.)
3. We cannot, therefore, predict the future course of human history.
4. There can be no scientific theory of historical development serving as a basis for historical prediction.

Elsewhere (see Chapter Four, section 1), Popper states, as does Einstein, that every discovery of new knowledge is the biggest miracle in the world. As far as he is concerned, there is no order in the discovery of new information, and so there is no order in the stages of history. Therefore, there is no meaning in human history. The absurdity of life and the meaninglessness in the course of history are conclusions that arise from the secular approach.

What is our conclusion, that of believing men and women? In Chapter Four, we saw that every discovery of new knowledge is in fact a divine revelation. In other words, new knowledge enters consciousness of humankind via God and in accordance with His plan. God determines the meaning of life and the meaning of history in accordance with His plan. We, human beings, cannot penetrate the details of the divine plan. Our knowledge comes from divine revelations, from that which God bestows on us.

8. CONCLUSION: THE HISTORY OF HUMANKIND FROM THE JEWISH PERSPECTIVE

A consistent analysis brings us to the conclusion that according to the secular approach, the history of humanity has no meaning, but this does not mean that all secular philosophers agree with this conclusion. Marx, Engels and their successors certainly would have disagreed with this statement. However, whatever any particular philosopher may state regarding his approach or his claims is not important. Rather, the results of a consistent and objective analysis of his views are important. In the previous section, it became clear that from the consistent secular perspective, history has no meaning or purpose. Similarly, from a secular viewpoint, there is no meaning in the creation of the world or in its development up to the historical age.

My point is that concepts such as meaning, purpose and progress are spiritual concepts that relate to spiritual entities. If we are talking about general things – including global matters, the development of nature, the evolution of life, history – only God can imbue meaning and purpose into these processes. Hence it is only consistent that the secular view, which denies God's existence, finds no meaning in historical developments.

As we have said, divine providence, the supervision of history and the realization of God's plan in history are concepts connected to the foundations of Judaism. The Bible and Judaism are the source of the idea that the course of human history has a purpose and a goal that exist above and beyond the individual events themselves, and that history or particular events within it are charged with meaning. The God of the Bible, who is the master of history, plans the course of history and makes it happen, and man is His partner in this endeavor.

This leads to another type of historiography, of writing history. The Jews created a new kind of historiography whose purpose was different from that of the work of Greek and Roman historians. The following is taken from the 1997 edition of the *Encyclopedia Britannica*:

> The Jews were the only people of antiquity who had the supreme religious duty of remembering the past because their traditional histories commemorated the working out of God's plan for his chosen people. By contrast, no Greek ever heard his gods ordering him to remember. It was the duty of every Jew to

be familiar with the Jewish sacred writings, which were ultimately gathered into what became the Old Testament. The writers of these biblical books only gave an authoritative selection of what everybody was supposed to know, and they were only concerned with the selection of such facts as seemed relevant in interpreting God's purpose.[9]

Let us think for a moment about the concept of history in general. We are familiar with many accounts of events that happened in the past. The reliability of these reports is always limited, and as a rule, accounts of events that took place a long time ago are less reliable than those of events that took place in recent memory. Of course, everything depends on the method of preserving the accounts of the events in question. This leads us to ask how the abundance of events can be linked together in order to create human history. A collection of facts on its own, without any particular principle connecting them, is not sufficient to give any meaning to human history. After all, the collection of accounts of events must be of some use to people who want to learn about their past in order to draw conclusions about the future.

Paul Johnson, a non-Jewish historian who wrote about the history of the Jews, relates to historiographical questions as follows:

> What are we on earth for? Is history merely a series of events whose sum is meaningless? Is there no fundamental moral difference between the history of the human race and the history, say, of ants? Or is there a providential plan of which we are, however humbly, the agents? No people has ever insisted more firmly than the Jews that history has a purpose and humanity a destiny. At a very early stage in their collective existence they believed they had detected a divine scheme for the human race, of which their own society was to be a pilot.[10]

The Bible is the quintessential archetype of Jewish historiography – Jewish writings about human history. In the history presented in the Bible, the connection with God is a major theme. The historical processes related in the Bible take place under divine supervision. Human history is an integral

---

9. *Encyclopedia Britannica* (1997), "The Study of History – Early Christian Era."

10. *A History of the Jews*, 2.

part of the history of the world. In contrast to the naturalistic explanation of the development of the world, life and humanity – which does not include God or any spiritual dimension – the Torah describes the history of the world as a spiritual process: God is the creator and supervisor of everything.

In order for us to understand this, we needed divine revelation. I will now be so bold as to relate my own personal experience of reaching an understanding of the uniqueness of our nation.

In June 1941, the war between Germany and the Soviet Union broke out. My family – my mother, father and I – were living at that time in Kiev, Ukraine, and the Germans arrived very quickly. In July 1941, we fled to Caucasia, and when the Germans entered Caucasia in the spring of 1942, we managed to flee to Turkmenistan in central Asia. At a fairly young age, I received a concentrated lesson in Jewish history. All the refugees who left with us were Jewish. We knew perfectly well that if the Germans caught us, it would mean certain death. I wondered about many things: what is unique about the Jewish people? Why were we chosen from all the other nations for this fate? Eventually, we settled in a relatively safe place far away from the front line, in the city of Stalinabad (Dushanbe), where I began to visit the public library and read every book available about Jewish history. But I did not find the answer to the question that was so much on my mind.

Why did the books that I found in the public library not answer my questions about the uniqueness of the Jewish people, a uniqueness that we felt so strongly at the time? The answer is simple. The history books belonged to secular historiography, and therefore did not speak about meaning at all. They were simply a collection of historical facts connected by one concept or another. This was history that did not include God.

It is important to stress that the Jews never identified God with nature (we discussed this kind of approach in Chapter Three, section 5). History is not a separate entity, nor does it have its own internal meaning. It is God, the ultimate spiritual entity, the source of spirituality, who endows history with meaning. The Torah is clear about the difference between the idolatrous nations who worshipped nature and idols and the Jews who prayed to God:

> ... and lest you lift up your eyes unto heaven, and when you see the sun and the moon and the stars, even all the host of heaven, you shall be drawn away and worship them, and serve them, which the Lord your God has allotted

to all the peoples under the whole heaven. But the Lord has taken you and brought you forth out of the iron furnace, out of Egypt, to be unto Him a people of inheritance, as you are this day. (Deuteronomy 4:19–20)

In a way, we can see the Bible as a book that provides us with a large and complex spiritual message, and which uses historical events as a means of conveying this message.

In sections 5 and 6, we saw that historical development can be expressed by Rabbi Akiva's statement: "**Everything is foreseen, yet the freedom of choice is given.**" The partnership between man and God in the development of human history is accomplished through very subtle interaction. Man has free will, but God's plan is carried out – "the counsel of the Lord will stand."

In Chapter Six, section 6, we saw that the stage of the evolution of life could not be explained solely as a derivative of the laws of nature. The life of man can be an appropriate paradigm for this stage. During his life, man makes choices and decisions using his free will, while the laws of physics, chemistry and biology operate at the same time. What characterizes this paradigm is the concept of creation, which assumes the existence of creation *ex nihilo* or change due to the action of an external active party on the development as a whole, namely divine providence. Of course, all of this can be attributed to the historical stage, to human history.

If historical developments can be compared with the life of man, then human history can be compared with the history of the life of man, to his biography. When I consider the various stages of my life, I see a number of facts. If I were to include all the facts of my life in my biography, I would end up with a jumble of facts instead of a coherent book that could be of use to other people. Here I would like to mention Albert Einstein, who wrote his *Autobiographical Notes*, which he defined as a kind of obituary, at the age of sixty-seven. In this document, he focused specifically on his thoughts. This is how he justified this approach:

> "Is this supposed to be an obituary?" the astonished reader will likely ask. I would like to reply: essentially yes. For the essential in the being of a man of my type lies precisely in what he thinks, not in what he does or suffers. Consequently, the obituary can limit itself in the main to the communicating of thoughts which have played a considerable role in my endeavors.[11]

---

11. *Albert Einstein: Philosopher–Scientist*, 33.

Here, too, we see Einstein's preference for things spiritual. The most important events, both in the history of a person and in the history of a nation and humanity, are connected to new creations, new ideas, in which divine involvement and providence can be discerned. In Chapter Four, we linked the appearance of new knowledge with divine revelation. The Bible meticulously relates encounters between human beings and God and mentions the effect of these encounters on people's lives. Therefore, I too wish to emphasize, in modern history, scientific discoveries and their implications on the lives of man. Besides, these discoveries open up a whole new understanding of the world in which we live.

To conclude this section, I would like to touch on another subject connected to history. We, as a nation, are used to serious self-criticism, especially when we returned to the Land of Israel after two thousand years of exile. But it is sometimes worth viewing the history of our nation through the eyes of an objective, external observer. Above, we quoted Paul Johnson who wrote *A History of the Jews*. In the Epilogue, he writes:

> One way of summing up 4,000 years of Jewish history is to ask ourselves what would have happened to the human race if Abraham had not been a man of great sagacity, or if he had stayed in Ur and kept his higher notions to himself, and no specific Jewish people had come into being. Certainly the world without the Jews would have been a radically different place. Humanity might eventually have stumbled upon all the Jewish insights. But we cannot be sure. All the great conceptual discoveries of the intellect seem obvious and inescapable once they have been revealed, but it requires a special genius to formulate them for the first time. The Jews had this gift. To them we owe the idea of equality before the law, both divine and human; of the sanctity of life and the dignity of the human person; of the individual conscience and so of personal redemption; of the collective conscience and so of social responsibility; of peace as an abstract ideal and love as the foundation of justice, and many other items which constitute the basic moral furniture of the human mind. Without the Jews it might have been a much emptier place.[12]

I included this long quotation in order to present an outsider's view, although this does not mean that I agree with everything Johnson says here. While Johnson mentions God, in actual fact he supports, perhaps

---

12. *A History of the Jews*, 585.

unconsciously, the anthropocentric view of history. From our point of view, the Jewish nation did not enter the stage of history by chance. God, who manages human development, chose one nation through which he brought these ideas to the world. He used, and continues to use, the Jewish people as a conduit for his providence. It is good to be a chosen people, even if it is not always easy.

9. CONCLUSION OF PART III: THE HISTORY OF THE WORLD

It is a commonly-held notion, and not just among uneducated people, that the world's development can be explained solely using the laws of physics. A study of the three chapters in Part III: The History of the World leads us to a different conclusion. Careful scrutiny of the world's development leads to the conclusion that the process of change in the world is accompanied by freedom from the precise observance of the laws of nature – "the release of the world from the tyranny of the laws of nature." I would even go as far as to say that the development of the world is accompanied by its redemption.

We can identify three distinct eras in the development of the world: from the creation of the world to the creation of life; from the creation of life to the creation of man; and from the creation of man until the present day. These three eras took place during very different time periods, each of which has a different level of importance. The first era lasted for ten billion years and the second for three and a half billion years, while the third era – the historical era – has so far only lasted approximately ten thousand years – which is around 10^{-6}, or 0.0001 percent, of the total time that the world has existed thus far. We can also talk about the different levels of importance of these three eras. Suffice it to say that the Torah devotes only a few pages to the first and second eras together, while almost the entire Torah, Bible and Talmud are devoted to the historical era.

Nevertheless, during the first era, several things occurred that are of supreme importance by any standard. First, there was the creation of the world – arguably the most important event of all, since without it no other events could have taken place. The creation of the world entails both the creation of the physical world and of the spiritual world – "**the heaven and the earth**." The spiritual world contains the laws of physics which determine the movements of matter. These laws have a special structure.

They are compatible with the life that is to be created at a later stage (the anthropic principle), and simple enough for the people who are be created in the future understand and use. Perhaps most important of all, they must be compatible with divine providence and human will. As we have seen (Chapter Three, section 8), not every system of laws, is compatible with man's free will, including the deterministic laws of classical physics.

We can call the first age the physical era. During that time, for more than ten billion years, the laws of physics were the principal tool of divine providence in the world's development. Our current level of scientific knowledge does not permit me to say with absolute (scientific) certainty that the development of the universe – which began with the Big Bang and continued with the formation of galaxies, stars and planets – can be explained solely and exclusively by the laws of physics. However, it is reasonable to assume that the cosmic systems operate in accordance with the laws of physics. For example, we understand today that our sun and other stars act as enormous thermonuclear furnaces.

Modern physics has not yet reached the state of being perfect science; there are still gaps. We do not yet have a plausible theory that combines quantum theory with the general theory of relativity. We can assume that in the future, a more complete theory will materialize, but it is also possible that we will never be able to achieve a perfect theory. The laws of nature – that is, physics – exist objectively, with no connection to our knowledge of them. It is reasonable to assume that, like the modern theory of physics, a more complete theory will also be a statistical theory. It will not be able to predict every future development based on knowledge of the initial data. In a non-deterministic world, certain occurrences, such as the appearance of a particular galaxy or of the solar system, are absolutely compatible with the laws of physics, but it is possible that they are not exclusively derived from them. This does not prevent physics from providing a fairly precise prediction in certain cases, even if it is never one hundred percent accurate. While bearing these reservations in mind, we can nonetheless claim that during the physical era, from the creation of the world until the creation of life, the laws of physics were the principal tool of divine providence.

From the creation of life, a new era began that lasted until the creation of man. From this point onward, we define the era according to its appearance in a particular place in the universe. Thus, it is possible that life has only been created in our solar system, and that the whole, enormous, perhaps even infinite, universe remains without any signs of life. Even though the whole universe, other than the solar system, remains in the pre-life era, the new era has already begun. A new thing has been created that changes the nature of the world. The importance of this new era is measured not only by the size of the universe, but by the qualities of the new phenomenon. We mentioned earlier that any living creature, even the tiniest fly, is more complex and sophisticated that the entire inanimate universe.

Living creatures have qualities that differentiate them from inanimate objects. Their movements cannot be described, even approximately, by physical equations. One need only watch the behavior of a cat. Its movements are not determined by the laws of physics, but by something else. It has particular goals that motivate it, such as the search for food. One cannot use the causality of the inanimate world to describe the cat's behavior even on a qualitative level. In the inanimate world, the cause always precedes the effect. While an inanimate object's movements are determined by its initial position, the cat's movements are determined by its future position – by the goal to be achieved. Final causes determine the effect.

Now we come to a rather weighty subject. It seems that the cat's behavior that is determined according to a goal contradicts modern science. More than two thousand years ago, Aristotle differentiated between different types of causes, one of which he termed the final cause. We can say that the cat's behavior is determined by a final cause. This situation contradicts what might be said to be the central feature of science – "the objectivity principle." According to this principle, one cannot attribute any purpose or meaning to objects, and when we carry out a scientific study we must commit to this principle *a priori*. Clearly, the objectivity principle does not come from science itself, but is a pre-condition for scientific work. Jacques Monod[13] sees the contradiction between the purposeful behavior of animals and the objectivity principle as the central problem of biology. His thesis is that the solution to this problem lies in the theory of natural selection. He seems to suppose that when billions of years of evolution are taken into account (in a sequence of processes connected by initial causes), one can arrive at the seemingly purposeful behavior of animals. Monod and other

---

13.   In his book, *Chance and Necessity*.

naturalist thinkers start from the hypothesis that in the end, everything is determined by physical forces and the laws of physics. From their point of view, the physical world, world one, is closed. In contrast to this, we saw (Chapter Three, section 9) that **macroscopic systems, such as our bodies or the bodies of animals, can move arbitrarily without obeying the classical deterministic laws and without breaching the laws of physics. The structure of modern physics is compatible with the involvement of our wills (and that of God) in the physical system without break**ing its laws.

I should stress that the compatibility of the laws of nature according to modern physics with the physical world's openness to divine and human involvement is a metaphysical, religious principle that stems from the Torah. It is good that science has reached the stage in which it is compatible with this principle, but this does not prove the metaphysical principle at the foundation of Judaism. What we can say is that the principle of the openness of the material world is a metaphysical foundation of all the sciences.

The physical world, world one, is not closed. It is open not only to divine providence and the free will of human beings, but also to the goals of living creatures. The new stage – the era of life – is the era of **instincts and purposefulness**. It is the instincts of living creatures, not the laws of physics, that determine their purposeful behavior. But that is not all. The development of the world, its evolution, is only partially determined by the laws of physics. In the era of life, the space in which Providence operates is growing. In the second half of the twentieth century, scientists gained a great deal of knowledge about the mechanism of heredity. Paradoxically, the evolution of life cannot happen when the heredity mechanism is working perfectly. When this happens, the hereditary characteristics are passed down without any changes. The change that forms the basis of evolution takes place because of random disturbances – in other words, because of a lack of lawfulness. Divine providence operates both with law-based tools (of the laws of nature) and in the law-free realm.

What about the spiritual world? In the physical era, the spiritual world contained,[14] primarily, the laws of nature and the details of the initial posi-

----

14. We must be clear that in the physical era, the laws of nature in the spiritual world were mainly used. We cannot know what the spiritual world contained – only what it was used for.

tion of the universe. In contrast, during the era of life, the spiritual world was expanded by the addition of hereditary information (or the use of this information; see note 14). We can imagine the expansion and development of the spiritual world in the era of life as follows. Everything started three and a half billion years ago. Something new was created, a new creature, which carried a plan for its own reproduction. This creature was able to reproduce, passing its structure to future generations. The information that was written in its genetic code is a particular text written in letters made out of certain molecules. The information contained in this text was extremely primitive. From this point onward (up to but not including the creation of man), the development of the spiritual world occurred through the expansion of the genetic code of living creatures.

The creativity of the divine spiritual world is constantly growing. The genetic pool of the animal world – the collection of the genetic texts of living creatures – is expanding. New species of ever-increasing complexity are being created. The creation of every new species is first and foremost an event that happens in the spiritual world and then in the physical world. During this whole period, approximately two million species were created. It is important to note that the creation of new and more sophisticated species reflects divine activity, the implementation of God's plan. But from an atheistic standpoint, the expansion of the genetic pool and the creation of new genetic texts is all just a result of randomness, of absolute purposelessness. From a logical perspective, one cannot deny the possibility that coherent, complex and sophisticated texts could be formed randomly. Even though the probability of each of these events is equal to zero and it is akin to a miracle from an atheistic standpoint, one cannot prove that such a miracle is impossible. However, to believe that such miracles really happened is something else entirely – it is an atheistic belief. There is an unbridgeable gap between this belief and a scientific proof.

The historical era began with the creation of man. This era is a continuation of the redemption process – the ongoing release from the necessity dictated by the laws of nature. Animals are characterized by their purposeful behavior; their **instincts** are what determine their goals. While one cannot deny the importance of instinct in man's behavior, the revolution that took place with the creation of man was the appearance of his **free will**. Human behavior is generally determined by free will, not (or not only) by instincts.

God's command, rather than human instincts, should be the basis of human behavior: "It shall be unto you for a fringe, that you may look upon it and remember all the commandments of the Lord and do them; and that you go not about after your own heart and your own eyes, after which you use to go astray" (Numbers 15:39). However, the freedom of choice is given; man is free to obey, or disobey, God's command.

In the historical era, for the first time after the billions of years since the creation of the world, God has a partner: Man was created in God's image and given the ability to communicate with Him. This does not happen all the time, nor does it happen for everyone, but the ability to connect with God is what sets the human soul apart. Earlier (Chapter One, section 1), we discussed the uniqueness of man. There is an enormous difference between the first creation – the physical universe – and the creation of man, God's partner. The physical universe takes up such a huge expanse that we can barely comprehend it, and just understanding the laws that govern the physical universe is the pinnacle of human thought. But man, with his soul and his free will, is infinitely more complex and sophisticated than the entire physical universe.

With all of man's many qualities and characteristics, his ability to communicate with God – albeit only a potential ability and one which is rarely realized openly – is the peak of divine creation. As we saw in Chapter Four, human creativity is dependent on connection with God. We have learned in this book about the special quality that we human beings have been given – our ability to connect to the spiritual world. We have distinguished between two types of connection: a **primary connection**, which is actually direct communication with God, and a **secondary connection** to the accessible spiritual world, once it has already been revealed to pioneers of the spirit such as prophets and great scientists.

The connection between God and His creations is not only through the prophets. It is true that the historical processes are carried out by human beings, but the divine plan is what actually happens – *everything is foreseen*, despite man's free will – *yet the freedom of choice is given*. In way that we cannot understand, divine providence directs all human beings, with their different thoughts and goals: "There are many devices in a man's heart; but the counsel of the Lord, that shall stand" (Proverbs 19:21).

So far, the historical era has lasted for only 0.0001 percent of the time that the world has existed, from creation to the present day. However, the importance of this era cannot be measured by the duration of its existence, just as the importance of life is not measured by the volume of space it fills. We talk about physical time, which is measured by particular cyclical physical processes, such as the time it takes for the earth to rotate on its axis. For us, the rotation period is a measure of time – one day. We also use clocks that split the day into smaller parts – seconds, minutes and hours. But maybe we can suggest another measure of time. Let us take two important events, two new creations, *ex nihilo*. Let us also assume that no other important event occurs between them. Let us now take this pair of events as a new unit of time – a spiritual moment. This new unit of time may be very long in terms of ordinary physical time, if a long time passed between the two events. On the other hand, the events may be extremely close to one another, in which case the new unit of time would be very short in terms of ordinary time.

We can call ordinary time "physical time" because it is defined and measured using physical processes. The new time can be called "spiritual time," since it is defined according to events that take place in the spiritual world. In the story of creation, the writer uses the word "day" to indicate new creations, starting from the first one – that of the world. These creations are primarily events that are part of a divine plan in the spiritual world. The period of time between a pair of creations – the creation of the world and the creation of light – is defined by the Torah as "one day." Although we cannot measure spiritual time with the precision with which we measure physical time, the use of the concept of spiritual time can help us understand the significance of various periods in the history of the world and of humanity.

Let us look at the three eras – the physical era, the era of life and the historical era – using the concept of spiritual time. From the perspective of spiritual time, the physical era is the shortest. A small number of new things were created during this period, including the world, the laws of nature, and time and space. From a physical perspective, this was by far the longest period, more than ten billion years. According to the laws of physics, the development that takes place from the first creation until the next one can last a very long time, even billions of years. However, the period of spiritual time between two consecutive creations is very small. It is a single spiritual moment.

The spiritual duration of the era of life is much greater. During this period, life was created together with its genetic code, and some two million new species were created also. We can say that this era lasted for at least two million spiritual moments.

However, the historical era is the longest era by far. As we have mentioned, in terms of physical time it has lasted, so far, approximately 0.0001 percent of the time that the world itself has existed – a tiny layer in the time dimension of the universe. But the spiritual duration of this era is immeasurable. It is a period of ceaseless creativity. The creativity of the Creator is now expressed in both divine providence and human creativity. In fact, the appearance of every new soul in the world is a new creation, *ex nihilo*, which contains enormous creative potential that, regrettably, is not always realized. But *the freedom of choice is given*. "If a man never creates, never brings into being anything new, anything original, then he cannot be holy unto his God," Rabbi Soloveitchik wrote in *Halakhic Man*.[15] He also emphasizes the "... obligation to participate in the renewal of the cosmos. The most fundamental principle of all is that man must create himself. It is this idea that Judaism introduced into the world."[16]

But we must not delude ourselves. Most of the time, we are immersed in the routine of our lives. This is the case even with people who are involved in creative pursuits such as science or art. They, too, have only rare moments of illumination that lead to creativity. Nevertheless, it is creativity that gives meaning to our lives. Each time we create, we fulfill our role in the world. Whether we are aware of it or not, we realize our connection with God by creation and innovation. This is true not only in the realms of Torah, science and art, but most of all in our lives, which are our most important creations.

We cannot fully comprehend the divine plan, our role in it or each person's part in it. But it is clear that unless we engage in innovation, we are not fulfilling our role. Therefore, it is also worthwhile for us to evaluate our lives using spiritual time units – moments of creation and innovation. Then, figures such as Moses and Abraham, rather than Jared and Methuselah, will emerge as the longest-living people in history. It will also become clear that

15. *Halakhic Man*, 108.
16. Ibid., 92.

one year in Albert Einstein's life – 1905 – was much longer than the entire lives of many other scientists.

True longevity lies in creation. While moments of creativity may be few and far between, the aspiration to creativity gives our lives meaning. "Righteous people are considered alive even in death,"[17] for they leave behind an eternal legacy.

17.   BT *Berakhot* 18a–b.

The Believer versus the Atheist

WE HAVE FINALLY REACHED THE END OF OUR LONG and sometimes tiring journey. Now we can summarize what we have achieved and the insights that we have gained. Our subject is the world's structure, laws and development. When I talk about understanding the world, I am not talking about a partial understanding such as, for example, from a purely scientific perspective, but a comprehensive understanding – including of humanity, the human soul and God's supervision of the world.

At the start of our journey, we encountered an issue which, in my opinion, attracts an inordinate amount of attention: the discrepancy between the literal interpretation of the Torah, particularly of the story of creation, and what is considered to be the conclusions of science. Over time, a secular world view has grown that apparently draws its conclusions from the achievements of science. In the past, Jewish philosophers such as Maimonides, Rabbi Yehuda Halevi and Nachmanides, and modern thinkers such as Rabbi Kook and Rabbi Soloveitchik, were not disturbed by the seeming discrepancy between the literal meaning of the story of creation, together with the various *midrashim* and science or philosophy. In the Preface to this book, I quoted Rabbi Soloveitchik, who wrote, "I have never been seriously troubled by the problem of the Biblical doctrine of creation vis-à-vis the scientific story of evolution at both the cosmic and the organic levels, nor have I been perturbed by the confrontation of the mechanistic interpretation of the human mind with the Biblical spiritual concept of man."

In his *Guide of the Perplexed*, Maimonides identifies three different types of people who read the Scriptures and the *midrashim*, and come across places "where the external sense manifestly contradicts the truth and departs from

307

the intelligible. They are all parables."[1] The first type includes people who lack basic knowledge of reality: ". . . if an ignoramus among the multitude of Rabbanites should engage in speculation on these *midrashim*, he would find nothing difficult in them, inasmuch as a rash fool, devoid of any knowledge of the nature of being, does not find impossibilities hard to accept."[2] The second group is comprised of those who have a certain amount of knowledge, understand the *midrashim* as legends, and hence reject them out of hand. "[H]e can take the speeches in question in their external sense and, in so doing, think ill of their author and regard him as an ignoramus."[3] A person who belongs to the third group, with which Maimonides himself identifies, understands that there is hidden meaning in these passages "whether or not the inner meaning of the saying is clear to him."[4]

Several centuries later, the non-Jewish philosopher Francis Bacon (1561–1626) expressed the same idea: "Certainly a little Philosophie inclines mans minde to Atheisme, but depth in Philosophie brings men about to Religion."[5] (One should bear in mind that at that time, philosophy was synonymous with knowledge of the world.)

Thus, we can distinguish three stages of understanding, and the three groups of people are classified in accordance with their level of knowledge and understanding. The first group includes people who believe and observe the commandments, but who understand little of the world in which they live. It is arguable that to a great extent, their faith is a product of their ignorance. They have no problem accepting the literal translation of the story of creation. They experience no conflict with the general knowledge that is currently available about the structure of the world and its development simply because they do not possess this knowledge.

Members of the second group are fairly similar to those of the first in terms of their level of knowledge. They call themselves intellectuals, but their knowledge is actually superficial. Everything is second-hand. They believe every scrap of science that comes to them from all sorts of sources,

---

1. *Guide of the Perplexed*, 9.
2. Ibid., 10.
3. Ibid.
4. Ibid.
5. *The Works of Fr. Bacon,* Vol. VII. London, 1826, 48.

and have never put any effort into understanding the world in which they live. They believe that a person can call himself modern and intellectual without basic knowledge of the foundations of modern science or of modern thinking. The people of this group reject faith and religion out of sheer ignorance. Unlike the first group, the ignorance of the second group is concealed beneath the veneer of a modern, intellectual person.

I do not say that anyone who has true scientific knowledge, or even any-one who is a scientist by profession and works in the field of science, must necessarily be a believing person. Perhaps such a person lacks knowledge about the structure of the world – information that we have presented in this book. Many people assume that anyone who possesses a good degree, or any scientist with a good reputation in his field, also knows about the structure of science and the logic of scientific discovery. However, we should not assume that every scientist who is an expert in a specific field is also knowledgeable about topics that have to do with the structure of the sci-ences, such as the theory of scientific cognition. The bottom line is that scientists who presume to draw conclusions in the area between religion and science must know the limits of science and its logical basis. Only then can they analyze the problem in a professional manner while avoiding an amateurish approach. In the Preface, I quoted Maimonides: "If, however, you have understood the natural things, you have entered the habitation and are walking in the antechambers. If, however, you have achieved perfection in the natural things and have understood divine science, you have entered in the ruler's place *into the inner court* and are with him in one habitation. This is the rank of the men of science; they, however, are of different grades of perfection."[6] In other words, knowledge of physics is not enough. One must also comprehend the metaphysical structure of reality – and that is the subject of this book.

Now I would like to explain the substantial difference between the periods in which Maimonides and Francis Bacon lived and our own era. Both Maimonides and Francis Bacon talk about the believer who is liable to lose his faith because of superficial knowledge and might return to his faith once he achieves a deeper understanding. Maimonides, in his *Guide of the Perplexed,* talks about "one who has philosophized and has knowledge

---

6.   *The Guide of the Perplexed* III, 51, 619.

of the true sciences, but believes at the same time in the matters pertaining to the Law and is perplexed as to their meaning because of the uncertain terms and the parables."[7] Here, Maimonides is explaining to those who are believers and yet are still "perplexed" the true, though hidden, content of the parables in the Torah.

This is not the case in our day. In the modern era, a generation gap was created between people who were believers and their non-believing children.[8] Today, when the non-believers are happy with their lot and many believers feel threatened by scientific accomplishments, there are quite different areas in the realm that lies between religion and science that require clarification other than those which appear in Maimonides' *Guide of the Perplexed.* My goals in this book include exposing people's preconceptions about the role of science and its limitations, while at the same time providing a complete picture of our world, its laws and development. By "a complete picture" I mean one that includes both the scientific and providential aspects.

In this book, I have presented a worldview that is based on Jewish sources and is contrary to the worldviews that do not include God. A worldview cannot be proven either logically or empirically. It is located in the realm of metaphysics or perhaps in the realm of faith, and there is a substantial difference between Jewish metaphysics and other metaphysics. The source of the Jewish world view is divine revelation, while other world views have no specific source. It is not true that there is a conflict between faith and science. There is no contradiction, nor can there be, between the foundations of science and its equations and the foundations of faith. However, there may be a contradiction between a particular worldview that seems to be based on the accomplishments of science and the worldview that is based on the Torah. It is actually a conflict between faiths – a conflict between secular faith (such a thing indeed exists) and Jewish faith: faith versus faith!

This is where the complexity of the problem lies. One cannot compare two claims, one religious and one scientific, as most people assume. One

---

7.   Ibid., Introduction, 10.

8.   The enormous achievements of science in the modern era, together with the overconfidence of scientists, particularly in the nineteenth century, in their ability to explain everything using science and their lack of understanding of the limits of science, have contributed greatly to the lack of faith.

can only compare two metaphysical, religious claims. The metaphysical nature of the claims means that there is no possibility of proving, logically or scientifically, the truth of some and the falsity of others. But this does not prevent us from talking about metaphysical standpoints, comparing them, deciding that they are contradictory and concluding that we prefer one over the other.

In fact, throughout this book, we have been dealing with the conflict between two opposing worldviews, the Jewish and the atheistic. Now, let us look at these two worldviews and compare them more systematically. Here I would like to summarize the analysis and the key conclusions. Let us put the **believer against the atheist.**

The foundation of the world. The atheist and the believer put forward opposing foundations. From the atheist's point of view the foundation of the world and everything in it is *materia*. Everything in the world, including human beings, their souls and their creations, is derived from *materia*. This is the basis of the view called materialism. Of course, the truth of the materialist view cannot be proven, but we can prove that it is not compatible with rationality. In Chapter One, section 9, we quoted the conclusion that Karl Popper reached in his work, *The Self and Its Brain*, which he co-authored with John Eccles:

> I do not claim that I have refuted materialism. But I do think I have shown that materialism has no right to claim that it can be supported by rational argument – argument that is rational by logical principles. Materialism can be true, but it is incompatible with rationalism, with the acceptance of the standards of critical argument; for the standards appear from the materialist point of view as an illusion or at least as ideology.[9]

Conversely, from the believer's point of view, the world and everything in it have a spiritual, rational foundation: God is the source and master of everything. Maimonides expresses it as follows:

> The foundation of all foundations and the pillar of wisdom is to know that there is a Primary Being who brought into being all existence. All the beings of the heavens, the earth, and what is between them came into existence only from the truth of His being. If one would imagine that He does not exist, no

---

9. *The Self and Its Brain,* 81.

other being could possibly exist. If one would imagine that none of the entities aside from Him exist, He alone would continue to exist, and the nullification of their [existence] would not nullify His existence, because all the [other] entities require Him and He, blessed be He, does not require them nor any one of them.[10]

While the world was created by God, He is not identical with it. "God created the world as a separate object, but He did not grant it independent existence. **The world exists because it is nurtured by some of the infinite being of God.**"[11] "All of our knowledge of God comes to us from His revelations."[12]

These are the two opposing world views. One regards matter as the source of all things, while the other sees this role as being fulfilled by God's spirit.

Law and order in the world. One of the most fundamental phenomena in the world that require an explanation is the existence of law and order. From a materialistic perspective, law is fundamental. In Chapter Three, section 4, we quoted physicist-scientist Professor Ginsburg as follows: "My atheist view is the intuitive claim that there is nothing but nature and the laws that govern it."[13] Law is immanent, inherent in nature, a derivative of nature. Matter and its laws are the foundation of everything in the world, including human beings. This point of view is simple, and it seems to be its simplicity that attracts large numbers of people to it. In fact, from the atheist's point of view, there is no need for any explanation for the presence of law and order in nature. From a purely logical perspective, there is nothing wrong with assuming that nature and its laws are an absolute, ultimate entity from which everything is derived.

However, the laws of nature are not sufficient to define this entity. One must also assume an infinite amount of information regarding the initial conditions. The world according to the view presented here is only a physical system. As we saw above (Chapter Two, section 3 and Chapter Three, section 6) the development of a physical system is determined by two factors

10. *Mishneh Torah, Sefer ha-Mada, Hilchot Yesdoei ha-Torah*, 1:1–3.

11. *And From There You Shall Seek*, 104.

12. Ibid., 142.

13. Мои атеистические убеждения (это) интуитивное суждение о том, что существует лишь Природа и управляющие ею законы . . . (В.Л. Гинзбург, О науке, о себе и о других, 486).

– the laws of physics and the initial position. From a certain perspective, the data of the initial position are much more important than the laws themselves. In a deterministic system all the information is contained in the initial position, while the laws themselves do not actually add anything new. We might say that the physical laws effect a transformation: they change the form of the information that the system contained in the beginning and simply transfer it from one time to another (random quantum processes affect the fidelity of this transfer and disrupt it somewhat).

Reality is not simple at all. It is just our routine, everyday thinking that prevents us from discerning the wonder in the world. The laws of nature are a complete collection of commands that instruct matter as to how it must change over time. Scientists have discovered complete texts written or denoted by mathematical symbols – physical laws, the laws of nature. Where do these texts come from? What or who is their source? The materialist's answer to this question is that nature itself determines these laws. But this is not an explanation. The materialist professes to explain the complexity of our world using the actions of the laws of nature. But the laws of nature alone are not enough of an explanation, since we also need the infinite catalog of initial conditions. In order to explain the world as it currently stands, the materialist must assume the existence of a world that was no less complex at another time – at the moment of creation, or prior to infinite time if he denies creation.

According to our sources, the texts of the laws of nature and the initial conditions are part of the divine spiritual world. Moreover, they are evidence of the presence of a divine entity that operates in the world – God.

The problem of the uniformity of the laws of nature. The materialist, atheist view of the laws of nature creates several problems that cannot be solved within the framework of that approach. One problem is the uniformity of the laws of nature – that exactly the same laws operate everywhere in the universe. Why should there be the exact same laws in a place that is millions of light years away from earth? If one believes that the laws of nature are a derivative of nature, then there is no reason for nature to "produce" the same laws in different places. We quoted Karl Popper, who reached the conclusion that "the structural homogeneity of the world seems to resist any 'deeper' explanation: it remains a mystery." The atheist's world view contains no rational explanation for the uniformity of the laws of nature.

In the Jewish way of thinking, however, the situation is different. The laws of nature belong to the divine spiritual world. They are part of a spiritual entity that is not dependent on matter. The laws of nature are not dependent on anything in the physical world, and hence they are identical everywhere in the universe.

The creativity of the world. In the secular way of thinking, we must assume that *materia* or nature, has almost unlimited creative power. The atheist, too, is a product of this entity. The greatest problem in the atheistic world view is the fact that over the course of the development of the world, new things are created *ex nihilo*. In Chapter Four, section 7, we quoted Karl Popper on the subject of the creativity of the world: "I would even suggest that the greatest riddle of cosmology may well be neither the original big bang, nor the problem why there is something rather than nothing . . . but that the universe is, in a sense, creative: that it created life, and from it mind – our consciousness – which illuminates the universe, and which is creative in its turn . . . ."[14]

This problem does not exist at all in the Jewish world view, according to which God is the creator.

The intelligibility of the world. The atheistic approach has failed precisely in the area where it should shine. From the atheist's point of view, science is the exclusive source of our knowledge of the world. But in a world without God, the existence of science is almost miraculous. In Chapter Four, section 1, we quoted Karl Popper and Albert Einstein regarding the fact that human knowledge is the greatest miracle in our universe. We devoted Chapter Four to the subject of understanding the world, and we reached the conclusion that science is divine revelation, and therefore in an (imaginary) world that is devoid of God, there is also no place for science.

A scientific picture of the world? Is this really true? One of the most common preconceptions, both among laymen and countless intellectuals and scientists, is that there is something that might be called a "scientific picture" of the world. This means that the development of the world from its very first moment (if, indeed, there was a first moment), the creation of life, the evolutionary development of life and the development of human society can all be explained scientifically, by the laws of physics. From this

---

14. *The Self and Its Brain*, 61.

viewpoint, the appearance of new things during the course of the development is only illusion. Deeper scrutiny must always reveal a scientific causal action. In that kind of world, there is no place for man's free will or for any kind of creativity. In fact, is there really any possibility of a scientific explanation of the world in general? Can an understanding of the world as a whole be based solely upon the laws of science? The answer is an unequivocal no. As we made clear above, the laws of nature on their own are not enough to describe or explain the world, since we also need information regarding the initial position. The quantity of this information is enormous. In fact, it is infinite. A scientific explanation is impossible without knowledge of the initial position of the world, but this information does not come from science. Therefore, a scientific explanation of the world is impossible. In order for this to be possible, one would have to assume that nature "produces" not only the laws that govern it but also an infinite amount of information regarding the initial position. There has to be a limit to the arbitrariness of the assumptions we can make. Rabbi Soloveitchik is sharply critical in his discussion of this phenomenon:

> Although even skeptics cannot deny that which is wondrous and hidden from them, they enjoy their mental and spiritual torment. A mania of masochism masters them utterly. They want to remain alone, by themselves, in a mechanical world without meaning or purpose, bereft of joy and hope. Atheists wander along the paths of an absurd existence. They are lost in their absurd, cruel agony and madness.[15]

* * *

In Part III: The History of the World, we took a detailed look at the various stages of the development of the world. We mentioned that from our point of view, the laws of nature are one of the conduits of divine providence. In the various stages of the world's development, the relationship between God's direct involvement and the action of the laws of nature changes. In the historical stage, together with the laws of nature and providence, human free will starts to be a factor in the development. We have gradually reached a picture of development under divine providence. This picture, which continues to improve over time, is dependent on our level of understanding

---

15. *And From There You Shall Seek*, 159, n. 6.

both of the principles of Judaism and of science. In the twentieth century, there was a revolution in science. Our understanding of the laws of nature, of the structure of the universe and its development improved, reaching a new level. I have tried to provide the reader with an up-to-date picture of the universe.

In fact, it is impossible to explain any stage in the development of the world using solely scientific tools. The physical era, from the creation of the world until the creation of life, contains the creation of the world, the laws of nature, and time and space. These entities cannot be explained by science, since we are talking about the creation of science itself, or, to be more precise, about the creation of things (such as the laws of nature) that constitute the subjects of the scientific description. As we saw in Chapters Six and Seven, it is absolutely impossible to describe the era of life and the historical era solely using scientific tools without the principle of divine providence.

Nevertheless, we have a particular interest in the stage of the development of life. The atheistic, materialistic argument focuses primarily on the materialistic "scientific explanation" of the evolution of life. This is not logical. The physical era preceded the era of life. If the era of life has some semblance of an explanation – the theory of natural selection – there is not even a hint of an explanation for the law and order found in the inanimate world.

The theory of evolution – an irrational belief. In Chapter Six, in which we discussed the development of life, we saw that there is no scientific theory that describes the development of life. There is no law of nature that determines the development of life. Darwinism has the status of a metaphysical hypothesis, a belief, and we also showed that it has no rational basis. A belief based on the creativity of the laws of nature – or to be more precise, the creativity of processes that combine necessity in accordance with law and randomness due to the absence of law – is thoroughly implausible.

Karl Popper summarized this as follows:

There exists no law of evolution, only the historical fact that plants and animals change, or more precisely, that they have changed. The idea of a law which determines the direction and the character of evolution is a typical nineteenth-century mistake, arising out of the general tendency to ascribe to the 'Natural Law' the functions traditionally ascribed to God.[16]

---

16. *Conjectures and Refutations*, 340.

Man's free will and scientific causality. In an argument between a believer and an atheist, the issue of free will takes a fairly central position. This seems to be an unsolvable problem. How can one reconcile man's free will and scientific causality? Immanuel Kant defined this problem as an antinomy: two contradictory views that can both be proven to be true. On the one hand, a person's body is made up of physical parts, and hence all his movements must exclusively obey the laws of nature. On the other hand, Kant was certain that human beings have free will, and hence a person's actions are controlled by his will.

The solution to the problem lies in the recognition that the world of matter, the physical world, is not closed, but is **open to divine and human will.**

A world open to the divine and human will. It is only with this in the background that the fundamental principles of Judaism – divine providence and free will – can be reconciled with the lawfulness of the world of matter. A comprehensive analysis of the principles of science was required (see Chapter Three, section 8) in order to understand that modern physics truly fulfills the necessary conditions of the openness of the world of matter. It is important to note that not all physical theories fulfill these conditions. For example, the deterministic world of classical physics is closed to the influence of the spirit. Only modern physics is flexible enough to permit spiritual involvement. However, we emphasized in Chapter Four, section 8, that the openness of the material world to human and divine involvement is a religious, metaphysical principle that comes from the Torah, and with which modern science is compatible. But this is not a "scientific" proof of the metaphysical principle that underlies the foundation of Judaism. On the contrary, the principle of the openness of the material world must be a metaphysical foundation of all the sciences. If classical physics does not fulfill this principle, this points to a flaw in classical physics, but it does not prevent us from using it to a particular approximation and within certain limitations.

The distinction between belief in the God of nature – deism – and the belief in a living, transcendental, personal and normative God. At the beginning of this epilogue, I quoted Francis Bacon: "Certainly a little Philosophie inclines mans minde to Atheisme, but depth in Philosophie brings men about to Religion." David Hume interpreted this as follows: ". . . [T]hey discover . . . that the course of nature is regular and uniform, their whole faith totters, and falls to ruin. But being taught, by more reflection, that this very regularity and uniformity is the strongest proof of design and of a supreme intelligence, they return to that belief, which they had deserted; and they are now able to establish it on a firmer and more durable foundation."[17]

However, we need to understand that the detection of design and supreme intelligence in law and order in nature does not necessarily lead to the recognition of a living, transcendental, personal and normative God – to a belief in the God of Abraham, Isaac and Jacob. We can see a belief in a transcendental God that is derived intellectually from law and order in nature as a stage on the way to belief in a God that involves Himself in worldly matters. However, there are many people who remain at the earlier stage and do not progress to the more comprehensive belief. The belief that sees God as the foundation of the world but denies His involvement in and His providence over it is called deism – unlike theism, the belief in a personal God, the Creator of the world, who sustains it and directs it.

The belief in a God who is involved in worldly matters is derived primarily from the divine revelation documented in our sacred writings. However, during the development of modern science, while it was at the stage of classical determinism, the problem arose regarding how both divine and human involvement can be understood in a world controlled by scientific causality, which allows no deviation from the lawfulness that fixes the development of the world. We mentioned above that a look at the structure of modern science brings us to the metaphysical principle of the material world's openness to divine and human involvement. As we said, modern physics is compatible with this principle. It does not contradict it. Thus the new kind of divine revelation, science, brings us to a deeper understanding of the world that is open to involvement by both divine and human free will.

History. Perhaps the most substantial difference between the secular view and the Jewish view lies in the approach of each to humanity's development. From our point of view, the development of humanity has meaning and purpose. Human history is the arena for God's actions. He manages and supervises the development of humanity, and determines history's purpose and goals. We saw in Chapter Seven (sections 5 and 6) that the essence of

---

17. *The Natural History of Religion*, 51.

historical development can be summarized in Rabbi Akiva's famous statement: "**Everything is foreseen, yet the freedom of choice is given.**" Divine and human participation in human history take place in highly delicate interactions. While human beings have free will, God's plan is carried out – "**the counsel of the Lord will stand.**"

Conversely, a coherent analysis of the secular view (Chapter Seven, section 7) leads to the conclusion that according to this view, human history has no meaning. This does not mean that all secular philosophers agree with this conclusion. There is no doubt that Marx, Engels and their successors disagreed with the conclusion that history has no meaning. The results of an objective, coherent analysis of a particular philosopher's views are important – not what that philosopher says about those views. According to these results, the secular thinker cannot ascribe any meaning or purpose to history. Likewise, from a secular perspective, the creation of the world has no meaning, nor does the world's development up to the historical era.

We have mentioned (Chapter Seven, section 8) that the concepts of meaning, purpose and progress are spiritual concepts that belong to spiritual entities. If we are talking about general, global, universal things such as the development of nature, the evolution of life and history, then it is God who instills meaning and purpose into these processes. Therefore, it is only logical that the secular view, which denies God's existence, finds no meaning in historical developments.

Foreign influences on Jewish thought. My guideline for this book is to extract the metaphysical principles from the Jewish sacred writings. Metaphysical premises that are at the basis of any philosophical approach cannot be logically or scientifically proven. This leads us to ask: how can we choose between the many different philosophical schools? Which one is true? Which one should form the basis of our world view? The reasonableness of the approach alone cannot guide us. What one person finds reasonable may be thoroughly unreasonable to another. Philosophers – all of them highly educated, capable people – have come up with a great many philosophical approaches, all of them different.

I believe that true Jewish philosophy should not rely on foreign philosophical approaches, nor need it reconcile itself to them. The source of Jewish metaphysics is in our sacred writings. However, Jewish philosophers do not always behave according to this principle. Medieval philosophers saw fit to confront the philosophies of Plato, Aristotle and other Greek philosophers. Likewise, modern Jewish philosophers choose to reconcile their philosophy with Kant's teachings. In Chapter Four, section 3, we quoted Rabbi Soloveitchik criticizing this trend: "The most central concepts of medieval Jewish philosophy are rooted in ancient Greek and medieval Arabic thought and are not of Jewish origin at all. It is impossible to reconstruct a unique Jewish world perspective out of alien material."

He also comments on the same trend in modern times: "Since the time of the great medieval philosophers, Jewish philosophical thought has expressed itself . . . upon premises, which were more non-Jewish than Jewish. The most characteristic example is to be found in Hermann Cohen's philosophy of religion. . . . There are many truths in his interpretation, but the main trends are idealistic Kantian and not Jewish."[18] The Sages expressed a similar view: "If a person tells you there is wisdom among the nations of the world, believe him. If a person tells you there is Torah among the nations of the world, do not believe him."[19]

However, foreign influences did not pass Rabbi Soloveitchik by either. In Chapter Four, section 7, we cited his opinion on Kant's theory of cognition.

> The transcendental consciousness of man . . . can reveal what reason cannot. Kant's doctrine, despite all the difficulties that it came up against, did not move, in this area, from its place. Reason does not film the 'data' but adapts it to its needs. It adapts it with the stylus of the categorical concepts in order to make it fit with a scientific view . . . . [Reason's] achievements are not the description of the 'data' as is, as the realists from the time of Aristotle believed, but idealistic constructions and symbols. It is here that the fathers of modern physics are in agreement with Kant . . . .

In his book *Halakhic Man*, which is considered a fundamental contribution to Jewish thought, Rabbi Soloveitchik places Kant's theory of cognition as a basis of the theoretical structure of his work:

> [Cognitive man] constructs an ideal, ordered, and fixed world, one that is perfectly clear and lucid; he fashions an a priori, ideal creation with which he is greatly pleased . . . . This latter approach is that of mathematics and the

---

18. *The Halakhic Mind,* 101.
19. *Eichah Rabbah* 2:13.

mathematical, natural sciences, the crowning achievement of civilization. It is both a priori and ideal – i.e., to know means to construct an ideal, lawful, unified system whose necessity flows from its very nature, a system that does not require, as far as its validity and truth are concerned, precise parallelism with the correlative realm of concrete, qualitative phenomena.[20]

However, this declaration of his adherence to Kant's teachings did not significantly harm the Rabbi's treatise, *Halakhic Man*. In fact, Rabbi Soloveitchik did not even need Kant's theory of cognition. The validity of the theoretical structure of halakha comes not from Kant's theory but from the fact that it is divine revelation: "When halakhic man approaches reality, he comes with his Torah, given to him from Sinai, in hand . . . . The essence of the Halakha, which was received from God, consists in creating an ideal world and cognizing the relationship between that ideal world and our concrete environment in all its visible manifestations and underlying structures."[21]

There is a significant difference between knowledge of the laws of nature (see Chapter Four) and knowledge of halakha. Scientific theories are revealed in stages, and at each stage they must be tested to see whether they fit with our experience. In contrast, there is no need to test the compatibility between halakha and reality – the laws of halakha do not determine the case is, but rather what it should be – the rules of ethics. This is the divine command to man, but man is also capable of not obeying God's command: the freedom of choice is given.

Nevertheless, Rabbi Soloveitchik's adherence to Kant's theory of cognition leads him to a false conclusion in his essay "And From There You Shall Seek." The point of departure is Maimonides's teaching regarding the identification of the "intellectually cognizing subject" and the "intellectually cognized object" with God. Maimonides writes in *Hilchot Yesodei ha-Torah:* "He is simultaneously the One who knows, the One who is known and the knowing itself, all as one" (2:10). God both knows and creates the knowledge. His knowledge is also the creation of the laws of the world. However, according to Kant's teachings, man also create the laws through the process of cognition. Rabbi Soloveitchik agrees with Kant:

---

20. *Halakhic Man*, 18–19.
21. Ibid., 19.

When a person grasps the intelligible essence of the entity, he strives towards it and is united with it. In the place of cognition as an action of capturing foreign objects which continue their independent existence and stability even after they have been grasped (like the ancient formulation of realism), comes active and creative cognition; it penetrates into the object's domain, conquers the others, takes it captive, and unites with it."[22]

But this is not so. Aviezer Ravitsky writes in his book, *Herut al ha-luhot* (*Freedom Inscribed*):

> Scientific cognition does not create the world for itself, but it faithfully reveals God's world. However, unfortunately, this solid basis of rational enlightenment in the universe is lost to modern man. It is definitely lost to a philosopher such as Rabbi Soloveitchik, who inclines towards theories of cognition and philosophy of science that are a great distance from the Aristotelian theory of existence".
> (187, my translation)

However, since the time of Aristotle, our understanding of the world has changed in many ways. David Hume showed that human beings cannot derive the laws of nature solely from a study of nature. We saw in Chapter Four that scientific knowledge does not create a world for itself, but reveals the divine spiritual world (the area of the laws of nature). Nonetheless, entry into the spiritual world is not free. God controls access to it. This is one of the channels of God's providence.

Another important aspect of knowledge of the world is that we human beings understand the laws of nature and the laws of ethics as two completely separate, unrelated entities. But there need not be such an absolute separation between the two areas of knowledge. Both of them belong to the same divine spiritual world.

Moreover, there is a certain advantage in looking at the world from the point of view of a theoretical physicist as it teaches us intellectual humility. We saw in Chapter Two that no effort to understand or imagine the essence of the tiniest particles, such as an electron or photon, can lead to a reasonable result. We cannot grasp the essence of a quantum particle using concepts that we know. If the understanding of a tiny particle evades us,

---

22. *And From There You Shall Seek*, 198.

how self-assured must a person be to think he can grasp the essence of the Creator of the world!

The spiritual world, its substance and its objectivity. One of the topics that comes up repeatedly in this book is the matter of the spiritual world, its substance and its objectivity – its non-dependence on human beings. Recognition of the existence of a divine spiritual world leads to a solution of several of the issues that remain unsolvable by the various secular approaches. It is worth pointing out that the spiritual reality is well anchored in Jewish tradition. Major concepts in Judaism such as God, the soul, providence, commandments and free will are concepts of a spiritual reality. As is written in *Ethics of the Fathers*, "With ten utterances the world was created."[23] If so, a spiritual reality – the utterances mentioned in the text – precedes the creation of the material world. The source of the reality is the word of God, God's thought. God turned the word into reality: "God said, 'Let there be light,' and there was light."[24] In the Torah, only the process of creation has the appearance of order out of chaos. God created order and lawfulness, which are also spiritual entities.

At this point, I would like to return to what we learned in the conclusion of Part II: The Laws of Nature (Chapter Four, section 8). **Unless God operating a given spiritual entity – namely, the laws of nature – on nature, nature itself does not exist.** This may explain the following verse: "The earth was without form and void." From a scientific perspective, it is impossible to define matter without the order inherent in the laws of nature. In fact, physical objects are law-like structures – entities that exist only because of the laws of nature. Without them, matter would not exist.

We have reached the conclusion that spirit precedes matter. This is the opposite conclusion to that which the majority of people generally believe, and to that which is at the foundation of materialism – the precedence of matter over spirit. In Chapter One (section 11) we quoted Rabbi Dessler, who defines the situation precisely: "The plan and purpose of creation is its spiritual content. Everything that exists in the physical world has a spiritual source. Its development, its activity, how it affects other things and is affected by them . . . ."

---

23. 5:1.
24. Genesis 1:3.

However, the world does not operate only according to the laws of nature. The laws of nature are only one of the tools of divine providence. We have seen that the physical, "natural" world is open both to divine providence and to the free will of human beings. It is only because of people's ignorance and preconceived ideas that they cannot see the wonder of the world developing under divine supervision. With my limited abilities, I have tried to refute this ignorance and these preconceptions.

Each of us bears a great responsibility to be God's partners in the perfection of the world. God said: "Let us make Mankind in our image, after our likeness: and let them have dominion over the fish of the sea and over the birds of the air, and over the cattle, and over all the earth, and over every creeping thing that creeps on the earth."[25] Man's creativity is the expression of his partnership with God.

---

25. Genesis 1:26.

Bibliography

𝕰𝖓𝖌𝖑𝖎𝖘𝖍

ATLAS, SAMUEL. *From Critical to Speculative Idealism: The Philosophy of Solomon Maimon.* The Hague: Martinus Nijhoff, 1964.

BARROW, JOHN D., and FRANK J. TIPLER. *The Anthropic Cosmological Principle.* Oxford: Oxford University Press, 1996.

BELL, JOHN S. *Speakable and Unspeakable in Quantum Mechanics.* Cambridge: Cambridge University Press, 1993.

BEN SHLOMO, YOSEF. *Lectures on the Philosophy of Spinoza.* Translated by Shmuel Himelstein. Tel Aviv: Ministry of Defense, 1992.

БЕН-ШЛОМО, ЙОСЕФ. Введение в Философию Иудаизма, Тарбут, Иерусалим, 1994.

BERGMAN, SAMUEL H. *The Philosophy of Solomon Maimon.* Translated from the Hebrew by Noah J. Jacobs. Jerusalem: Magnes Press, 1967.

BERKOVITS, ELIEZER. *Faith after the Holocaust.* New York: Ktav Publishing House, 1973.

BERKOVITS, ELIEZER. *God, Man and History.* Jerusalem: Shalem Press, 2004.

BORN, MAX & ALBERT EINSTEIN. *The Born-Einstein Letters: Correspondence between Albert Einstein and Max and Hedwig Born from 1916 to 1955, with Commentaries by Max Born.* London: Macmillan, 1971.

BUBER, MARTIN. *I and Thou.* New York: Collier Books, 1958.

BURTT, EDWIN A. *The Metaphysical Foundations of Modern Science.* Atlantic Highlands, N. J.: Humanities Press, 1996.

CAMPBELL, LEWIS & WILLIAM GARNETT. *The Life of James Clerk Maxwell.* London: Macmillan, 1884.

CARMELL, ARYEH & CYRIL DOMB, EDS. *Challenge: Torah Views on Science and Its Problems.* New York: Feldheim, 1978.

DARWIN, CHARLES. *On the Origin of Species.* London: John Murray,1859; New York: Bantam Classics, 1999.

DESCARTES, RENÉ. *Key Philosophical Writings.* Hertfordshire: Wordsworth Classics, 1997.

DESSLER, RABBI ELIYAHU. *Strive For Truth.* Translated from the Hebrew (*Michtav me-Eliyahu*) by Aryeh Carmell. Jerusalem/NewYork: Feldheim, 1978.

EINSTEIN, ALBERT. *Ideas and Opinions.* New York: Wings Books, 1954.

EINSTEIN, ALBERT, and LEOPOLD INFELD. *Evolution of Physics.* Cambridge: Cambridge University Press, 1938.

EINSTEIN, ALBERT. *Cosmic Religion.* New York: Covici-Friede, 1931.

FACKENHEIM, EMIL L. *God's Presence in History.* New York: New York University Press, 1970.

FACKENHEIM, EMIL L. *Quest for Past and Future,* Boston: Beacon Press, 1968.

FACKENHEIM, EMIL L. *The Jewish Return into History: Reflection in the Age of Auschwitz and a New Jerusalem.* New York: Schocken Books, 1978.

FACKENHEIM, EMIL L. *What Is Judaism?* New York: Summit Books, 1987.

FACKENHEIM, EMIL L. *To Mend the World.* New York: Schocken, 1982.

FAIN, BENJAMIN. "Comprehensibility of the World: Jewish Outlook." *BDD* [*Be-khol derakhekha daehu*] *Journal of Torah and Scholarship,* 9:5–21.

FAIN, BENJAMIN. *Creation Ex Nihilo.* Jerusalem/New York: Gefen, 2007.

FAIN, BENJAMIN. Вера и Разум, Маханаим, Иерусалим, 2007.

FAIN, BENJAMIN. *Evolution and Providence in Divine Action and Natural Selection* (edited by J. Seckbach and R. Gordon). New Jersey/Singapore: World Scientific, 2009.

FAIN, BENJAMIN. *Irreversibilities in Quantum Mechanics.* Dordrecht, Netherlands: Kluwer Academic Publishers, 2000. (See specifically chapter 6, "Quantum Measurement and Irreversibility.")

FAIN, BENJAMIN, and MERVIN F. VERBIT. *Jewishness in the Soviet Union: Report of an Empirical Survey.* Jerusalem: Jerusalem Center for Public Affairs/Tarbut, 1984.

Bibliography

FEYNMAN, RICHARD. *The Character of Physical Law.* London: Cox and Wyman Ltd, 1965.

FEYNMAN, RICHARD, ROBERT B. LEIGHTON & MATTHEW SANDS. *The Feynman Lectures on Physics, Vol. 1.* London: Addison-Wesley, 1963.

FUKUYAMA, FRANCIS. *The End of History and the Last Man.* London: Penguin Books, 1993.

GALILEI, GALILEO. *Dialogue Concerning the Two Chief World Systems.* Berkeley: University of California Press, 1953.

GALILEI, GALILEO. *Two New Sciences: Including Centers of Gravity and Force of Percussion.* Madison, Wisconsin: University of Wisconsin Press, 1974.

GOULD, STEPHEN J. *Wonderful Life: The Burgess Shale and the Nature of History.* London: Penguin Books, 1989.

ГИНЗБУРГ В.Л.: О науке, о себе и о других, Физматгиз, Москва, 2003.

GUTTMANN, JULIUS. *Philosophies of Judaism.* Translated by David Silverman. New York: Schocken Books, 1973.

GREENE, BRIAN. *The Elegant Universe: Superstrings, Hidden Dimensions, and the Quest for the Ultimate Theory.* New York: W. W. Norton, 1999.

HALDANE, JOHN B.S. *The Inequality of Man.* Harmondsworth, Eng.: Penguin Books, 1937.

HARDY, ALISTER. *The Living Stream.* London: Collins, 1965.

HERNECK, FRIEDRICH. *Albert Einstein.* Berlin: Buchverlag der Morgen, 1967.

HESCHEL, ABRAHAM J. *Between God and Man: An Interpretation of Judaism.* London: The Free Press, 1959.

HUME, DAVID. *The Natural History of Religion and Dialogues concerning Natural Religion.* Oxford: Clarendon Press, 1976.

HUME, DAVID. *A Treatise of Human Nature.* Edited by L.A. Selby-Bigge. Oxford: Clarendon Press, 1888 (Russian translation, 1996).

ISH-SHALOM, BENJAMIN. *Rav Avraham Itzhak Ha-Cohen Kook: Between Rationalism and Mysticism.* Albany: State University of New York Press, 1993.

JOHNSON, PAUL. *A History of the Jews.* New York: Harper Perennial, 1988.

KANT, IMMANUEL. *Critique of Practical Reason.* Chicago: University of Chicago Press, 1949.

Bibliography

KANT, IMMANUEL. *Critique of Pure Reason.* London: Macmillan, 1923.

KANT, IMMANUEL. *Prolegomena to Any Future Metaphysics.* New York: Liberal Arts Press, 1950.

KOLITZ, ZVI. *Confrontation.* Hoboken, New Jersey: Ktav, 1993.

LAMM, NORMAN. *Torah Umadda: The Encounter of Religious Learning and Worldly Knowledge in the Jewish Tradition.* Northvale, NJ: Jason Aronson, 1990.

LAUE, MAX VON. *Geschichte der Physik.* Bonn: Athenaum-Verlag, 1950.

LEVI, YEHUDAH. *Torah and Science.* Jerusalem/New York: Feldheim Publishers, 2006.

LUZZATTO, RABBI MOSHE HAYYIM. *The Way of God.* Translated by Aryeh Kaplan. Jerusalem: Feldheim, 1983.

MAIMONIDES, MOSES. *The Guide of the Perplexed.* 2 vols. Translated by Shlomo Pines. Chicago: University of Chicago Press, 1963.

MAYR, ERNST. *One Long Argument: Charles Darwin and the Genesis of Modern Evolutionary Thought.* Cambridge MA: Harvard University Press, 1993.

MONOD, JACQUES. *Chance and Necessity: An Essay on the Natural Philosophy of Modern Biology.* London: Penguin Books, 1997.

NEWTON, ISAAC. *Optics.* New York: Dover, 1952.

PENFIELD, WILDER. *The Mystery of the Mind.* Princeton: Princeton University Press, 1975.

PENROSE, ROGER. *The Emperor's New Mind: Concerning Computers, Minds and The Laws of Physics.* London: Vintage, 1990.

PLATO. *Apology. The Laws. Meno. Phaedo. The Republic. Timaeus.*

POPPER, KARL R. *Conjectures and Refutations.* London: Routledge, 2000.

POPPER, KARL R. *Knowledge and the Body-Mind Problem.* London: Routledge, 2000.

POPPER, KARL R. *The Logic of Scientific Discovery.* London: Routledge, 1992.

POPPER, KARL R. *Objective Knowledge: An Evolutionary Approach.* Oxford: Clarendon Press, 1981.

POPPER, KARL R. *The Open Society and Its Enemies. Vol. 1: The Spell of Plato. Vol. 2: The High Tide of Prophecy: Hegel, Marx, and the Aftermath.* London: Routledge, 1999.

Bibliography

Popper, Karl R. *The Open Universe*. London: Routledge, 1995.

Popper, Karl R. *The Poverty of Historicism*. London: Routledge, 1999.

Popper, Karl R. *Quantum Theory and the Schism in Physics*. London: Routledge, 1995.

Popper, Karl R. *Realism and the Aim of Science*. London: Routledge, 1994.

Popper, Karl R. *Unended Quest*. London: Routledge, 1993.

Popper, Karl R., and John C. Eccles. *The Self and Its Brain*. London: Routledge, 1995.

Russell, Bertrand. *A History of Western Philosophy*. New York: Simon and Schuster, 1945.

Russell, Bertrand. *Human Knowledge: Its Scope and Limits*. London: George Allen and Unwin, 1948.

Schilpp, Paul A., ed. *Albert Einstein: Philosopher-Scientist*. The Library of Living Philosophers. New York: Tudor Publishing, 1951.

Scholem, Gershom. *Major Trends in Jewish Mysticism*. Jerusalem: Schocken, 1941.

Schrödinger, Erwin. *Mind and Matter*. Cambridge: Cambridge University Press, 1961.

Schrödinger, Erwin. *What Is Life?* Cambridge: Cambridge University Press, 1948.

Schroeder, Gerald L. *Genesis and the Big Bang*. New York: Bantam Books, 1990.

Schroeder, Gerald L. *The Science of God*. New York: The Free Press, 1997.

Simpson, George G. *The Meaning of Evolution*. New York: New American Library, 1951.

Soloveitchik, Joseph B. *And From There You Shall Seek*. Translated from the Hebrew by Naomi Goldblum. New York: Ktav Publishing House, 2008.

Soloveitchik, Joseph B. *Halakhic Man*. Philadelphia: Jewish Publication Society of America, 1983.

Soloveitchik, Joseph B. *Halakhic Mind*. London: Collier Macmillan Publishers, 1986.

Thorpe, William H. Biology, *Psychology and Belief*. Cambridge, Cambridge University Press, 1961.

THORPE, WILLIAM H. *Purpose in a World of Chance.* Oxford: Oxford University Press, 1978.

WESTFALL, RICHARD S. *Never at Rest: A Biography of Isaac Newton.* Cambridge: Cambridge University Press, 1980.

WHITEHEAD, ALFRED N. *Adventures of Ideas.* New York: The Free Press, 1961.

WHITEHEAD, ALFRED N. *Science and the Modern World.* New York: Macmillan, 1935.

WIGNER, EUGENE. "The Unreasonable Effectiveness of Mathematics in the Natural Sciences." In *Communications in Pure and Applied Mathematics* 13/3. New York: John Wiley and Sons, 1960.

𝕳𝖊𝖇𝖗𝖊𝖜

AGASSI, YOSEF. *Toldot ha-filosofiah ha-hadashah* [The history of modern philosophy]. Tel Aviv: Tel Aviv University, 1993.

AVINER, RABBI SHLOMO. *Sefer ha-kuzari: perush* [The Kuzari: A commentary]. Bet-El: Sifriat Chava, 2003–2007.

BEN SHLOMO, YOSEF. *"Shirat ha-hayyim": Prakim be-mishnato shel ha-Rav Kook* [Song of life: Selections from the teachings of R. Kook]. Tel Aviv: The Ministry of Defense, 1989.

BUBER, MARTIN. *Be-sod siah* [In the secret of dialogue]. Jerusalem: Mossad Bialik, 1959.

DESSLER, RABBI ELIYAHU. *Michtav me-Eliyahu* [Letter from Eliyahu]. Tel Aviv: Sifriati, 1995.

ELDAD, ISRAEL. *Hegyonot yisrael* [Reflections on Israel]. Tel Aviv: Ha-midrasha Ha-leumit/Yair, 1980.

FAIN, BENJAMIN. *"Evolutziah shel ha-hayyim"* [The evolution of life]. *Asia* 77–78 (January 2006): 38–64.

FAIN, BENJAMIN. *Hok ve-hashgaha* [Law and Providence]. Machon Har Bracha, 2009.

FAIN, BENJAMIN. *Yesh me-ayin* [Creation Ex Nihilo]. Jerusalem: Rubin Mass, 2004; Second Edition: Machon Har Bracha, 2008.

HALEVI, RABBI YEHUDA BEN SHMUEL. *Ha-Kuzari. Be-ha-takato shel Rabbi Yehuda Ibn Tibbon* [The Kuzari: translated by Rabbi Yehuda Ibn Tibbon]. Tel Aviv: Hamenorah, 1984.

Bibliography

KOOK, RABBI AVRAHAM YITZHAK HA-KOHEN. *Orot ha-kodesh* [Lights of holiness]. Jerusalem: Mosad HaRav Kook, 1992.

LEIBOWITZ, YEHAYAHU. *Guf ve-nefesh: Ha-be'ayah ha-psycho-fisit* [Body and mind: the psychophysical problem]. Tel Aviv: The Ministry of Defense, 1989.

LEIBOWITZ, YEHAYAHU. *Sihot al mada ve-arachim* [Discussions on science and values]. Tel Aviv: The Ministry of Defense, 1989.

LEIBOWITZ, YEHAYAHU, AND YOSEF AGASSI. *Sihot al ha-filosofia shel ha-mada* [Conversations concerning the philosophy of science]. Edited by Chemi Ben-Noon. Tel Aviv: The Ministry of Defense, 1997.

MAIMON, SOLOMON. *Ha-masah al ha-filosofiah ha-transzendentialit* [Essay on transcendental philosophy]. Translated and edited by Shmuel H. Bergman and Nathan Rottenstreich. Jerusalem: Hebrew University, 1941.

MAIMONIDES, MOSES. *Hakdamot le-perush ha-mishneh, hakdamah le-masechet avot* [Introduction to the commentary on the Mishneh, introduction to Ethics of Our Fathers]. Jerusalem: Mossad HaRav Kook. 1961.

RAVITSKY, AVIEZER. *Herut al ha-luhot: kolot aherim shel ha-mahashavah ha-datit* [Freedom Inscribed: Diverse Voices of Jewish Religious Thought]. Tel Aviv: Am Oved, 2000.

SCHOLEM, GERSHOM. *Devarim be-go* [Explications and implications]. Tel Aviv: Am Oved, 1990.

SCHWEID, ELIEZER. *Ha-filosofim ha-gedolim shelanu* [Our great philosophers]. Tel Aviv: Yediot Aharonot, 1999.

SCHWEID, ELIEZER. *Toldot filosofiat ha-dat ha-yehudit ba-zeman he-hadash* [The history of the philosophy of the Jewish religion in modern times]. Volumes 1–4. Tel Aviv: Am Oved, 2001–2006.

SOLOVEITCHIK, JOSEPH B. *Ha-adam ve-olamo* [Man and his world]. Jerusalem: Eliner Library Department of Religious Education and Culture in the Diaspora, 1998.

SOLOVEITCHIK, JOSEPH B. *Ish ha-emunah* [Man of Faith]. Jerusalem: Mosad HaRav Kook, 1992.

SOLOVEITCHIK, JOSEPH B. *Ish ha-halakhah: galui ve-nistar* [Halakhic man: revealed and hidden]. Jerusalem: Ha-histadrut ha-tzionit ha-olamit, 1992 (See specifically "U-vikashtem mi-sham" [*And From There You Shall Seek*]).

About the Author

Professor Benjamin Fain, a world-renowned physicist, has published numerous scientific books and articles. Recently he has been devoting his time to the relationship between Torah and science. His previous book, Creation Ex Nihilo, has been translated into English and Russian and has been well received.